Agro Processing Methods Equipment Operation and Maintenance

About the Author

Tejas Ashok Bhosale completed his Bachelor of Technology (B. Tech.) from Mahatma Phule Krishi Vidyapeeth (MPKV), Rahuri, Maharashtra. He qualified for the Junior Research Fellowship (JRF) examination conducted by the Indian Council of Agricultural Research (ICAR). Subsequently, he earned his Master of Technology (M. Tech.) from G.B. Pant University of Agriculture and Technology (GBPUAT), Pantnagar. He has also qualified for the ICAR Agricultural Scientists Recruitment Board National Eligibility Test (ICAR-ASRB-NET). With over 12 years of teaching experience in State Agricultural Universities (SAUs), Tejas is currently serving as an Assistant Professor at Veer Chandra Singh Garhwali Uttarakhand University of Horticulture and Forestry (VCSGUUHF), Bharsar, Pauri Garhwal, Uttarakhand. He is a DGCA-certified drone pilot, specializing in the application of drones within the agricultural sector. Tejas has published 7 research papers, 5 popular articles, 1 book chapter, and 1 book. He has handled one project as Principal Investigator (PI) and another as Co-Principal Investigator (Co-PI). Additionally, he possesses administrative experience in various capacities within SAUs. His areas of specialization include agricultural mechanization, precision agriculture, the use of drones in agriculture, and the design and development of intercultural and harvesting machinery. Tejas's expertise and contributions significantly enhance agricultural technology and education.

Agro Processing Methods Equipment Operation and Maintenance

Tejas Ashok Bhosale
Assistant Professor
Agricultural Engineering
Department of Natural Resource Management
College of Horticulture
Veer Chandra Singh Garhwali Uttarakhand University of Horticulture and Forestry,
Bharsar, Pauri Garhwal, Uttarakhand

CV CONTENT VIBES
PUBLISHERS • PRINTERS • AGGREGATORS

CV CONTENT VIBES
PUBLISHERS • PRINTERS • AGGREGATORS

1168, Sector 13, Urban Estate
Karnal-132 001, Haryana
Tel: 91-84470 75807, 18440 41168
Email: contentvibesppa@gmail.com
www.contentvibes.in

Print ISBN: 978-93-67551-92-9

ebooks ISBN: 978-93-6755-585-9

Preface

In the value chain of agricultural production, agro processing is essential because it transforms raw agricultural materials into products that are marketable, usable, and consumable. As a way to increase food security, add value to agricultural commodities, and prolong the shelf life of food products, the field has grown significantly in importance. This book, "Agro Processing Methods, Equipment Operation and Maintenance," is designed to provide a comprehensive overview of the essential processes involved in agro processing, with a special focus on the machinery and equipment used in these operations.

The book explores a wide range of processing methods, from traditional techniques to the more advanced technologies currently being implemented in the industry. Every processing technique is covered in detail, giving readers a clear grasp of how to use it and how it relates to various agricultural products. In a market that is becoming more and more competitive, this knowledge is essential for increasing processing efficiency, guaranteeing product quality, and satisfying customer demand.

In addition to the methods, the book delves into the operation of the various equipments used in agro processing. The importance of proper equipment operation is emphasized, as it directly impacts the quality of the processed products and the overall performance of the facility. Detailed sections on equipment maintenance ensure that readers understand the significance of routine checks and the necessity of preventive maintenance to avoid costly breakdowns and extend the lifespan of machinery.

Designed for both students and industry professionals, this book aims to serve as a practical guide to understanding agro processing from the ground up. Whether you are involved in food production, agricultural processing, or machinery maintenance, the knowledge imparted through this book will help optimize operations and improve product outcomes. The integration of operational practices and maintenance techniques provides a holistic approach to agro processing that is vital for sustainable development in the agricultural sector.

—Author

Content

1

Acquaintance with Different Unit Operations Involved in Agro-Processing

Agro processing involves a diverse range of unit operations aimed at converting raw agricultural products into value-added goods. These processes serve to enhance the shelf life, quality, and overall appeal of agricultural commodities while also boosting their nutritional content and market value. The unit operations employed in Agro processing are determined by the specific characteristics of the product and the desired outcome. Common steps include cleaning, sorting, peeling, grinding, and milling. Preservation methods such as blanching, fermentation, drying, and freezing play a crucial role in preparing products for consumption or further manufacturing. Furthermore, operations like extrusion, canning, juicing, and packaging are essential for producing a variety of processed food items, while proper storage and warehousing ensure the long-term availability and sustainability of these goods. Each unit operation is designed to contribute toward creating high-quality, market-ready products, minimizing waste, and ensuring optimal utilization of raw materials. By combining these processes effectively, Agro processing maximizes the potential of agricultural resources and strengthens the overall food industry.

OVERVIEW OF MATERIAL HANDLING

Materials handling encompasses a broad spectrum of activities, including mechanical harvesting on farms, transportation of live animals, refrigerated transport of perishable goods, and pneumatic conveying of flour from rail cargo to bakery storage facilities. It is important to minimize product losses during these operations while maintaining the quality of raw materials, such as preserving vitamin content and physical appearance, ensuring sanitary conditions, reducing bacterial growth, and optimizing the timing of transfers to avoid delays that could compromise both the economy and product quality.

The journey of agricultural produce from farms to processing areas often results in significant transformations. For instance, grapes are transported via tractors, trucks, or trailers to juice plants or wineries, where they are graded, washed, and processed further. However, there are limitations on the size of transport vehicles and the duration fruits and vegetables can be held. Since these are living, respiring products, prolonged storage can increase batch temperatures to levels that encourage spoilage.

Handling dry materials like sugar and flour presents unique challenges. Sugar, when transported to processing facilities via trucks or rail, is pneumatically conveyed to storage tanks. Without proper management of storage duration, temperature, and humidity, sugar tends to cake. Additionally, improper handling can lead to dusting and static electricity buildup, which poses a risk of explosion due to the highly combustible nature of sugar particles. Similar issues arise in the flour industry, where poor handling may cause safety hazards and losses in product quality. Proper handling methods also help preserve desirable volatile compounds in spices, prevent irritation to personnel, and avoid flavor contamination between different spices.

Food processing plants employ a variety of equipment for efficient materials handling, including screw conveyors, bucket conveyors, belt conveyors, and vibratory conveyors. These systems are very important for managing the diverse range of food materials that require precise and safe handling during processing.

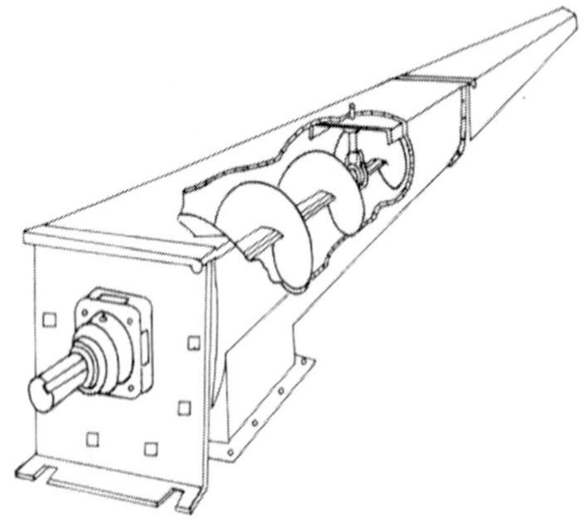

Figure.: 1.1 Screw conveyor

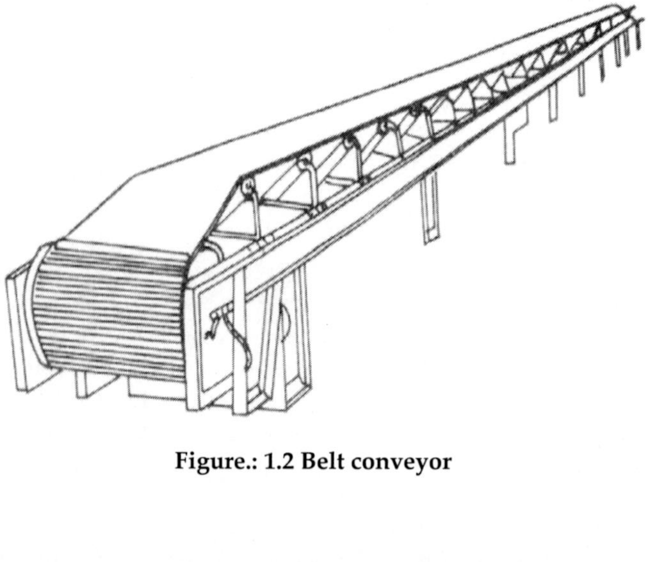

Figure.: 1.2 Belt conveyor

The primary aim of material handling are centered around ensuring efficiency, safety, and quality in the movement and processing of products. These objectives include maintaining acceptable product quality by preserving the physical and nutritional attributes of the material, ensuring proper sanitation to prevent contamination and uphold hygienic standards, minimizing holding time to reduce delays that could affect product freshness and efficiency, minimizing product loss to ensure cost-effectiveness and reduce waste, and limiting bacterial growth to maintain food safety and extend shelf life. Achieving these goals is critical for optimizing material handling processes across various industries.

Selection and Receiving of Raw Materical

- Fruits and vegetables should be ripe but firm, evenly matured, free from blemishes, insect damage and malformation.
- Harvesting at proper maturity is an important step in selection of raw material.
- Most of the fruits are harvested at soft ripe stage.
- Vegetables except peas, beans etc are harvested at mature stage to enable them to withstand cooking during sterilization.
- Some vegetables like green beans, greens peas, ladies finger should be tender and free from soil, dirt etc.

Pumping

This unit operation involves the transfer of liquids from one processing step to another using pumps, with single screw and gear pumps being commonly utilized. In the food industry, pumping liquids between locations or processes is a frequent operation, requiring pumps suited to the specific properties of the food being handled. Rotary gear pumps are widely used, where inner gears rotate to draw food into the pump housing and then expel it. These pumps require tight clearances for mechanical efficiency, making them effective for liquids and pastes but unsuitable for chunkier foods, as they can crush them into purees. Conversely, single screw pumps, also called progressing cavity pumps, are ideal for handling foods with larger suspended pieces without causing damage. Their design features large clearances between the rotor and housing, allowing food like corn kernels, grapes, and small shrimp to be transported gently without physical harm. Centrifugal pumps are usually employed for moving liquids to plate heat exchangers, ensuring pressure does not build excessively within the plates. An important feature of food pumps is the ability to disassemble them easily for thorough cleaning. Modern sanitary stainless steel pumps can often be taken apart within minutes using a single tool, facilitating maintenance and hygiene.

Cleaning

All foods are naturally grown or available in the open environment, necessitating thorough cleaning before consumption. This process can range from simple dirt removal on fruits and vegetables using abrasive brushes to more advanced methods like microfiltration for eliminating bacteria from milk.

Grains are typically cleaned of stones through screening, which may involve vibrations. Cleaning techniques vary depending on the product and the type of dirt or contaminants present and may include water, steam, pressurized air, brushes, vacuuming, magnetic separation for metal contaminants, and mechanical separation.

For instance, the soft drink industry requires exceptionally pure water, exceeding typical drinking water standards. Any impurities, such as dust, colloidal particles, or certain inorganic salts, can interfere with carbonation by reducing carbon dioxide solubility and encouraging gas escape. To achieve this level of purity, processes such as controlled chemical flocculation, sand filtration, carbon purification, microfiltration, and de-aeration are employed, making it a comprehensive cleaning process rather than a simple operation.

Specific cleaning methods are also influenced by surface characteristics. For example, high-pressure water jets are used to remove dirt from the grooves of pineapples' asymmetric surfaces. Similarly, different food products require specialized cleaning equipments and techniques. In cleaning equipment, walls, and floors in food plants, the chemical and physical properties of the surfaces and the type of soil determine the cleaning approach. Mild alkaline detergents suffice for most soils, while strong alkalis are needed for stubborn fat or protein deposits. Hard salt soils formed during heating often require strong acids to clean the heating surfaces effectively.

Cleaning is a unit operation aimed at removing contaminants from food to prepare it for further processing. This process can be carried out using wet or dry methods, depending on the product and the type of dirt.

Wet cleaning methods include soaking, spraying, flotation, washing, and ultrasonic cleaning, while dry cleaning methods include separation through air, magnetic attraction for metal contaminants, or physical means. Typically, fruits and vegetables are washed with water to remove dust, dirt, and surface microflora. However, certain fruits like peaches and apricots, which undergo lye peeling, are not washed before peeling to prevent nutrient loss. Washing food after peeling should be avoided, as it can strip away vitamins and minerals.

Common washing techniques involve soaking or agitating in water, using cold or hot water sprays, or employing mechanical washers that tumble or agitate the food on moving belts or revolving screens while immersed in water or sprayed with water. High-pressure water sprays are usually effective for cleaning. Detergents are often added to wash or rinse water for better results. For disinfection, vegetables may be soaked in dilute solutions of potassium permanganate or chlorine (25-50 ppm), ensuring thorough cleaning and safety.

Mixing

Mixing is a versatile process where various combinations of materials—solids with solids, liquids with liquids, liquids with solids, or gases with liquids—are blended using specialized mixers tailored to the nature of the materials involved. For instance, a conical blender is ideal for mixing dry ingredients, such as those in baking powder. The tumbling action in the blender bowl, lasting 10–20 minutes, ensures a homogeneous mixture.

For preparing a dry cake mix, shortening must be cut into flour, sugar, and other dry ingredients to achieve a fluffy, uniform blend. In this case, a ribbon blender is recommended. This equipment features a horizontal trough with rotating mixing elements, and its efficiency depends on selecting the appropriate ribbon-like mixing element for the task.

When mixing solids into liquids, a propeller mounted within a stainless-steel vat is the preferred choice. Various designs of propellers, turbines, and paddles are available, each suitable for specific mixing needs, ensuring effective and consistent blending.

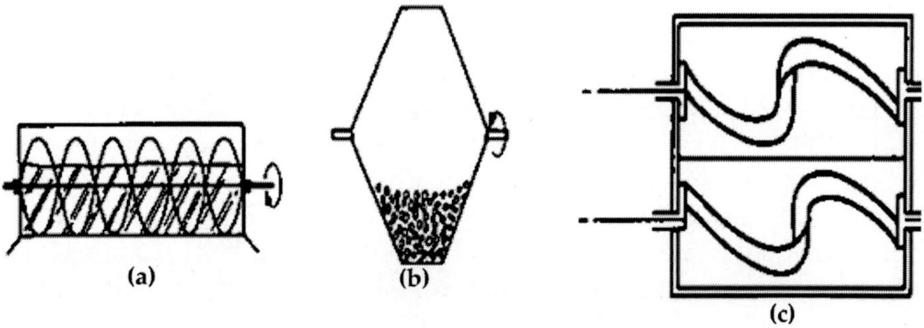

Figure.: 1.3 Mixers- (a)Ribbon blender,(b)Double-cone mixer,(c)Kneader

All mixers perform a similar function of blending materials, but they often generate some heat during the process, which is generally controlled to prevent undesirable effects. For heavy and viscous materials, specialized mixers are employed, such as those with arms designed for kneading dough or paddles for working butter. These mixers are precisely engineered to maximize efficiency and minimize energy consumption, ensuring an optimal mixing or working process.

Certain mixers are specifically designed to incorporate air into the product during mixing. A notable example is the scraper-beater used in ice cream freezers. In this setup, the dasher rotates within the freezer cylinder, scraping the mix from the surface to accelerate freezing and achieve uniformity. Simultaneously, it introduces air into the mix, resulting in the desired volume increase (overrun) and a smooth texture in the final ice cream.

Different types of mixers are selected based on the nature of the materials being mixed, whether they involve solids with solids, liquids with liquids, liquids with solids, or gases with liquids. Each type is tailored to meet specific processing needs efficiently.

- For simple mixing of dry ingredients, a conical blender may be used.
- A ribbon blender with rotating mixing elements is used to mix sugar with other dry components to produce fluffy dry mix.

- Propeller type agitator mounted within stainless steel vat is used for mixing solids into liquids to dissolve them as in case of salt and sugar solution.

Separation Process

Separation processes in the food industry involve isolating different components based on their physical or chemical properties. This may include separating solids from solids, such as peeling potatoes or shelling nuts; separating solids from liquids, such as filtering or pressing juice from fruit; or separating liquids from liquids, such as centrifuging oil from water. It can also involve removing gases from solids or liquids, as in vacuum canning to air from canned food.

Hand sorting and grading, once a common practice, are now being replaced by mechanical and electronic sorting systems due to labor costs. For example, photocells can detect color differences to identify and reject discolored or moldy products at high speeds. In peanut butter production, each peanut passes through a light beam, activating an air jet to remove discolored peanuts. Similarly, eggs with blood spots are identified and rejected through light scanning, while size-based sorting of fruits and vegetables is achieved using screens with different openings.

Peeling processes, such as lye peeling, are used for fruits like peaches and apricots. The fruits are treated with a heated lye solution to soften their skins, which are then removed using mechanical fingers or water jets. The density difference between the fruit and its skin allows the skin to float away.

Oil extraction is another key separation process. For instance, corn oil is obtained by first separating the germ from the kernel through milling and then applying high pressure to the germ in an oil press. Similar methods are used for extracting oil from peanuts, soybeans, and cottonseeds, with fat solvents employed to recover residual oil from the pressed cake. The separation of oil and solvent is then achieved using distillation equipment.

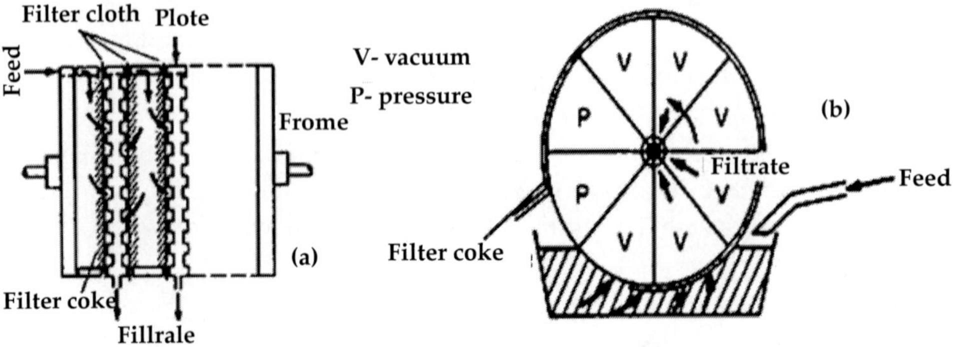

Figure.: 1.4 (a) Plate and frame press (b) Rotary vaccum filter

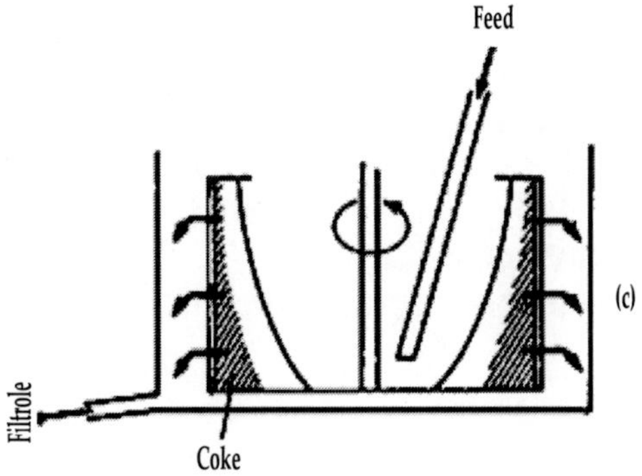

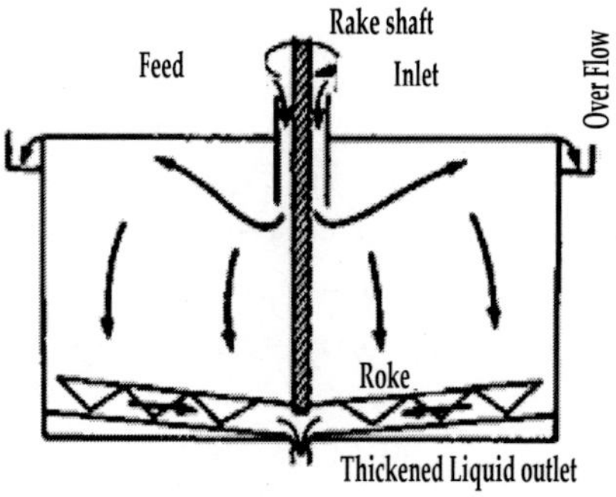

Figure.: 1.5 (c) Centrifugal filter (d) Continuous-sedmentation plant

Crystallization is a separation process usually used to extract substances like salt from seawater or sugar from sugarcane juice. By evaporating part of the water, the solution becomes supersaturated, leading to the formation of crystals. Since these crystals are pure, the process also serves as a method of purification. Once the crystals form, they are separated from the remaining liquid using centrifugation.

Recent advances in separation techniques include the use of manufactured membranes with specific porosities or permeabilities designed to separate colloidal and macromolecular components. One such method is ultrafiltration, which uses membranes that allow water and small molecules, such as salts, acids, and bases, to pass through, while larger molecules like proteins and sugars are retained. This process can be conducted at ambient temperatures, preventing the heat damage to sensitive food components that often occurs during evaporation. Additionally, removing acids and salts from water helps prevent their accumulation, which could otherwise harm the sensitive solids being retained.

It involve separating a solid from a solid like peeling of potatoes, separating a solid from a liquid as in filtration or a liquid from solid as in pressing of juice from a fruit. It might involve the separation of a liquid from a liquid as in centrifugation of oil from water. It might also involve removing gas from a solid or liquid as in vacuum removal or air from canned food during canning. Common separating methods used in fruit and vegetable processing are discussed below:

- **Grading:** After preliminary sorting, the fruit and vegetables are graded to obtain uniform quality with respect to size, colour etc. Grading can be done either manually or with the help of mechanical graders. Different types of mechanical graders include screen grader, roller grader, rope or cable grader, conveyor grader etc.
- **Sorting:** Sorting is the separation of foods into different categories on the basis of a measurable physical property. Sorting and grading ensures the removal of inferior or damaged commodity. For sorting, inspection belt can be used, in addition to trained personnel who detect poor quality produce unsuitable for canning. Automatic colour sorters can be used for sorting to reduce labour cost.

- **Peeling, coring and pitting:** These are the primary unit operations for preparing fruit and vegetables for processing.
    - Peeling of fruit and vegetables is carried out to remove unwanted or inedible material and to improve the appearance of the final product.
    - The main consideration for peeling is to minimize cost by removing as little of the underlying food as possible and reducing energy, labour and material cost to a minimum.
- The peeled surface should be clean and undamaged.
- Depending upon the commodity, peeling and coring methods can be selected such as:
    - Hand or knife peeling
    - Machine/abrasive peeling
    - Flash steam peeling
    - Lye (caustic) peeling
    - Lame peeling.
- Cores and pits in fruits like apple, peach, apricot etc are removed by hand or by machine (de-corer).

Reduction of Size

Size reduction is the process of breaking large solid particles into smaller pieces without altering their chemical properties. In the process industries, solids are reduced in size and shape through various methods, depending on the intended purpose. This is typically done mechanically, with large particles being crushed or reduced to a more manageable size. Achieving uniformity in the size and shape of the particles is often a challenge, but it is desirable in many applications. Reducing the size of solids increases their reactivity, facilitates the separation of unwanted ingredients, and decreases the bulk of fibrous materials, making them easier to handle.

Usually the equipments used for size reduction in agricultural products includes crushers and grinders. The performance of these machines is usually evaluated based on ideal operational standards, considering factors such as the amount of power required and the uniformity of the particle size. While the ground product typically consists of a range of particle sizes, some equipment allows for control over the largest particles, such as with a hammer mill, although controlling fine particles is often difficult.

There are several methods for reduction of size, with four commonly used techniques.

- Compression
- Impact
- Attrition or rubbing
- Cutting

For example, compression is used for coarsely reducing hard solids, with relatively few fines produced; impact can result in coarse, medium, or fine products; attrition produces very fine products, particularly from soft, nonabrasive materials; and cutting provides specific particle sizes and shapes, with minimal fines.

Crushing

When a material is subjected to an external force that exceeds its strength, it fails by rupturing in multiple directions. The particles produced from this crushing process tend to be irregular in shape and size. Crushing is commonly used in the production of food grain flour, grits, and meal, as well as ground feed for livestock. Additionally, crushing is employed to extract oil from oilseeds and juice from sugarcane

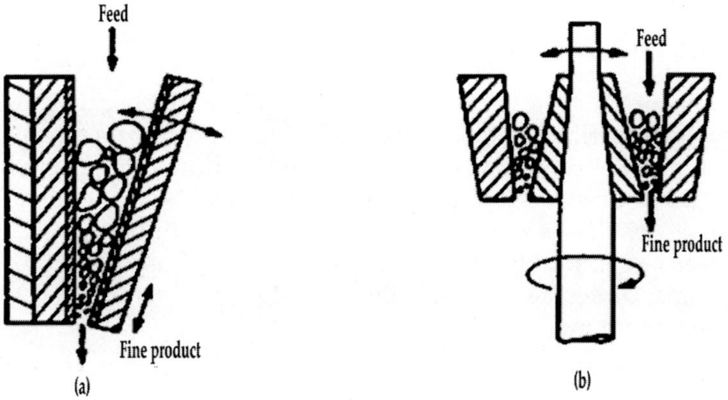

Figure.: 1.6 Crushers:(a) Jaw (b)Gyratory

Impact

When a material experiences a sudden blow of force that exceeds its strength, it fails, similar to how a nut cracks when struck with a hammer. The operation of a hammer mill is an example of applying dynamic force through the impact method.

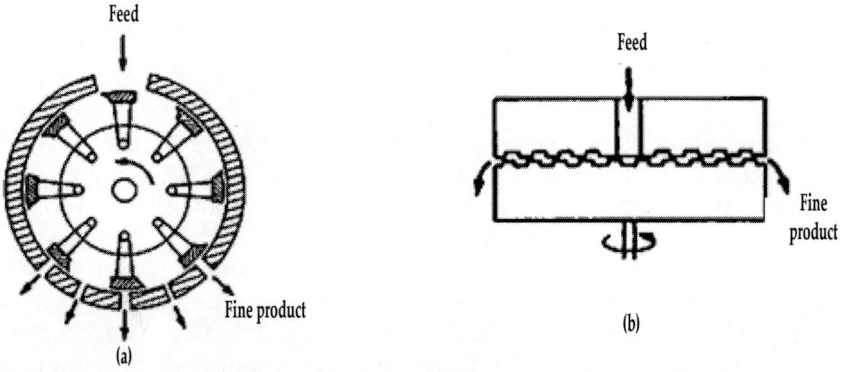

Figure.: 1.7 Grinders : (a) hammer mill, (b) plate mill

Cutting

In this method, size reduction is accomplished by forcing a knife through the material, where minimum deformation and rupture of the material is achieved. An ideal knife is of excellent sharpness and as thin as practicable. The size of vegetables and fruits are reduced by cutting by knives.

Shearing

It combines cutting and crushing and consist of units like a knife and a bar. In an ideal shearing unit the clearance between the bar and the knife should be as small as practicable and the knife as sharp and thin as possible.

HEATING OF FOODS

Heating of foods is performed to eliminate microorganisms, preserve the food (as in pasteurized milk and canned peas), and improve texture and flavor (as in cooking). Foods are heated through conduction, convection, radiation, or a combination of these methods. Since many foods are sensitive to heat, prolonged exposure can result in off-flavors, darkened colors, or nutrient loss. Therefore, it is ideal to heat foods quickly and cool them promptly. Various methods such as hot water toasters, direct steam, direct flame contact, or microwave cookers are used for heating or cooking.

- **Blanching:**Treatment of fruit and vegetables by dipping in boiling water or steam for short periods followed by immediate cooling is called blanching. The key objectives of blanching are:
    - Inactivation of enzymes, to cleanse the product initially to decrease the microbial load.
    - To preheat the product before processing.
    - To soften the tissue for facilitating compact packing in the cans.
    - To expel intercellular gases in the raw fruit.
    - To prevent excessive pressure built up in the container.
    - To allow improved heat transfer during heat processing.
    - To ensure development of vacuum in the can and
    - To reduce internal can corrosion.
- **Pasteurization:**Pasteurization is a mild heat treatment process used to heat food below 100°C, with the goal of eliminating specific vegetative microbial pathogens and inactivating enzymes. For liquid foods like fruit juices, milk, milk products, and liquid eggs, pasteurization is typically carried out in a continuous heat exchanger. The product is quickly heated to the desired pasteurization temperature in the first heat exchanger, held for the necessary duration in holding tubes, and then rapidly cooled in a second heat exchanger. Viscous fluids require a swept surface heat exchanger (SSHE) to increase heat transfer and prevent surface fouling.

  Package pasteurization is similar to traditional thermal processing but is done at lower temperatures. The required heat treatment for stabilizing a food is determined by the D value, which refers to the time required to kill the most heat-resistant microorganism or enzyme in the food. For example, in milk pasteurization, the D60 value indicates a 12-log reduction of Coxiella burnetti, while liquid whole egg pasteurization involves a 9-D reduction in Salmonella seftenberg.

The High Temperature Short Time (HTST) method is used to preserve the nutritional and sensory quality of foods since color, flavor, and vitamins also have D values. For milk, the HTST process typically operates at 71.8°C for 15 seconds, which causes fewer changes in flavor and retains more vitamins compared to the Low Temperature Long Time (LTLT) process, which operates at 63°C for 30 minutes. Flash pasteurization, which utilizes even higher temperatures for shorter times (such as 88°C for 1 second or 94°C for 0.1 second), is also applied to milk.

In milk pasteurization, the inactivation of alkaline phosphatase serves as an indicator of proper pasteurization. For liquid egg pasteurization, the activity of alpha-amylase is used as the primary indicator.

- **Processing:** Heat processing involves heating food in cans to a specific time and temperature combination to eliminate the risk of microbial spoilage. It is crucial to avoid overcooking, as it can negatively impact the texture, flavor, and appearance of the product.

  In continuous non-agitating cookers, cans are transported through boiling water in crates carried by overhead conveyors on a continuously moving belt. In continuous agitating cookers, the sealed cans are rotated by a mechanical device, which agitates the contents. This agitation helps reduce the overall processing time.

  For most fruits and acid vegetables, the standard heat processing is done at boiling water temperatures (100°C). Non-acidic vegetables, such as most non-tomato and non-rhubarb varieties, require processing at higher temperatures, generally between 115°C and 121°C, under pressure, to ensure proper preservation.

- **Sterilization:** Sterilization is a more intense heat treatment applied to food after it is packaged in a hermetically sealed container. The main goal of this process is to destroy both spoilage and pathogenic microorganisms to ensure the food's safety and shelf life. For acid and medium-acid foods (with a pH less than 4.5), the focus is on destroying heat-resistant vegetative microorganisms or enzymes.

  For low-acid foods, such as mushrooms, potatoes, peas, and other vegetables, sterilization is typically carried out at elevated temperatures between 115°C and 121°C to effectively inactivate microorganisms. On the other hand, acid foods, including peaches, pears, pineapples, and other fruits, are usually processed at 100°C or lower to adequately deactivate enzymes while preserving the food's quality.

COOLING PROCESS

Cooling is the process of removing heat energy added during food processing. This operation is crucial to lower the temperature of the food, which can range from chilling it to refrigerated temperatures or further cooling for freezing. In milk processing, cooling is typically achieved by passing the milk through heat exchangers or coolers, where cold water or refrigerants are pumped to absorb the heat.

Fruits like apple slices, berries, and cherries are often frozen to preserve their quality. Thawing of frozen foods can be done through heating or disintegration methods.

For freezing vegetables like peas, beans, and mushrooms, air blast freezers are used. These devices individually freeze the items to maintain quality. In the case of canned or packaged foods, freezing may be done by immersing the food in refrigerants to rapidly lower the temperature and prevent the formation of large ice crystals that could damage the food's texture.

Evaporation

Evaporation in the food industry is mainly used to concentrate liquids by removing water. This is achieved by boiling the liquid at lower temperatures under reduced pressure, which helps preserve the food's flavor, color, and nutrients while efficiently removing water. Vacuum evaporators are commonly used for this purpose, as they lower the boiling point, allowing water to be removed without applying excessive heat. Multi-stage evaporators further enhance the efficiency of this process by using several stages of evaporation, where the vapor from one stage is used to heat the next, making the process more energy-efficient. These techniques are widely used in the production of concentrated juices, milk powders, soups, sauces, and other liquid food products.

Drying Process

Drying is a process that removes water from food products, bringing the moisture content to around 97-98% solids while minimizing any damage to the food's texture, flavor, and nutritional value. While evaporators primarily concentrate foods by removing 2-3 times the amount of water, dryers take this process further, reaching nearly complete dryness. These dryers are essential for producing well-known products like milk powder and instant coffee.

The spray dryer is one of the most common methods for drying liquids. It atomizes the liquid into fine droplets using a nozzle, and then hot air is passed through to quickly dry the particles. Other methods of drying include sun and solar drying, atmospheric dehydration (kiln, tower, and cabinet dryers), and continuous processes like tunnel, continuous belt, fluidized-bed, and microwave-heated dryers. Vacuum dryers (shelf, belt, drum) and freeze dryers are also used for drying and dehydrating food products, particularly when preserving the food's quality is critical.

Before drying, fruits are often pretreated to maintain color, texture, and quality. This can involve sulfur fumigation or dipping them in a potassium metabisulphite solution to prevent oxidation and preserve their integrity during the drying process.

Extrusion

Extrusion cooking is a vital unit operation in industries like breakfast cereals and snack foods, where it plays a key role in shaping products such as cereals and snacks. The process involves the use of high pressure and temperature to force dough or batter through a die, creating characteristic shapes and textures. The dough consistency, pressure, temperature, and other variables are carefully controlled to achieve the desired outcome, such as puffed or flaked cereals.

This type of forming is not limited to cereals; it also includes shaping other food products like butter, snack bars, and cheese curd. For example, cheese curds are pressed into various shapes, bread dough is formed into loaves or rolls, and sausages are shaped through the extrusion process. The versatility of extrusion cooking allows for a wide range of product textures and forms, making it a cornerstone technique in the food processing industry.

FOOD PACKAGING

Food packaging is a critical step in preserving the quality and safety of food products. It serves to protect food from contamination by microorganisms, dirt, dust, light, moisture, and other environmental factors that could cause spoilage or degradation. Various materials such as metal cans, glass, plastic bottles, paper, metallic films, and pouches are commonly used for packaging, each offering different protective qualities depending on the type of food.

In modern food processing, automatic packaging systems have become increasingly prevalent. These systems are designed to form, fill, and seal containers automatically, streamlining the packaging process. The convenience of these systems extends to easy-to-open and dispose-of packages, making them consumer-friendly. Additionally, newer packaging technologies offer benefits like space-saving during food processing, transportation, and marketing.

The packaging process can be adapted to different scales of production, from batch processing to semi-continuous or fully automatic continuous processes. The choice of process depends on the available resources and the specific needs of the food product being processed, ensuring efficiency and sustainability across the food industry.

2

Cleaning and Grading of Agricultural Commodities

Fruits and vegetables are more perishable and generally have a higher value compared to cereals, making them very important in terms of minimizing waste and improving employability in the food industry. The losses in fruits and vegetables are significant, but through effective post-harvest processing, these losses can be reduced, and surplus produce can be better utilized. This processing involves a variety of techniques that prepare fruits and vegetables for conversion into processed foods. The food preservation and processing industry has evolved from being a luxury to an essential sector, playing a crucial role in conserving and enhancing the utilization of fruits and vegetables.

To prevent waste during peak seasons and ensure availability during off-seasons, modern methods of storage and processing are necessary. These techniques allow for both large-scale and small-scale processing, extending the shelf life of produce for better distribution. The ultimate goal of food processing is to apply systematic techniques to preserve, process, package, store, and distribute food in a way that ensures a steady supply of diverse and nutritious food options, thereby improving food intake and nutritional standards, particularly during periods of low availability.

For effective preservation and processing, key prerequisites include cleaning, grading, and sorting the produce based on its maturity level. This ensures that only the highest quality fruits and vegetables are used in the processing chain, maintaining food safety, nutritional value, and consumer acceptability throughout the year.

CLEANING OF AGRICULTURAL COMMODITIES

Blanching is a unit operation used in food processing to remove contaminating materials from food and prepare the surface for further processing. In vegetable processing, blanching serves the additional purpose of cleaning the product. This process involves briefly exposing the food to heat, typically by immersing it in hot water or steam, which helps to remove dirt, enzymes, and microbial contamination. By doing so, blanching not only improves the quality of the food but also prevents microbial growth during storage or delays in processing. This early removal of contaminants ensures that the remaining bulk of food is preserved and remains safe for consumption throughout its shelf life.

Grain Cleaning

Grain cleaning is a crucial process aimed at removing impurities such as dirt, rocks, sticks, and broken grains from freshly harvested crops. This process significantly enhances the quality, market value, and longevity of the grains during storage. By eliminating contaminants, grain cleaning helps to prevent spoilage, reduce the risk of mold and pests, and preserve the nutritional value of the grains. It also reduces the chances of infestations, which can lead to financial losses. The cleaning process usually involves mechanical techniques such as screening, aspiration, and magnetic separation. In more advanced applications, optical sorting technology is employed to accurately and efficiently remove unwanted materials, reducing the need for manual labor while increasing the overall effectiveness and speed of cleaning.

- **Dry cleaning:** Dry cleaning methods are typically used for products that are smaller, have greater mechanical strength, and possess lower moisture content, such as grains and nuts. These procedures help ensure that the surfaces of the food remain dry, which helps in preservation and prepares them for further drying or storage. The primary types of equipment used for dry cleaning include:
- **Wet cleaning**: Wet cleaning is a more effective method for removing soil, dust, and pesticide residues from root crops and soft fruits or vegetables. This method involves the use of water or other cleaning solutions to remove contaminants from the surface of the food. Unlike dry cleaning methods, wet cleaning is dustless, which makes it cleaner and more efficient. Additionally, wet cleaning causes less damage to delicate foods, such as fruits and vegetables, as it is gentler compared to abrasive dry methods. This process helps to ensure that the food is clean and safe for further processing or consumption while maintaining its quality.
- **Separators based on screening:** These machines use screens or meshes with different hole sizes to separate food products based on their size. This method helps in removing broken, damaged, or undersized particles from the main product.
- **Magnetic separators:** These are used to remove metallic impurities, such as iron or steel particles, from the food product. This ensures that the food is free from harmful contaminants that could pose risks to both consumers and processing equipment.
- **Air classifiers:** These devices use air streams to separate particles based on their size, shape, and weight. Lighter particles, such as dust or chaff, are separated from the food product, improving the cleanliness of the materials.

These dry cleaning methods are essential for maintaining food quality and safety, particularly for products like grains and nuts that need to remain dry to prevent spoilage and ensure effective storage.

- **Removing contaminants and foreign bodies:** Physical separation of contaminants from food is most effective when the food items have a regular, well-defined shape. For example, round foods can be separated from contaminants using their ability to roll. This can be achieved by placing the food on inclined or upward-moving conveyor belts. The round shape allows the food to roll smoothly, while irregularly shaped contaminants may not follow the same path, making it easier to separate them.This method is commonly used for sorting products like tomatoes, apples, or other spherical foods, where the consistent shape of the food can be leveraged to achieve separation. Other mechanical methods, such as vibrating screens or air blasts, can also be used in combination to further enhance the cleaning process.

PROCESS OF SORTING

Sorting is a critical process in food processing where products are categorized based on measurable physical properties to ensure uniformity for subsequent processing. The four main properties used for sorting foods are:

- **Size:** Foods are sorted by their size to ensure consistent processing. For example, grains or fruits may be sorted by diameter or length to standardize their treatment.
- **Shape:** Products with irregular shapes can be separated from those with more uniform forms. This is particularly important in products like vegetables or fruits where shape consistency is crucial for packaging or further processing.
- **Weight:** Sorting by weight allows for separation based on mass, which is important for products like nuts or packaged goods to ensure uniform portion sizes and packaging.
- **Color:** Color sorting is used to remove products that are overripe, under-ripe, or damaged. It's commonly employed in fruit and vegetable processing, where color is an indicator of ripeness and quality.

Employing sorting techniques early in the process helps ensure that the food items meet quality standards and are ready for the next steps in processing, leading to a more efficient and uniform final product.

- **Shape and size sorting:** Size sorting is a process which is used to separate solids into different fractions based on their particle size. The particle size distribution of a material is typically expressed either as the mass fraction of the material that is retained on each sieve or as the cumulative percentage of material that is retained. This allows for the classification of materials into different size groups, which can then be further processed or used for specific applications.

In size sorting, materials are passed through a series of sieves with progressively smaller openings. Larger particles are retained on the coarser sieves, while smaller particles pass through to the finer sieves. The sorted fractions are then collected and analyzed based on their size. This method is widely used in industries such as food processing, mining, and pharmaceuticals, where uniformity in particle size is crucial for consistent product quality or efficient further processing.

- **Color sorting:** Microprocessor-controlled color sorting equipment is an advanced method for sorting small particulate foods based on their color, shape, and size. In this system, particles are fed into a chute one at a time, where their velocity is controlled by adjusting the angle, shape, and lining material of the chute. As the particles move along the chute, they pass through photo detectors that measure the reflected color of each piece.The photo detectors compare the reflected color with preset standards to identify any defects in the food items, such as discoloration or foreign materials. If a defect is detected, a short burst of compressed air is used to separate the defective particles from the acceptable ones. This process allows for high-speed sorting, ensuring that only high-quality, uniformly colored products are passed on for further processing, while defective items are efficiently removed. This technology is widely used in the food industry to ensure product quality and improve sorting accuracy, especially for products like fruits, vegetables, and snack foods.

- **Weight sorting**: Weight sorting is a precise method for separating foods based on their weight, which makes it especially useful for more valuable food products. This technique ensures that the food items are sorted into accurate weight categories, leading to consistent product quality and uniformity. Weight sorting can be highly beneficial for high-end products where even slight variations in weight can affect the final product's quality, such as in certain packaged foods or premium products like nuts or dried fruits.

Aspiration and flotation sorting, on the other hand, depend on differences in density to separate food items. In aspiration sorting, air is used to blow away lighter particles, while heavier particles fall and are collected. Similarly, flotation sorting utilizes liquids or air to separate materials based on their buoyancy, allowing lighter contaminants to float while denser food particles sink.

Both aspiration and flotation sorting are similar in principle and operation to aspiration and flotation cleaning, as they take advantage of the physical properties of the food or contaminants to facilitate separation. These methods are especially useful when dealing with food items that may have light or irregularly shaped contaminants, helping to maintain food purity while minimizing the risk of damage to the products.

GRADING

Grading is also known as "sorting"but it specifically refers to evaluating the overall quality of food based on several attributes. Grading is typically performed by machines or trained operators who assess multiple factors simultaneously.

- Grading is the process of sorting agricultural produce into different categories based on their specific quality standards.
- This practice helps farmers adhere to quality specifications for their products, preventing exploitation by traders and ensuring they receive a fair price.
- Since graded products follow defined standards, there is little room for consumer deception. Grading benefits both farmers and consumers, safeguarding consumers from fraudulent practices.

Grain Grading Ensuring Uniformity and Quality

Grain grading is the process of evaluating crop quality and categorizing grains based on their size, weight, and degree of damage. This process is essential for determining the market value of the crops and maintaining quality consistency. Graded grain of higher quality generally commands better prices in the market, boosting profitability for agricultural businesses. Grading typically involves sorting grains by size, shape, and density, but it can also assess factors like moisture content, protein levels, and other nutritional attributes that impact the overall quality. While grading can be done manually, advanced technologies such as color sorting, image recognition, and computer algorithms facilitate faster and more precise grading.

Establishing Criteria for grade standards

Agricultural produces are graded according to the standardized grade specification. The quality specification parameters considered to grade the agricultural produce are known as standardized grade specifications.

Standardised grade specification of agricultural produce is the main source for classifying other respective products.

Standardization of grade specification

Grade specification considered for grading the agricultural produce need to be standardized. If these specifications are same from one place to other place and one period to anther period and also if it is acceptable by both buyers and sellers only then its called standardized grade specification. Standardised grade specifications can be classified as regional and national specifications.

Significance of Grading

- There is no doubt in obtaining a good price for the quality agricultural produce because of grading.
- Grading of agricultural produce is a benefit for farmers, traders and consumers of Agricultural Marketing System and even it is benefited to whole country.
- Farmers benefit from grading as they obtain proper price for their produce based on its quality, marketing of the produce will become easy for the traders and consumers to obtain a quality product for the spent money.
- Graded agricultural produce will create more and competitive demand for a good quality produce in the international markets and also its useful in earning foreign exchange which in turn is a inspiration for the country is development.

Various Levels of Grading

Grading of agricultural produce is done at different levels these include

- Grading for exports
- Grading for domestic purpose
- Grading at producer's level

Grading for Exports

Among the agricultural produces in India, the spices have huge demand in the International market.

As there will be more countries participating in the international market, there are more chances for Indian products to have lot of demand and also can earn more foreign exchange by obtaining a competitive price for the produce. This can be achieved by grading the exportable agricultural produce according the AGMARK standards of Export Quality Contol and Inspection order 1963.

This kind of grading done for exporting the produce is known as grading for exports.

Grading for domestic purpose

Grading of agricultural produce for export is mandatory where as for domestic purpose it is optional.

In order to retain the quality of the produce and welfare of the consumers has made the grading process necessary to such products according to the AGMARK Standards.

Since this grading is done for the welfare of the consumers it is optional and not mandatory.

Grading at producer's level

Farmers usually do not obtain the profits derived from grading the agricultural produce. In this regard, during the 3rd Five year plan, from 1963, a scheme was implemented for grading at producer's level with a purpose that the profits should reach the farmers directly.

Grading at producer's level were categorized into three sub levels and are followed below:

- Grading at farm level
- Grading at the Co-operative institutions
- Grading at the regulated markets

Advantages of Grain Cleaning and Grading

Grain cleaning and grading are essential to maintaining crop quality, extending storage life, boosting profitability, and minimizing waste. Properly cleaned and graded grain ensures consumer safety, increases the market value of crops, and supports sustainable agricultural practices. By adopting advanced grain cleaning and grading technologies, agricultural businesses can enhance productivity, reduce labor costs, and ensure consistent quality across their products. These technologies also help reduce the risk of contamination, pests, and infestations, contributing to overall food safety and efficiency.

Importance of Grain Cleaning and Grading

Grain cleaning and grading are important for agricultural businesses to maintain crop quality and consistency. Advanced technologies have transformed these processes, promoting sustainability and enhancing production efficiency. By investing in such technologies, agricultural businesses can optimize operations, minimize waste, and boost profitability while ensuring the production of safe, nutritious crops. In conclusion, grain cleaning and grading are vital for high-quality crop production. Technologies like optical sorting, color sorting, and computer algorithms help reduce contamination and pest risks while ensuring consistent quality. Agricultural businesses that prioritize these technologies can increase efficiency, reduce waste, and support healthy crop production, contributing to the sustainability and safety of the food system.

OPERATION AND MAINTENANCE OF DIFFERENT CLEANERS

Processing involve three steps that are mentioned below:

Step 1

- Pre- conditioning and pre- cleaning
- **Pre- conditioning:** Isolation of seed from plant parts with which it was harvested e.g. Shelling
- **Pre- cleaning :** Removal of external materials like trash, stones, clods which are either in larger size or lighter in weight. No pre- cleaning is required for hand harvested and winnowed seeds
- The machineries involved in this operation are:

Scalper

This process removes larger inert materials from the seeds. If it uses a single sieve, it is referred to as a scalper, and if it uses two sieves, it is called a rough cleaner. The unit typically consists of a vibrating or rotating screen or sieve with perforations large enough to allow the rough seeds to pass through easily.

Figure.: 2.1 Seed Scalper

Debearders

The machine features a horizontal beater with arms rotating inside a steel drum. As the seeds pass through, the beater rubs and clips the seeds, effectively removing husks, beards, and awns. It is used to thresh oats, debeard barley, thresh white caps in wheat, and de-hull certain grass seeds. Additionally, it helps in polishing the seeds.

Figure.: 2.2 Debearders

Huller scarifier

Have two rubber faced rough surfaces to rub the seeds. Dehulling (removal of outer coat or husk) and scarifier (scratching the seed coat) can be done simultaneously or separately.

Maize sheller

- High capacity power operated shellers - bulk
- Hand shellers – breeder or nucleus seed.

Step 2

Cleaning

The second stage of cleaning is carried out with air blasts and vibrating screens and is applicable to all kinds of seeds. It is Primarily the same as scalping but more refined. It is performed mostly by one machine known as air-screen cleaner.

Air-Screen Cleaner Cum Grader

The air-screen machine is a fundamental cleaning device in most seed processing plants, and it is typically the first step before meeting specific seed specifications. These machines come in various sizes, ranging from small, two-screen models used on farms, in breeder programs, or by experimental stations for small quantities, to larger industrial models with 7-8 screens.

The air-screen machine separates seeds based on differences in size and weight, making it more versatile than machines that rely on just one physical characteristic. It operates with three cleaning elements: an aspirator to remove light material from the seed mass, a scalper to drop good seeds through screen openings while larger debris is carried over the screen into a separate spout, and a grader to separate good seeds, which pass over the screen, from smaller particles that drop through.

Figure.: 2.3 Air screen cleaner

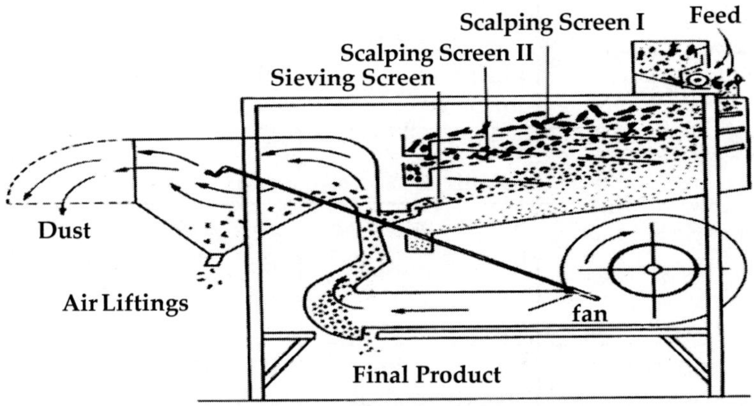

Figure.: 2.4 Gum glader

Step 3

Cleaning and Grading

To ensure the production of quality seed, it is crucial to clean the harvested seeds by removing impurities such as inert materials, weed seeds, other crop seeds, seeds from different varieties, and damaged or deteriorated seeds. Various seeds can be separated based on one or more physical characteristics. Common properties used to distinguish and separate seeds include size, shape, length, weight, color, surface texture, affinity for liquids, and electrical conductivity. The challenge, however, is to identify the most relevant property for separation and selecting the appropriate machinery that effectively utilizes this characteristic for optimal seed cleaning. Some of the identified properties and machines operating by following the properties are listed below:

Table.: 2.1 Identified properties and uses of machine operating

Name of the Separator	Property followed	Uses
Vibratory separator	Shape and surface texture	Removal of weed seeds
Spiral separator	Shape or the degree of its ability to roll	Separation of damaged/flat and wrinkled seeds from smooth seeds. Separation of mustard, rape, soybean and peas from wheat, flax, oats, etc., and round seeds from flat seeds.
Disk / Indented cylinder separator	Length	Dissimilar material like wheat, rye, mustard, barley from oats

Name of the Separator	Property followed	Uses
Electrostatic separator	Electrical property	Johnson grass from sesame seed
Electronic colour sorters	Colour / brightness	Separation of off coloured seeds
Inclined draper	Shape and surface texture	Separation of smooth or round seeds from rough flat or elongated seeds
Magnetic separator	Surface texture and stickiness	Removal of contaminating weed seed from clovers, alfalfa seeds and iron metals
Roll mill	Shape and surface texture	Separation of smooth clover seed
Gravity separator or Destoner	Density or specific gravity	Removal of badly damaged, deteriorated, insect damaged crop seed and stones from good seeds.

Upgrading

Seed lots require further cleaning treatment to remove adulterants that are similar to pure seed in size and shape, to be separated by air screen cleaner. Removal of seeds larger or smaller than required size (sizing) and removal of cracked, damaged or otherwise defective seeds (grading) is accomplished in this final stage of processing.

SPECIFIC GRAVITY SEPARATION

This method utilizes a combination of weight and surface characteristics to separate seeds based on their density. The principle of flotation is employed in this process. A mixture of seeds is introduced at the lower end of a sloping, perforated table, where air is forced upward through the deck by a fan. This stratifies the seeds into layers based on their density, with the lightest seeds and inert particles positioned at the top and the heaviest seeds at the bottom. The table oscillates, causing the seeds to move at varying rates across the deck. The lightest seeds float down under gravity and are discharged at the lower end, while the heavier seeds are pushed up the slope by the oscillating motion and are discharged at the upper end. This separation process is effective for sorting seeds of similar size but different densities, as well as seeds of the same density but different sizes.

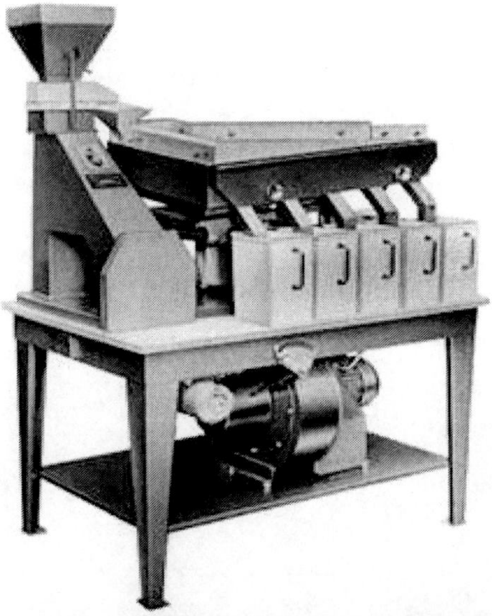

Figure.: 2.5 Specific gravity separator

INDENTED CYLINDER

This method separates seeds based on their length. The equipment consists of a slightly inclined, horizontally rotating cylinder and a movable separating trough. The interior surface of the cylinder is equipped with closely spaced, small hemispherical indentations. When the seeds enter the rotating cylinder, small seeds are pressed into these indentations due to centrifugal force, allowing them to be removed. Larger seeds, which do not fit into the indentations, flow toward the center of the cylinder and are discharged by gravity. This process efficiently sorts seeds by their length.

Magnetic separator

The magnetic separator sorts seeds based on their surface texture or related characteristics. Initially, seeds are treated with iron filings, which adhere only to those with a rough surface. The treated seed batch is then passed over a revolving magnetic drum, where the rough-surfaced seeds are attracted to the magnet and separated from the smooth, uncoated seeds. The addition of varying amounts of water during the mixing of the seeds and powder can enhance the process, depending on the seed type. The effectiveness of magnetic separation is greater when there is a significant difference in surface texture among the seed components.

Figure.: 2.6 Magnetic Separator

PRINCIPLE OF FUNCTION

Colour separator

The color separator is used to remove discolored seeds, which are typically of lower quality. Since the density and size of discolored seeds are often similar to those of healthy seeds, other separation methods are ineffective. Electronic color separation uses photocells to compare the seed color with a predetermined "background," which is selected to match the light reflection of good seeds. When the seed color differs from the background, the photocells detect the difference and generate an electric impulse. This impulse triggers an air jet, which blows away the discolored seeds.

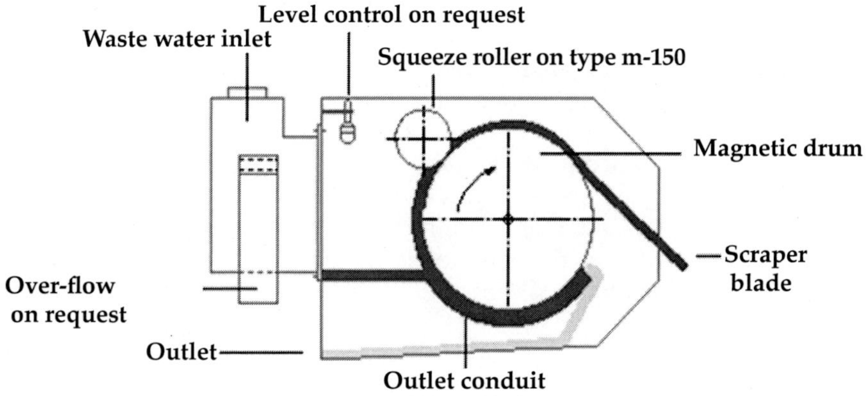

Figure.: 2.7 Colour separator

Separating Seed by Color

The color sorter uses an electronic eye that detects different colors based on machine settings. As the seeds fall through a chute, they pass in front of the electric eye. If the color of a seed does not match from the desired color, the eye triggers a burst of air that directs the discolored seed into a reject bin, while the remaining seeds continue to the collection bin.

Figure.: 2.8 Separating seed by color

Friction cleaning

Air-screen combinations are not effective at removing debris that has a similar size and density to the seeds. However, if the debris has a different surface texture, it can be separated using friction cleaning. In this process, objects that roll or slide over a sloping surface experience friction based on their texture and the texture of the surface. The separation occurs on a velvet cloth or rubber belt with adjustable inclination, ensuring that the slope required for the seeds to run off differs from that needed for the debris. As the belt moves upward, the debris is removed, while the seeds roll downward.

Spiral separator

The separator that classifies seeds based on shape and rolling ability consists of sheet metal strips arranged in a spiral around a central axis, resembling an open screw conveyor placed vertically. The seeds are introduced at the top of the inner spiral. Round seeds roll faster down the incline compared to flat or irregularly shaped seeds, which tend to slide or tumble. As round seeds gain speed, they orbit around the axis and eventually roll over the edge of the inner flight into the outer flight, where they are collected separately. Slower-moving seeds do not gain enough speed to escape the inner flight. Many spirals feature multiple inner flights stacked above one another to enhance the capacity.

Figure.: 2.9 Spiral separator

Liquid flotation

Cleaning by flotation relies on the principle that the density of the seed of a given species is specific both for filled and ill filled seed. In this method, liquids with a density or specific gravity between that of the full and empty seed are used. The specific gravity of the liquids used is such that the full seed sinks and the empty seed and light debris float.

OPERATION AND MAINTENANCE OF GRADERS

Grading Machinery

Grading size and quality is vital for marketing fruits and vegetables. Sizing machines are generally categorized into two types: those that grade based on diameter and those that grade by weight. Machines that grade by diameter come in various designs and sizes, offering higher output than those grading by weight. Roller feed conveyors are commonly used for quality sorting of fruits and vegetables. A well-designed weight grader has multiple benefits—it is adaptable to different shapes, easy to adjust, and suitable for crops prone to blemishes. Grading by weight tends to be more accurate than grading by diameter.

Grading involves the quality separation of food products, with the term 'quality' having different meanings depending on the commodity and the significance of its material properties. Essentially, grading involves a comprehensive assessment of all attributes that impact a product's acceptance both as food and as a raw material for further processing. Almost every grading methods assess multiple properties simultaneously, making mechanical grading more complex, which is why manual grading is often preferred. The separation typically occurs based on size, shape, and color to categorize products into different quality grades.

- **Grading method:** In general the properties of food product which determine its quality may be shape, size, maturity, texture, flavour, and colour and contaminants. Grading may be done manually or with the help of specialized machines, which are discussed below:
- **Manual grading**: Grading of fruits, vegetables, eggs, and similar food products is primarily carried out manually. The grader makes a holistic judgment based on the overall quality and physically separates the food into various quality categories. For example, apples may be graded using color cards that assess characteristics like the proportion of the surface displaying the correct fruit color, rusting, and surface imperfections. Cherries are graded by comparing them to plastic models, while eggs are manually graded by a process called candling. This non-destructive method involves spinning the egg in front of a strong light in a dark room, allowing the grader to assess the egg's quality. Candling enables the operator to grade thousands of eggs per hour into 3 to 4 categories.

While manual grading remains widespread, especially in India for fruits like mangoes, oranges, and kinnow, it does have its drawbacks. The process is labor-intensive, requiring a significant amount of manpower, making it less efficient compared to automated methods. Nonetheless, manual grading is still preferred in many cases due to its effectiveness in assessing the subtle qualities of food products.

- **Machine grading:** Grading machines are available for cereals and fruits and vegetables separately. Machine grading for cereals is of two types viz. rotary screen grain cleaner and grader and spiral separator.
- **Grading machines for fruits and vegetables:** There are four types of grading machines for fruits and vegetables. They are screens, roller grader, and diverging belt grader and weight grader.
- **Screens**: A variety of fruits and vegetables are graded using vibrating screens made of materials like copper, stainless steel, or plastic, which do not react chemically with the products. The material to be graded is passed over a vibrating or rotary screen that is perforated to allow the smallest material to pass through first, followed by medium-sized and then the largest material. This method effectively sorts fruits such as apples, oranges, and kinnow, as well as vegetables like potatoes and tomatoes, into different grades. The material that passes through the top of the screen can be rescreened to further separate new fractions, ensuring accurate and efficient grading.

Roller graders are fast, accurate, and cause minimum amount of damage to fruit, making them extensively used in the fruit industry. In these machines, each roller rotates counterclockwise, ensuring that each fruit registers its minimum dimension with the available space. Fixed spacing between the rolls is used to remove small fruit, twigs, and leaves.

The diverging belt grader is widely used and consists of two belts that gradually increase the distance between them. As the fruit moves along the belts, smaller pieces fall through the widening gap earlier, while larger pieces travel further and fall later.

Weight graders are accurate, quick, and reduces the damage to fruits and vegetables. They are used for large-size products like apples, oranges, mangoes, potatoes, tomatoes, and eggs. The product is placed in individual cups, and as the cups pass through the sorter, they are indexed by spring-loaded trips. The tension of the springs weakens progressively, ensuring heavier fractions discharge first, followed by lighter fractions.

The expanding pitch rubber spool potato sizer uses two driving rollers with helical grooves to move rods with rubber spools. The progressive increase in pitch allows for various grades of potatoes to be obtained. The system is designed to support parallel running driving helixes and an endless sizing conveyor, with an adjustable collecting platform to suit different potato grades. It can grade 2-3 tonnes of potatoes per hour with minimal mechanical damage to the tubers.

Figure.: 2.10 Expanding pitch rubber spool potato sizer

Root Crop Combines : Mechanized Harvesting for Efficiency

Self-propelled potato combines are commercial machines designed for efficient potato harvesting. These machines are equipped with a pointed blade that splits the ridge, an elevator conveyor to lift and shake off the soil, and agitator sprockets to provide sufficient agitation to the material being conveyed. The rotary cage wheel elevates and cleans the tubers, while a bagging platform ensures the potatoes are filled into bags after cleaning. This machine can harvest, separate, clean, and bag potatoes in a single operation, covering about 0.6 hectares per day.

However, the losses associated with this machine can be significant, ranging from 15-20% or even higher in some cases. Factors influencing these losses include soil moisture and type. Potatoes harvested from soil with lower moisture content tend to suffer less damage than those harvested in higher moisture conditions. Additionally, potatoes harvested from sandy loam soil generally experience less damage compared to those harvested from heavier soils.

SEED PROCESSING EQUIPMENTS

Air screen cleaner

This machine is the most important component in every cleaning plant. It utilizes screens and aspiration (air blow) to achieve two types of separation. A coarse upper screen eliminates larger material, while a fine lower screen retains the seeds and allows finer matter to pass through. The seed fraction is then subjected to a transverse or nearly vertical air stream that eradicates light impurities like empty or partly filled seeds, husks, and glumes. Typically, a series of sieves with different sized perforations is used, and the cleaning process involves progressively removing smaller particles. Key factors that influence the quality and quantity of cleaned seeds include: (i) the size of the perforations, (ii) the precision of the perforations, (iii) the angle at which the sieves operate, (iv) the amplitude and speed of sieve movement, and (v) proper cleaning and maintenance of the equipment.

Cleaner cum grader

The dried seeds should be cleaned and graded with help of a cleaner cum grader.

It consists of the following parts:

- A hopper in the top for seed filling
- A flutted roller below the hopper to regulate the seed flow to the screen
- Screen (or) sieves: Perforated metal sheet with specific size of perforation in which there are two types
- Rectangular perforations for paddy
- Round perforations for seed other than paddy
- Screen shaking unit for oscillating the sieves to move the seeds on the screens
- Screen brushes to remove the blocked seeds
- Air blower with adjustments for air outlet
- Collecting outlet
- Air duct for directing the blown up light particles to outside
- Collecting bins

Working Principle

The seeds are first fed into the hopper and directed on to the initial sieve. This first sieve is a scalping screen that removes foreign materials larger and heavier than the seeds, allowing the entire seed quantity to pass through. The second sieve is a cleaning sieve, which eliminates unwanted particles larger than the seeds. The third sieve, callled the grading sieve, sorts the seed lot by size, ensuring uniformity, while also screening out undersized, shriveled, and immature seeds, as well as dust and dirt. Finally, the seeds are rolled and passed through an air column, where light chaff and other materials are removed by the blowing air.

Adjustments Flutted roller

The speed of this roller can be adjusted so as to increase (or) decrease the flow of seeds to the hopper of the sieves.

- Slope (or) inclination of the screen

The angle of inclination of the screens can be adjusted according to the nature of seeds.

- Rate of vibration of sieve

This can be adjusted either to increase or to decrease the speed of the rolling seeds on the screen.

- **Volume of air flow:** By increasing (or) decreasing the air inlet.
- **Choice of screens**: According to variety we have to change the screen
- Screen dams

Small check dams, which can be provided here and there on the screens so that the seeds can be stopped a while and takes the charge either to pass or to roll.

Types of seed cleaner cum grade

- Crippen model cleaner cum grader
- Clipper model cleaner cum grader
- Petkas cleaner cum grader

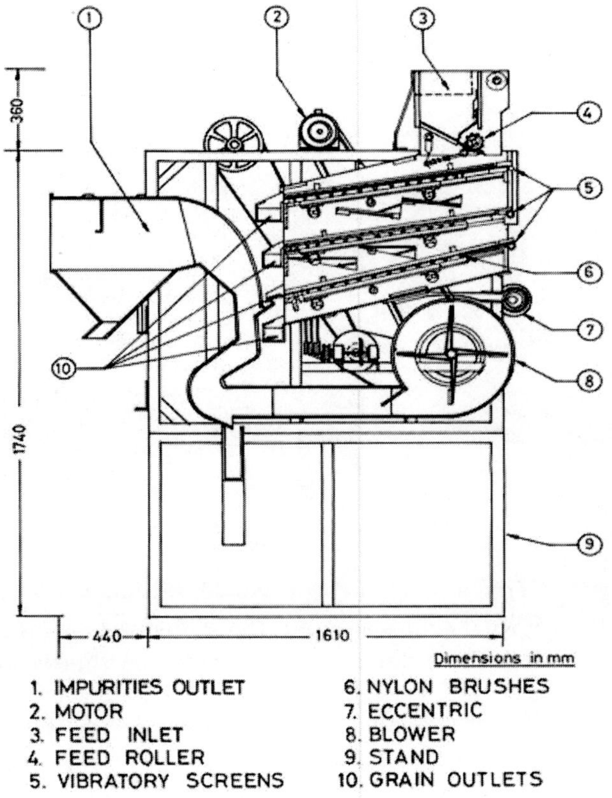

Figure.: 2.11 Adjustments Flutted roller

Disc Separator

The machine consists of a series of discs that rotate together on a horizontal shaft inside a cylindrical body. Each disc has multiple undercut pockets. Seeds enter the intake end of the separator and move through the open centers of the discs towards the discharge end. As the discs rotate through the seed mass, the pockets lift out short seeds, while rejecting longer seeds. The longer seeds are moved by flights attached to the disc spokes towards the discharge end, where they exit through the tailings gate. The rate at which seeds travel through the open centers of the discs is controlled by a conveyor or blades connected to the spokes. The disc separator provides precise separation, with seed length and shape being the only factors influencing the separation. Flexibility is achieved by adjusting the size of the pockets.

Indented Cylinder Separator

The indented cylinder separator consists of a rotating, nearly horizontal cylinder with adjustable, horizontal separating mechanisms mounted inside it. The interior surface of the cylinder features indentations. As the cylinder rotates, the seed mass is turned, allowing each seed a chance to fit into the indentations. Short seeds are lifted out of the mass and dropped into the lifting mechanism, whereas longer seeds remain in the cylinder and are discharged through a separate spout at the end

Figure.: 2.12 Indented cylinder separator

As the cylinder rotates, centrifugal force helps hold the seeds in the indentations. Short seeds remain in the indent until the cylinder rotates to a point where the indent is inverted enough for gravity to release the seed. The size, shape, and surface texture of the seeds determine how they fit into the indent, allowing them to be lifted out of the seed mass. The cylinder's speed generates centrifugal force, which holds the seeds in the indent as they are lifted. Consequently, the shape and size of the seeds cause some to fall out after being lifted only a short distance, while others are lifted higher before falling out.

Figure.: 2.13 Working principle of the indented cylinder separator

As the seeds enter the cylinder, the small, short, easy to separate seeds are quickly removed. The center cylinder section removes the intermediate sizes of seeds still in the cylinder. All indents in a cylinder are the same size, only the progressively declining amount of material to be lifted causes this difference in separating action.

Adjustments

- Cylinder speed
- Size of the indent
- Trough setting
- Tilt of the cylinder
- Adjustable retarder.

Specific Gravity Separator

Seeds of the same size and general shape can often be separated because they differ in specific gravity or relative weight. This difference is very useful in removing light, immature seeds or heavy sand and rocks to improve the purity and germination of crop seeds.

Figure.: 2.14 V. Specific gravity separator

Lab Model

If seeds which differ in specific gravity (relative weight / unit of volume) are placed on substrate of intermediate density, seeds of higher specific gravity will fall down through the substrata, while seeds of lower specific gravity will be buoyed up the substrata. Here air is used as separation substrata.

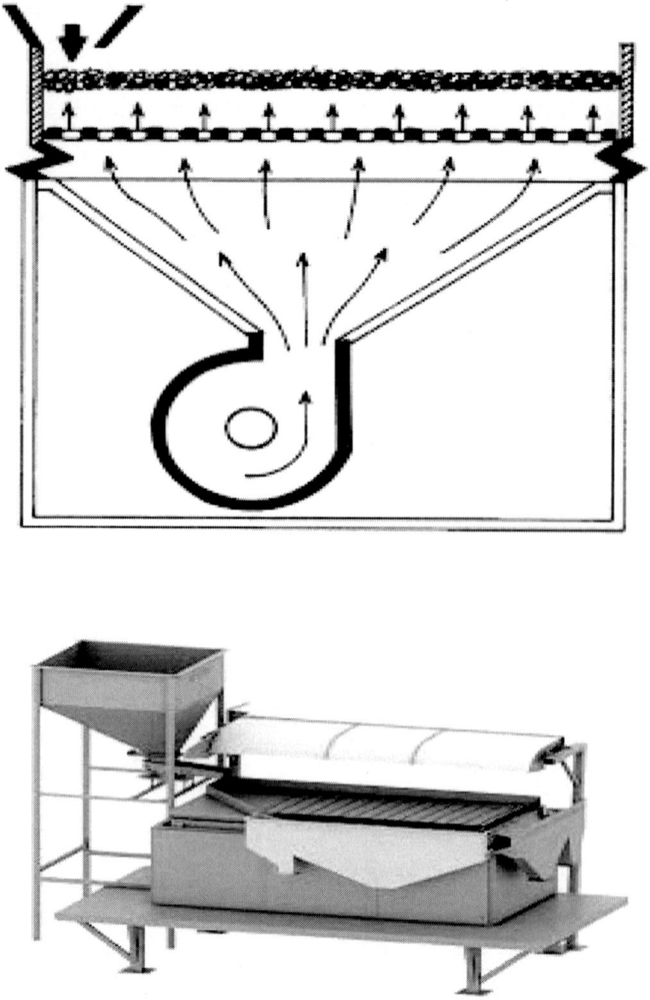

Figure.: 2.15 Separation substrata

Operating principle of the specific gravity separator

As seeds move across the deck of the gravity separator, they pass through an upward air column rising from the porous deck surface. The air pressure and the terminal velocity of the rising air can be precisely controlled to separate seeds based on specific gravity. The air is adjusted so that only the lighter seeds are lifted off the deck, which cause them to float. Heavier seeds, having a velocity greater than the air, remains on the deck surface. This process results in the stratification of the seed mixture into vertical zones, with the heavier seeds at the bottom and the lighter seeds elevated at the top of the seed mass.

Adjustments

- Feed rate
- Air flow
- End slope
- Side slope
- Deck oscillation speed
- Deck speed.

ROLL MILL /DODDER MILL / VELVET ROLL MILL

This separator is designed to separate seeds based on their surface texture and shape. It should only be used after the seeds have been thoroughly cleaned and separated from the chaff. The separator is particularly effective in distinguishing seeds with rough seed coats or angular shapes from those with smooth surfaces.

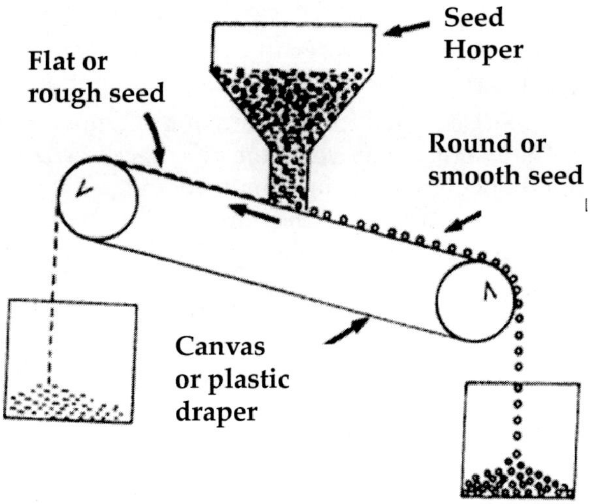

Figure.: 2.16 Seed coats or angular shapes from those with smooth surfaces

Working Principle of the Roll Mill

The roll mill consists basically of two roller, covered with flannel or velvet, placed side by side, so that they touch each other down their entire length. The rollers are mounted on an incline and they turn in opposite directions. A curved adjustable shield is mounted above the rollers.

Separating action

The mixture of smooth and rough seeds is fed into the machine at the high end, where the rollers touch each other. As the rollers rotate, seeds with rough surfaces or sharp edges are caught by the fabric covering the rollers. These seeds are then propelled upwards and strike the curved shield at an angle, causing them to bounce back down to the roller and strike the shield again. In contrast, smooth seeds are unaffected by the fabric roller covering, and they simply bounce down the inclined surface, moving forward between the rollers and discharging at the lower end of the machine.

- Adjustments
- Rate of feed
- Speed
- Clearance between shield and rolls
- The angle of inclination of rolls.

Understanding Magnetic Separator

The separation process relies on the seeds' affinity for liquids. Since seeds contain no free iron and are not magnetically attracted, they are first pretreated with a magnetic material such as finely ground iron powder. Rough or cracked seed coats, dirt, chaff, or seeds with sticky residues will absorb the liquid and become sticky, causing the iron powder to adhere to them. In contrast, smooth-coated seeds do not absorb the liquid, so no iron powder attaches to them.

After the seeds are discharged from the mixing chamber, they pass through a powerful magnet. The magnet removes the iron-coated seeds by attracting them to a revolving drum that generates a high-intensity magnetic field. The seeds with iron powder adhere to the drum until they are brushed or scraped off, while the seeds without iron powder fall into a separate discharge spout.

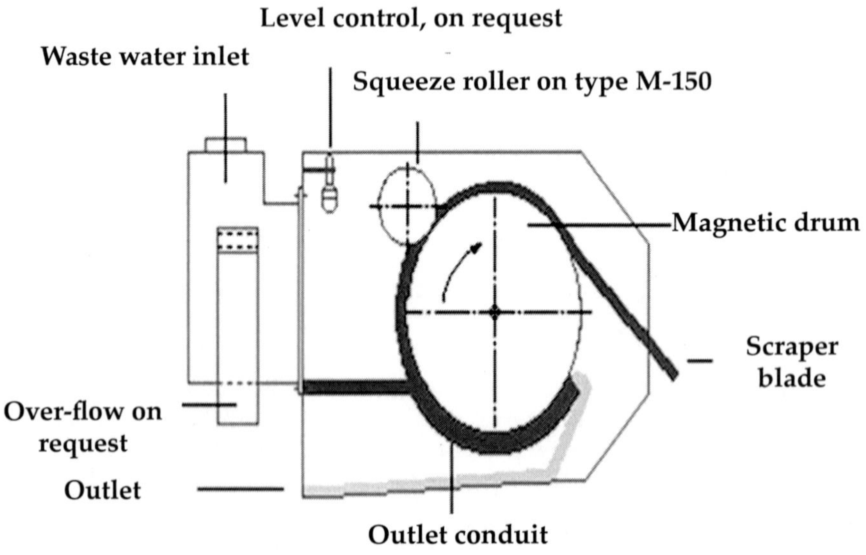

Figure.: 2.17 Magnetic Separator

Seeds which are relatively free of iron powder are not attracted by the magnet and will fall into a separate discharge spout.

For successful magnetic seed separation, it is necessary that the seeds to be separated exhibit distinct differences in their seed coat characteristics. The crop seeds should have a smooth surface, while the seeds to be removed should possess a rough surface that retains liquid and allows the iron powder to adhere. The effectiveness of the separation depends on the extent of the seed coat differences and the thoroughness with which the moistened seeds are mixed with the iron powder.

Colour Separator

Large crop seeds, like peas and beans, often exhibit color variations between different varieties, as well as due to factors like immaturity or disease. Electronic color sorting machines are capable of separating these seeds based on color differences and can also remove mud balls and discolored seeds in a single operation.

Figure.: 2.18 Color separator

The electronic color sorter uses photoelectric cells to inspect each seed individually. Each seed is compared with a predefined background or color range, and is then discharged accordingly. Seeds that match the desired color are directed to the good seed spout, while those that fall within the reject range are deflected by a blast of compressed air into the reject discharge spout. While the machine is highly sensitive, its capacity is low since it examines each seed individually. However, it offers a low operating cost and is particularly useful for large-seeded crops, despite its high initial cost.

Spiral Separator

The separator, which classifies seed according to its shape and rolling ability, consists of sheet metal strips fitted around a central axis in the form of a spiral. The unit resembles an open screw conveyor standing in a vertical position. The seed is introduced at the top of the inner spiral. Round seeds roll faster down the incline than flat or irregularly shaped seeds, which tend to slide or tumble.

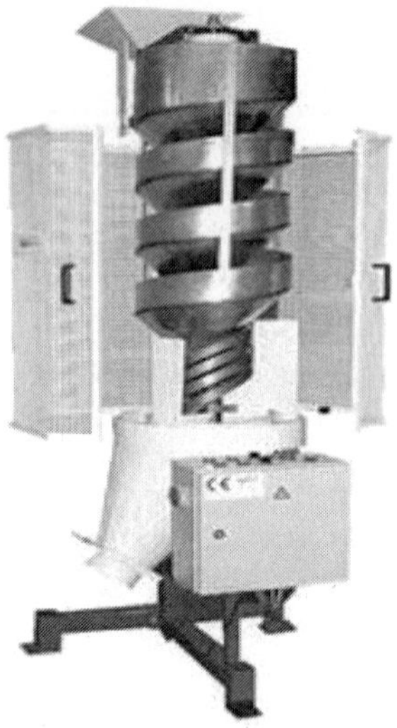

Figure.: 2.19 Tend to slide or tumble

The orbit of round seed increases with speed on its flight around the axis, until it rolls over the edge of the inner flight into the outer flight where it is collected separately. The slower moving seed does not build up enough speed to escape from the inner flight. Most spirals have multiple inner flights arranged one above the other to increase the capacity. Processing equipments used for improving the quality of the seed From the time of harvest to the final stage of seed storage, seeds must go through various processing equipment tailored to their specific needs. However, certain equipment, such as dryers and seed cleaner-cum-graders, are used universally for all types of seeds. The following outlines the processing machinery and equipment used in seed handling.

OPERATION AND MAINTENANCE OF DESTONERS

Destoners are used in industries such as grain processing, rice mills, and seed cleaning to remove stones, dirt, and other impurities from grains and seeds. The process helps improve the quality of the final product and reduces wear on downstream machinery.

Operation of Destoners

Destoners work by utilizing differences in the density and specific gravity between stones (heavier) and grains or seeds (lighter). They typically involve air currents and mechanical vibration to separate the lighter material from the heavier stones. Below are the common working steps of a destoner:

Key Components

- **Airflow System:** Provides air to separate lighter grains from heavier stones.
- **Deck (Screen):** The material to be cleaned passes over a screen or deck with vibrating motion.
- **Vibration System:** Vibrates the deck to move the grains in a specific direction.
- **Heavy and Light Material Collection:** Separate sections to collect stones and other impurities from grains.

Working Steps

- **Feeding Material:** Grains are fed into the destoner through a hopper or conveyor.
- **Vibration & Airflow:** The material is spread over the vibrating screen, while air flows through it.
- **Separation of Stones:** The stones, being heavier, drop to the bottom of the deck, while the lighter grains are carried away by the airflow or the vibration.
- **Discharge of Clean Material:** The clean grains or seeds are collected in a separate container or bin.
- **Discharge of Stones:** The stones and impurities are collected and discharged in a different compartment.

Proper upkeep of Destoners

To ensure efficient operation and prolong the lifespan of destoners, regular maintenance is necessary. Proper maintenance includes both preventative and corrective actions.

Maintenance Activities

- Cleaning and Lubrication
    - **Cleaning:** Regular cleaning of screens, air channels, and discharge outlets is important to prevent clogging and ensure optimal airflow.
    - **Lubrication:** All moving parts, including motors, vibrators, and bearings, should be lubricated as per the manufacturer's recommendations to reduce wear and tear.
- Inspection and Adjustment
    - **Vibration Mechanism**: Inspect the vibration system regularly to ensure the motor, springs, and counterweights are functioning correctly. Incorrect vibration can affect separation efficiency.
    - **Airflow System**: Check the air supply to ensure it is working at optimal pressure and volume.

- **Screens:** Inspect the screens for wear, damage, or clogging. They should be replaced if they are damaged or excessively worn.
- **Seals and Gaskets:** Ensure all seals and gaskets are intact to prevent air leakage, which could affect the efficiency of separation.
- **Alignment of Components:** Ensure that all parts of the machine, including the deck and motor, are correctly aligned to avoid unnecessary strain on components.

- Motor and Electrical Components
  - **Check Electrical Connections:** Inspect electrical components and wiring for any signs of damage or wear.
  - **Motor Maintenance:** Periodically inspect the motor for overheating, noise, and vibration. The motor should be cleaned, and any worn-out parts should be replaced.
  - **Control Panel:** Ensure that the control panel is functioning correctly and is free from dust and moisture.
- Troubleshooting
  - **Ineffective Separation:** If stones are not being separated efficiently, check for improper airflow, incorrect vibration frequency, or clogged screens.
  - **Excessive Vibration or Noise:** This could indicate a misalignment or worn-out components. Check the vibration system, motor, and bearings.
  - **Motor Failure:** In the case of motor failure, check the electrical system, circuit breakers, and motor windings for damage.
- Calibration:
  - Ensure that the destoner is properly calibrated according to the type of grain or seed being processed. The separation settings (airflow, vibration) may need to be adjusted depending on the material.

Safety Protocols

- **Electrical Safety:** Ensure all electrical components are correctly insulated and grounded to prevent electrical hazards.
- **Protective Guards:** Ensure that protective guards around moving parts, including the vibrating screen and motor, are in place to prevent injury.
- **Dust Control:** Grains and seeds can produce dust. Implement a dust collection system to protect workers and prevent explosions in high-dust environments.

Quick Fixes and Solutions

- **Excessive wear of the screen:** Often caused by the presence of large stones or hard materials. Solution: Check for any irregularities in the material feed or screen type.
- **Inconsistent separation:** This could be caused by improper air volume, vibration frequency, or clogged air passages. Solution: Clean air ducts and adjust the airflow and vibration settings.

- **Motor overheating:** This can result from excessive load, improper voltage, or worn-out bearings. Solution: Inspect and replace faulty components, ensure proper motor ventilation.

Concluding Remarks

Proper operation and upkeep of a destoner ensure efficient grain cleaning and enhance the lifespan of the equipment. Regular checks of air systems, screens, vibrations, and the motor are important for smooth and reliable operation.

UPKEEP OF AGRICULTURAL PROCESSING LINES

Need of Regular Maintenance

Regular maintenance of agricultural processing lines is crucial for ensuring operational efficiency, maintaining product quality, and safeguarding safety. Scheduled maintenance helps detect and resolve problems before they become serious, reducing the likelihood of unplanned downtimes. Additionally, it prolongs the life of the machinery, leading to a better return on investment.

- **Operational Efficiency:** Routine inspections and maintenance keep machinery running smoothly, minimizing disruptions and ensuring production schedules are met, all while controlling operational costs.
- **Product Quality:** Regular upkeep guarantees that machines operate at their optimal levels, producing products that adhere to industry standards for quality.
- **Safety:** Properly maintained equipment lowers the risk of accidents, protecting workers and ensuring compliance with safety protocols.

Daily Inspections

Daily inspections are important for the smooth operation of processing lines. These checks play a major role in detecting potential issues early and preventing disruptions.

Main Components to Inspect Daily

- **Belts and Chains:** Inspect for wear, alignment problems, and proper tension. Worn or misaligned belts can cause machinery to operate inefficiently or break down.
- **Lubrication Points**: Verify that lubrication points are properly greased. Insufficient lubrication can lead to excessive friction and premature wear.
- **Safety Guards and Emergency Stops:** make sure that safety guards are intact and operational. Test emergency stops to Make sure they work correctly.
- **Temperature and Pressure Gauges:** Monitor temperature and pressure levels to ensure they are within the specified ranges. Any deviations could signal underlying issues.
- **Cleanliness**: Ensure the processing line is free from debris and contaminants. Regular cleaning prevents blockages and other operational problems.

Monthly Inspections and Maintenance

Monthly inspections involve more detailed checks to assess machinery and identify parts that may require replacement, ensuring the processing line operates smoothly.

Main Components to Inspect Monthly

- **Motors and Bearings:** Listen for unusual noises or vibrations, indicating issues with bearings or motors. Lubricate bearings as needed and ensure smooth motor operation.
- **Electrical Components**: Check wiring, connectors, and control panels for wear, corrosion, or damage. Test the electrical systems to ensure proper functioning.
- **Hydraulic and Pneumatic Systems:** Look for leaks, pressure drops, and proper fluid levels. Examine hoses and seals for wear and replace as necessary.
- **Conveyors and Rollers:** Check for misalignment, wear, and proper operation. Ensure rollers rotate freely and conveyors move smoothly.
- **Sensors and Actuators:** Test sensors and actuators for responsiveness and accurate data transmission. Clean or replace malfunctioning sensors as needed.

Annual Maintenance Shutdowns

Annual shutdowns provide a comprehensive overhaul of processing lines, allowing for thorough inspections, repairs, and part replacements.

Crucial Components to Inspect During Annual Shutdowns

- **Structural Components:** Examine frames, supports, and other structural parts for signs of damage, fatigue, or corrosion. Reinforce or replace any compromised components.
- **Gearboxes and Drives**: Disassemble gearboxes to check for wear in gears and bearings. Replace worn parts and reassemble with fresh lubrication.
- **Heat Exchangers and Cooling Systems:** Clean heat exchangers to prevent buildup that could affect efficiency. Inspect cooling systems for leaks and ensure proper operation.
- **Pneumatic and Hydraulic Cylinders:** Disassemble and inspect cylinders for wear or damage. Replace seals and gaskets as required.
- **Software and Control Systems**: Update software and firmware, and test control systems to ensure they are functioning properly and making accurate adjustments.

Scheduling Inspections and Upkeep

The success of a maintenance program relies on careful scheduling of inspections and tasks. A well-organized schedule ensures maintenance is evenly distributed throughout the year, preventing overloads on the maintenance team and ensuring reliable machine performance.

Benefits of a Scheduled Maintenance Program

- **Reduced Downtime**: By scheduling maintenance during off-peak periods, production disruptions are reduced. Planned shutdowns help avoid unexpected breakdowns that can lead to significant downtime.
- **Cost Savings:** Preventive maintenance is generally more cost-effective than reactive repairs. Early issue detection can avoid expensive emergency repairs and extend equipment lifespan.
- **Improved Safety:** Regular maintenance and inspections reduce the risk of accidents, ensuring worker safety and compliance with regulations, and avoiding legal issues.
- **Increased Productivity:** Well-maintained machines run more efficiently, increasing productivity and ensuring better quality products.

Implementing a Maintenance Schedule

- **Train Maintenance Staff:** Regularly train staff on new maintenance techniques and safety protocols. Well-trained staff can perform tasks accurately and safely.
- **Use Maintenance Management Software:** A computerized maintenance management system (CMMS) can help track tasks, schedule inspections, and maintain records of all maintenance activities.
- **Create a Maintenance Calendar:** Develop a calendar that outlines daily, monthly, and annual tasks. Ensure all team members are familiar with the schedule and their responsibilities.
- **Monitor and Adjust:** Continuously evaluate the effectiveness of the maintenance program and adjust as necessary. Gather feedback from staff and operators to identify improvement areas.

3

Operation and Maintenance of Dehusker, Dehuller, Degermer and Dryer

The operation and maintenance of dehusking, dehulling, degerming, and drying equipment are crucial in ensuring the efficiency and longevity of these machines in grain and seed processing industries. These machines play a vital role in removing husks, hulls, and germs from grains, as well as reducing moisture content to enhance storage stability. Proper handling and regular maintenance not only improve performance but also reduce downtime and operational costs.

Dehuskers are used to remove the outer husk from grains like paddy and millet. Their efficiency depends on factors such as roller pressure, feed rate, and machine alignment. Routine maintenance involves checking for wear and tear on rollers, adjusting pressure settings, and ensuring that all moving parts are well-lubricated. Similarly, dehullers remove the outer shell of seeds and grains, requiring careful calibration to avoid excessive grain breakage. Blade sharpness, motor performance, and sieve integrity should be regularly inspected to ensure optimal functioning.

Degermers are employed to separate the germ from the endosperm in grains like maize. This process enhances the shelf life of processed products and improves their quality. Regular maintenance of degermers involves inspecting the abrasion plates, checking the feed rate, and ensuring that airflow mechanisms are clear of obstructions. Any malfunction can lead to uneven separation, affecting the final product quality.

Dryers are essential in reducing the moisture content of grains to prevent microbial growth and spoilage. They require proper temperature control, uniform airflow, and regular cleaning of heat exchangers and drying chambers. Overheating or under-drying can compromise the grain quality and lead to storage losses. Timely inspections of sensors, air ducts, and burner efficiency help maintain effective drying operations.

A well-planned operation and maintenance routine ensures these machines function optimally, increasing productivity and product quality while reducing energy consumption and repair costs.

GRAIN DESTONER

A Grain Destoner is a specialized machine designed to clean and separate grains based on their viscosity. Its key function is to eliminate unwanted materials such as stones, heavy contaminants, and foreign particles from large quantities of grains. This process is important for enhancing the quality and safety of grains intended for consumption, as well as improving the efficiency of subsequent processing stages.

The working of the Grain Destoner Machine depends on the density differences between the grains and contaminants. By generating a controlled environment with airflow and vibration, the machine separates grains by their weight and size, effectively removing stones and other impurities.

Operation of a Grain Destoner Machine

Stages of Operation in Grain Destoner Machine

- **Feeding:** The grains are fed into the machine via a hopper. These grains may contain numerous amount of impurities such as stones, dust, and dirt, which need to be separated during the process.
- **Air Separation:** Once inside the machine, the grains are subjected to an airflow that separates lighter materials like dust and chaff from the heavier grains and stones. The airflow is meticulously controlled to ensure that only the unwanted particles are eliminated.
- **Vibration and Vibration Adjustment:** A vibrating screen system is used to enhance the separation of heavier contaminants like stones from the grains. The vibrations cause the heavier impurities to move downward, while the lighter grains rise upward, improving the overall separation efficiency.
- **Discharge:** Following the separation, the clean grains are discharged from the machine, ready for further processing, packaging, or storage. At the same time, the stones and foreign materials are expelled through a dedicated outlet.

Benefits of Using a Grain Destoner Machine

- **Enhanced Food Safety Standards:** One of the primary benefits of a grain destoner machine is its ability to remove harmful impurities, thereby enhancing food safety. By ensuring that stones and other foreign contaminants are eliminated during processing, it helps maintain adherence to stringent food safety regulations, as these contaminants can pose serious health risks if consumed.
- **Boosted Processing Efficiency:** A grain destoner machine significantly speeds up the grain processing cycle by automating the impurity removal process. This increases overall operational efficiency by reducing manual labor and improving throughput.

- **Cost-Effective Solution:** A high-quality grain destoner machine helps save money in the long term by reducing product waste and improving the quality of the processed grains. It also cuts down operating costs by eliminating the need for manual labor in sorting and cleaning.
- **Improved Storage and Extended Shelf Life:** By removing impurities, the machine enhances the storage conditions for grains. Clean grains are less susceptible to pests, mold, and other contaminants, ensuring that they remain fresh and have a longer shelf life during storage.

DEHULLER

The hulling machine is designed to remove the husk from grains or seeds while minimizing damage to the bran layer and preventing breakage of the grains as much as possible. Due to the varying surface characteristics of different grains, friction must be applied to effectively remove the husk. As a result, a nominal amount of percentage of broken grains is unavoidable during the hulling process. The machine's design, precise adjustments, and operation all play a crucial role in ensuring optimal performance and high efficiency, ultimately leading to the best quality of grain production.

Designs and Structure of Dehuller

The methods used to remove hulls from grains date back to the earliest days of grain cultivation. The need for hull removal arose with the cultivation of einkorn, which is thought to have begun in the Neolithic period. In more recent years, the focus has shifted to the creation of affordable dehulling machines for small-scale farmers in developing countries, particularly for crops like rice and sorghum.

A three-step process is required to remove the hulls from the grain kernel. Below are the three steps:

- The grain kernels are physically eliminated from their hulls.
- The mix of kernels and hulls are then separated by their different specific gravity—hulls are lighter than grains.
- Not all grain will have the hulls removed, so the remaining grains in hulls and grains without hulls need to be sorted into two separate streams. Kernels are smaller than hulls, so the sort is based on differences in size. Grains in the hulls are recirculated back to the beginning of the dehulling process.

Impact Dehullers

An impact dehuller works by propelling the hulled grain against a hard surface at high speeds, causing the hull to break apart. While this method can lead to a significant amount of chipped, cracked, or broken grain, it poses no issue if the grain is immediately cooked or milled. However, when the goal is to dehull the grain rather than turn it into flour, the impact force must be carefully controlled to avoid pulverizing the grain. Impact dehullers have continuously evolved in their design.

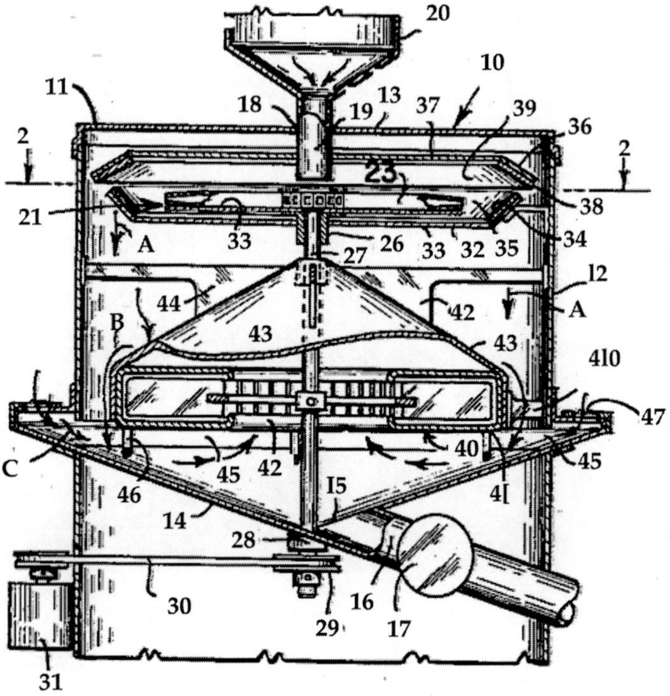

Figure.: 3.1Schematic for an Impact Dehuller.

The hammers used in these machines wear out over time and require regular replacement. They can also cause wear on other parts of the dehuller. For crops like spelt and barley, friction and a rolling motion enhance the dehulling process. Since einkorn hulls are more tightly attached to the seeds, impact alone is less effective at separating them compared to friction.

Friction Dehullers

Hulls can be removed from grains by applying pressure and rubbing the hulled grains together. The earliest friction dehullers were crafted from stone, similar to stone mills, but with the stones placed further apart than in traditional flour grinding.

A dehuller can be created by modifying a hand mill used for grinding flour. The design involves placing a rubber disk over the metal burrs. Different polymers can be used, but a food-grade rubber disk is typically mounted on the mill's grinding face. These rubber disks are commonly made of polyurethane. To increase friction and enhance the dehullingprocess, the rubber disk can be impregnated with sand.

Figure.: 3.2 Frictiondehuller disks.

Friction dehullers offer numerous amount of benefits. Their operating speed can be easily controlled by adjusting the angular velocity of the rotating shafts. The equipment is versatile and can be adjusted to process different types and sizes of grains. Additionally, various friction surfaces can be employed to meet specific needs without requiring changes to the mechanical system (Gauthier et al., 2012).

However, the main demerit of friction dehullers is that their components wear out quickly and require regular replacement. Maintenance and repair costs for friction dehullers can be higher compared to other alternatives. As the friction surface wears down, frequent adjustments are necessary to maintain proper spacing, ensuring the machine continues to effectively remove hulls. To maintain optimal performance, critical tolerances must be adhered to.

Abrasion Dehullers

Abrasion dehullers operate similarly to friction dehullers, with the separation process being driven by rubbing rather than impact. Additionally, the hulls are mechanically scarified by sharp points, which reduces the friction force required for separation. The most common design features rotating disks placed parallel to the ground, spinning in opposite directions. These disks are equipped with teeth that tear the hulls away from the kernels. The differing specific gravities of the seeds and hulls, combined with the centrifugal force of the counter-rotating disks, causes the hulls and seeds to move in opposite directions. While abrasion dehullers require a larger initial investment, their design enables higher-speed operation, greater throughput, higher yields, and overall better efficiency than impact or friction dehullers. However, scarification of the grain remains a challenge. Once scarified, the grain must be milled quickly to reduce degradation and mold infection.

Figure.: 3.3 Cornell Impact-Friction Dehuller

Figure.: 3.4 Detail of the impact mechanism

Separation

After the kernels are removed from the hulls, the edible grain and chaff must be separated. This is typically done using an air column, based on the principle that lighter materials, such as hulls, will float, while the heavier grains will fall. While a fan can be utilized for this process, it is less effective at collecting the hulls in one place. An aspirator or airlock in an enclosed column is more efficient at suspending the hulls, dust, and chaff compared to a fan.

Once the grain is separated by air, further separation can occur based on size and gravity. Screens of many sizes, both larger and smaller than the grains, help remove larger and smaller foreign materials. A gravity table can be used to sort the grains by mass. In some cases, the final step before bagging or milling spelt into flour involves passing the dehulled product over a gravity table.

Power Supply of dehullers

The earliest dehullers were powered by human labor or draft animals, and water and wind were also used before electric motors were invented. Hand-operated models, which are generally modified hand-cranked mills, remain available. These dehullers are low-cost, easy to assemble, and can be operated without electricity or fossil fuels. However, their capacity is limited, and they require considerable labor. Dehullers can also be powered by gas or diesel engines, which do not require proximity to electrical lines and can reduce installation costs. However, such models in the U.S. market are often custom-built or modified from electric-powered models. Gasoline-powered models were not included in this study.

For most on-farm applications, it is usually prefered to use a unit that runs on single-phase electricity. Some farms, do not have electricity which makes hand-cranked models desirable for smaller-scale operations. Single-phase power, operating on standard 110-120V, is generally sufficient for small- and medium-scale operations, though these systems are limited in power and may be more prone to overload. For calculations, single-phase 115V power is assumed unless noted otherwise. Farms that use 220V wiring for heavier equipment, like arc welding, may benefit from upgrading to 220V or three-phase power, which offers advantages in throughput and performance. Larger units, may require three-phase power systems to accommodate higher current and voltage. For units that lack a built-in method for separating kernels from hulls, additional equipment and connections are needed. The use of a variable frequency drive, which adjusts for grain conditions, can increase efficiency and quality.

Working Conditions

The efficiency of a dehuller is controlled by the condition of the grain, which varies based on weather, harvesting techniques, and other factors when the grain is harvested. Kernels tend to break cleanly when moisture content is 14% or lower. Moist grain is harder to dehull, but as it dries, it becomes more brittle and susceptible to cracking, chipping, and breakage. Grains need to be dried before they can be stored in bins.

It is very important to remove dirt, sticks, small rocks, and weeds before dehulling to ensure smooth operation. Most farms in the study use gravity tables, fanning mills, or paddy tables. A gravity table separates grains from heavier or lighter objects using vibration and forced air. A fanning mill utilizes forced air from fans to separate lighter particles from the grain. Paddy tables, initially designed for rice separation, depend on size and gravity but not air. Running raw grain through a magnet removes ferrous metals that could damage equipment or harm consumers. Grain cleaning equipment manufacturers include Codema and Ferrell-Ross (Clipper).

Larger operations have begun using color sorters. These machines sort items that cannot be removed by magnets or screened, such as weed seeds and rodent feces, based on color. While color sorters are still out of reach for most on-farm operations due to their cost, their prices are dropping as they become more widely used.

Dust is a significant concern during dehulling, as hull dust contains silica and is a health hazard. In high concentrations, it can lead to explosions. Mill dust can also reduce dehuller efficiency and limit the types of materials that can be used in the machinery. Dust collection systems need to be appropriately scaled to keep airborne dust at safe levels.

As high-speed dehullers approach their capacity, performance declines. The machines become more prone to clogging and malfunctions, grain quality worsens, and there is an increase in cracked or broken grain, higher heat, and more grain needing to be recirculated. While maximum output can be reached for most models, it typically cannot be sustained for more than an hour. Smaller models, especially electric ones, tend to overheat and back up, while hand-operated models cause operator fatigue. Although a modified Corona mill could theoretically achieve 25 lb/hr, a more realistic output is 5 lb/hr unless multiple people are involved. Due to these limitations, dehullers are generally operated at less than 100% capacity, typically around 50-80% depending on the model.

Upkeep and Repair

Dehullers, like all machinery, require regular service and upkeep to ensure efficient operation and prevent unexpected breakdowns. Components that experience frequent movement, impacts, or constant friction are the first to show signs of wear. Manufacturers typically recommend replacing certain parts annually to avoid failures during peak production periods. For impact dehullers, this often includes the impeller rings, which help increase the speed and force with which grains strike the surface used to break the hulls.

One manufacturer suggests allocating 4-5% of the initial purchase price for annual maintenance and repair. Other manufacturers provide a detailed schedule for routine maintenance and estimated replacement costs. Upkeep and repair costs for used equipment can be considerably higher. Moving parts are most susceptible to wear, whether they are exposed to impact or friction.

Due to dust buildup, worn components, and general debris, it is necessary to periodically disassemble, clean, and inspect the units for wear. If significant wear is found, the units should be reassembled using replacement parts. For instance, it is recommended that the Horn dehuller undergo a complete rebuild every ten years.

Purchasing used Equipment

Purchasing used equipment can offer savings on the initial cost, but this does not always imply in lower operating expenses. For used equipment to be functional, it must be in good working condition, which often requires time for restoration and repairs, as well as the cost of replacement parts. In many cases, newer models are equipped with electronic systems that can adjust the speed of grain flow, the return flow of unhulled grains, and the output, increasing efficiency.

With the increased interest in hulled grains, demand for used dehulling equipment has risen. However, it is essential to thoroughly inspect the equipment and assess its condition before making a purchase. Mechanical skills are crucial for maintaining and repairing used equipment, especially when dealing with outdated models that may require modifications.

Modified Equipment

Dehullers designed for other grains and seeds can be adapted to dehull spelt, emmer, and einkorn. For instance, oat, rice, barley, sunflower, and clover dehullers have been adjusted to work with spelt. However, each grain has specific requirements that necessitate different settings. Attempts to create a universal dehuller have led to designs that compromise optimal performance for any single type of grain. Even within spelt varieties, adjusting settings for different sizes is important.

Factors to Consider while Selection of a Huller

Factors that are to be considered in the selection of a huller are

- Capacity
- Energy requirement
- Efficiency of husk removal
- Extent of physical damage to beans
- Separation of loose husk
- Durability
- Ease of maintenance

Techniques for Milling/ Dehusking

Wet milling method

This method of processing is being adopted by comparatively smaller units. This method is practiced in southern india. The milling quality of this method was found to be good and on an average 72% recovery of grains

Dry milling method

This method of milling of pulses is mostly aodpted in the northern and central India. It varies widely from region to region. Dhal from dry milling method is said to have better cooking quality a wet milling.

Engle Berg Huller

This huller is the most widely used machine for paddy hulling in India. The main component of this machine is a ribbed cast iron roller that rotates on an axis within a large concentric cylinder. The inner roller is equipped with a spiral ribbed strip covering ¼ of its length, while the remaining ¾ portion features 4 to 6 straight ribbed strips. The roller spins at speeds ranging from 600 to 900 rpm. Paddy is introduced into the hopper and moves around the cylinder due to the rotational direction of the flutes, eventually reaching the outlet. Friction between the grains and the steel parts of the huller helps remove the husk and bran, with the machine performing both husking and bran removal simultaneously.

Under Runner Disc Huller

- The Under Runner disc huller consists of two horizontal cast iron discs, each partly covered with an abrasive layer, typically made of energy. The top disc is fixed to the machine body, while the bottom disc rotates. The rotating disc can be vertically adjusted, allowing the clearance between the two discs to be controlled. The clearance is determined based on the grain variety and condition. The state of the abrasive coating on the discs also influences the clearance. Over time, as the abrasive coating wears, the hulling action becomes concentrated in the center, causing a ridge to form around the outer ring of the coating.

Rubber–Roll Sheller

- A rubber-roll sheller consists of two rubber rolls that rotate in opposite directions at different speeds. A feeder uniformly distributes the feed into the machine, creating a thin layer of grain between the rotating rolls. One roll is fixed, while the other is adjustable to achieve the desired clearance between them. The differing speeds of the rolls generate a shearing force on the grain's surface, leading to the opening and breaking of the husk.

Husk Separator

This machine is utilized in separating husk from the mixture of shelled grains, husk, and unshelled grains produced by the huller or sheller. In the first stage, the husk, broken grains, germ, and bran are separated, which is achieved by the husk separator. The machine is simple, consisting of a fan and a system to evenly distribute the sheller output onto an oscillating sieve with fine perforations. This setup ensures that air flows evenly across the mixture, blowing away the husk. The perforations allow the broken grains, germs, and bran to pass through, while the immature grains are also blown away by the fan.

POPULAR INDUSTRIALISED DEHULLING SYSTEM

Hot Dehulling

The most commonly used dehulling system for today's high-protein, low-fiber meal market is Hot Dehulling System. This system can produce meal quality year-round, even with hard-to-dehull new crop beans, while ensuring hull fats remain under 1%. It is capable of processing high-moisture beans, up to 13.5%, directly from the field or within a few weeks of harvest, meeting the market's high-protein, low-fiber requirements. The Hot Dehulling system eliminates the need for costly, high-maintenance grain dryers, tempering silos, or rotary conditioners. Unlike a conventional system where beans are heated twice, the Hot Dehulling system heats the beans only once. A Vertical Seed Conditioner (VSC) gradually heats the beans to 140°F (60°C) and reduces moisture by over 2%, conditioning the beans consistently in just 30 minutes. The Jet Dryer is then used for the last phase of heating and drying.

Warm Dehulling

The Warm Dehulling System is designed for regions where imported beans are processed. Since these beans are harvested two to three months before processing, they undergo natural conditioning during the shipping process. There are two main differences between the Warm and Hot Dehulling systems. First, a slightly larger Crown Vertical Seed Conditioner (VSC) is used to heat the beans to the proper flaking temperature of 155°F (70°C) while also drying them by over 2%. The second difference is the elimination of the Jet Dryer, which reduces installation costs. Otherwise, the dehulling process closely resembles that of the Hot Dehulling system. The Warm Dehulling system still produces low-fiber, high-protein meal while maintaining hull fats near 1%. Additionally, it is designed so that customers can upgrade to a full Hot Dehulling system in the future.

Cold Dehulling

The Cold Dehulling System is good for plants that already have existing grain dryers and conditioners and wish to add dehulling to produce a lower fiber meal. This system takes advantage of the existing drying and conditioning equipment, while incorporating efficient, patented Aspirators to separate the free hulls and meats after the cracking and conditioning processes. The Cold Dehulling System is designed with the flexibility to be easily upgraded to a full Hot Dehulling system in the future. Regardless of the system selected, Crown's experienced technical expertise ensures the best solution tailored to your plant's layout.

DEGERMER

A grain degermer is a machine that eliminates the germ and bran from grains like corn and wheat:

Working of a Degermer

The grain is conditioned and passed through a chamber with a rotor that creates friction between the grains, removing the germ and skin. A pneumatic system then sucks the germ and peel away.

Merits

Grain degerming can improve palatability, reduce cooking time, and create food products.

Variants of grain degermers

Some types of grain degermers include:

- **Horizontal Maize Degermer Verdi:** Uses a semi-wet process to eliminate the germ and bran from corn grains
- **Degermer HSVBF:** A vertical maize degerming machine that decorticates and degerms all kernels
- **SATAKE Group:** A degerming chamber that can prodce evenly degermed maize with a higher yield

DRYER

Understanding the Dynamics of Drying

The drying process involves the diffusion of moisture from the interior of the grain to its surface. Hot, dry air comes into contact with the grain, heating the moisture inside, which then evaporates into the surrounding air. To simplify, the drying process can be divided into three key phases: In the first phase, water inside the kernel is drawn out towards the outer wall. In the second phase, this water evaporates into the air surrounding the kernels. In the third phase, the moisture-laden air is expelled externally. When the cereal enters the grain dryer, it initially has a uniform moisture content throughout. As the hot air starts to evaporate the moisture on the exterior, the internal moisture moves towards the outside to maintain a new balance of humidity. This process removes moisture from both the surface and the core of the seed, utilizing hot air currents and the porosity of the product.

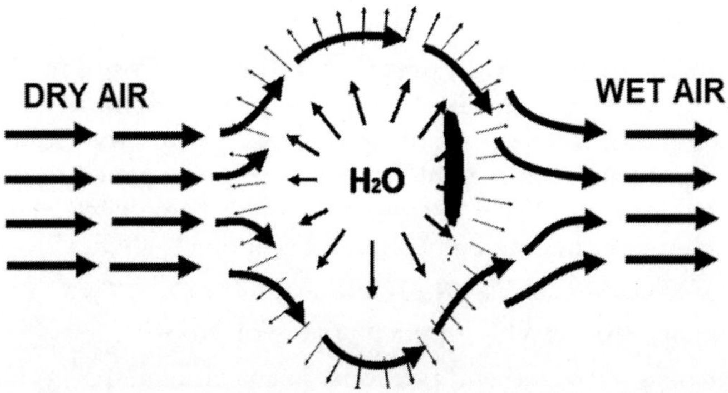

Figure.: 3.5 Dynamics of Drying

AIR HEATING

Hot air grain dryers exploit this principle of moisture diffusion from inside to outside and the continuous current of air that laps the grain allows to continuously remove the moisture that is released from the grain.

A correct balance of temperatures, air flows, pressures, and quantities of product to be treated allows to optimize the performance of the dryers.

Grain dryers typically consist of:-

- A heat generator with an aeration system for generating the flow of hot air
- A desiccant body that contains the cereal to dry, where the excess water evaporates
- A control panel with the control, regulation, and safety devices of the entire system
- Any complementary equipment designed for accumulating, cleaning, weighing, and handling the product.

Air heating systems are classified into direct and indirect systems based on how the air is heated. In direct heating systems, combustion gases are mixed with ambient air and directly introduced into the grain mass for drying. It is important to set the burners to the correct temperature to ensure complete fuel combustion. The main advantage of this system is its high efficiency, as all the heat generated by combustion is utilized for drying.

In contrast, indirect heating systems pass external air around the combustion chamber and the pipes that keep the combustion fumes separate from the drying air. The combustion products are expelled into the atmosphere, and the system's efficiency and fuel savings improve with larger heat exchange surfaces.

The last phase of the drying process is cooling, which is vital for proper storage of the product. The cooling method varies depending on the type of dryer. In batch dryers, cooling occurs at the end of the drying process using the same fan that was previously used to blow hot air. In continuous dryers, cooling happens in a dedicated section of the column or a separate cell. This phase is crucial to prevent condensation, mold formation, and fermentation.

Varieties of Dryer

The Preminent distinction in dryer operation lies in the method of drying, which can either be in batches or continuously. Batch drying, as seen in discontinuous or batch dryers (e.g., Mecmar mobile grain dryers), involves drying a full batch of product—equivalent to the machine's capacity—after which the batch is emptied, and the dryer is prepared for the next cycle. These dryers are often mobile, allowing them to be positioned wherever needed.

Discontinuous dryers are typically preferred for

- Small-scale operations with only a few tons of product.
- Drying the beginning and end portions (heads and tails) of continuous dryers.
- Providing drying services to third parties.

- Farmers who want to manage the drying of their crops while minimizing fixed plant costs compared to stationary dryers.
- Drying various types of cereals.

Continuous dryers operate by allowing the drying process to proceed without interruption. Wet grain is introduced at one end of the machine, while the dry and cooled product is released from the other end. These machines typically remain stationary and operate continuously for extended periods, ranging from several days to weeks.

Continuous dryers are particularly suited for

- Large drying operations that require the processing of 240 tons of grain per day or more.
- Farms that need to dry substantial quantities of grain daily.
- Users who need to dry large volumes of the same type of cereal.
- Operations with dedicated grain transport and storage infrastructure.

Theory of Drying

- Convection process in which moisture from a product is eliminated
- The water content of agro-product is given in terms of moisture content
- They gain or loose moisture as per the atmospheric conditions
- Moisture migration into or from a product is dependent on the difference of vapour pressure between atmosphere and product
- If the vapour pressure of grain is more than atmospheric vapour pressure, transfer of moisture from grain to atmosphere takes place
- If the atmospheric vapour pressure is more than grain vapour pressure, grain absorbs moisture from the atmosphere

Periods of Drying Rate

- Constant rate period
- First Falling rate period
- Second falling rate period

Constant rate period

- Moisture migration rate from inside of product to its surface equals the rate of evaporation of water from surface
- This period continues till critical moisture content is reached
- Critical moisture content is the moisture content of a product where constant rate drying ceases and falling rate starts
- This period is very short for agricultural products
- Drying of sand and washed seeds takes place in constant rate period

Falling rate period

- Most of the agricultural products are dried in falling rate drying period
- Movement and diffusion of moisture in interior of grains controls the entire drying process

First falling rate

- Unsaturated surface drying
- Drying rate decreases because of the decrease in wet surface area
- Fraction of wet surface decreases to zero, where first falling rate ends

Second falling rate

Sub surface evaporation takes place & it continues until the equilibrium moisture content is achieved.

Working Principle of Drying Process

- Movement of moisture takes place due to
  - **Capillary flow** : Liquid movement due to surface forces
  - **Liquid diffusion :** Liquid movement due to difference in moisture concentration
  - **Surface diffusion :** Liquid movement due to moisture diffusion of the pore spaces
  - **Vapour diffusion :** vapour movement due to moisture concentration difference
  - **Thermal diffusion :** vapour movement due to temperature difference
  - **Hydro dynamic flow :** water and vapour movement due to total pressure difference

Thin Layer Drying

- It is the process in which all grains are fully exposed to the drying air under constant drying conditions i.e. at constant air temp. & humidity. Up to 20 cm thickness of grain bed is taken as thin layer and all commercial dryers are designed based on thin layer drying principles. it is represented by Newton's law by replacing moisture content in place of temperature

  M-Me/Mo-Me = e -Kq

  M – Moisture content at any time q, % db

  Me- EMC, %db

  Mo – Initial moisture content, %db

  K – drying constant

  q - time, hour

Deep Bed drying

- Grains are not uniformly exposed to the same drying conditions.
- The drying air's condition varies over time and with the depth of the grain bed.
- The airflow rate per unit mass of grain is relatively low.
- The drying process in a deep bin can be seen as the sum of multiple thin layers.

- The humidity and temperature of the air entering and leaving each layer change over time.
- The volume of the drying zone depends on factors like the temperature and humidity of the entering air, the moisture content of the grain, and the airflow velocity.

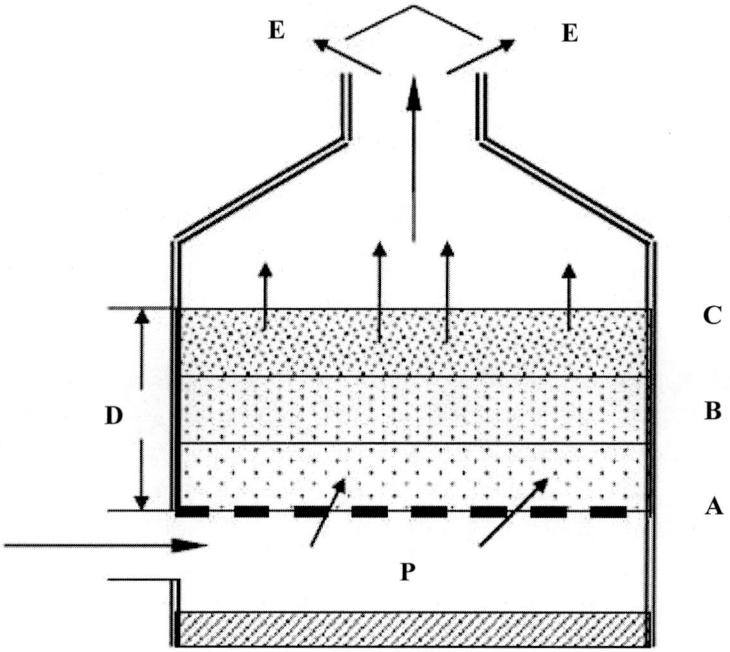

Figure.: 3.6 Deep bed drying zones of grains. D: bed height; P: plenum chamber; A: lower zone; B: middle zone; C: upper zone of grain and E: Exhaust (Moist) Air

Continuous Flow Dryer

- It is Columnar type dryer in which wet grains flow from top to the bottom of the dryer
- There are two type of the continuous flow dryer named:-
    - Mixing
    - Non-mixing

Mixing

- Grains are diverted in the dryer by providing baffles
- Use low air flow rates of 50-95 m3/min/tonne
- Zig-zag columns which are enclosed by screens are utilized to achieve mixing
- High drying air temperature of 65°C is used

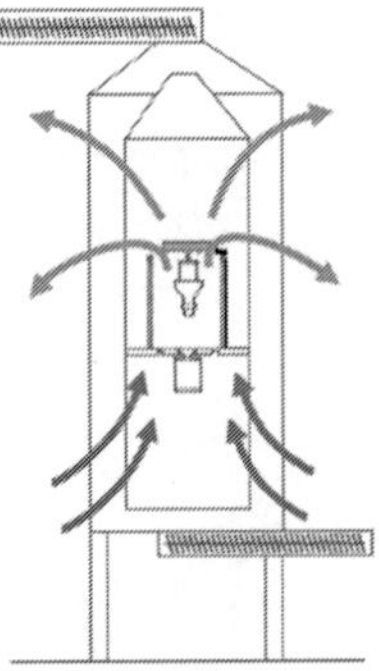

Figure.: 3.7 Continuos flow dryer Tell about "Non-mixing continuous how dryer" after that image

Baffle dryer

- A continuous flow, mixing-type dryer.
- It consists of a receiving bin, a drying chamber with baffles, and a plenum equipped with a hot air inlet.
- Baffles are used to divert the flow of air and mix the grain.
- The grain is fed at the top and moves downward in a zig-zag path, where it interacts with a cross-flow of hot air.
- A bucket elevator recirculates the grain until it reaches the desired moisture level.
- The result is a uniformly dried product.

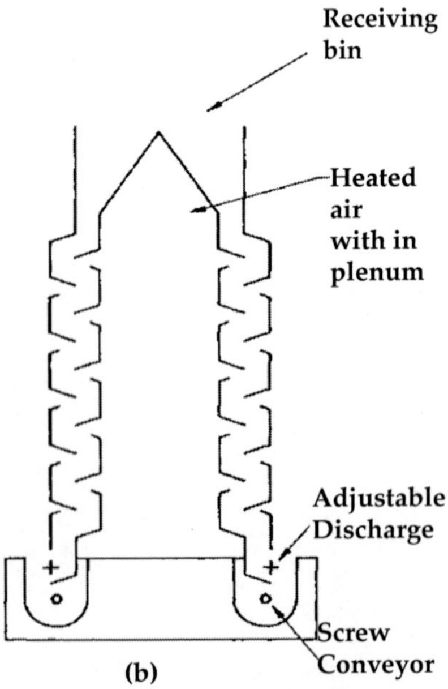

Figure.: 3.8 Baffle dryer

Mixing type Baffle Dryer

Non-mixing

- Grains flow in a straight path
- Baffles are not provided and drying takes place between two parallel screens
- High airflow rates can be used
- Drying air temp. of 54°C is used

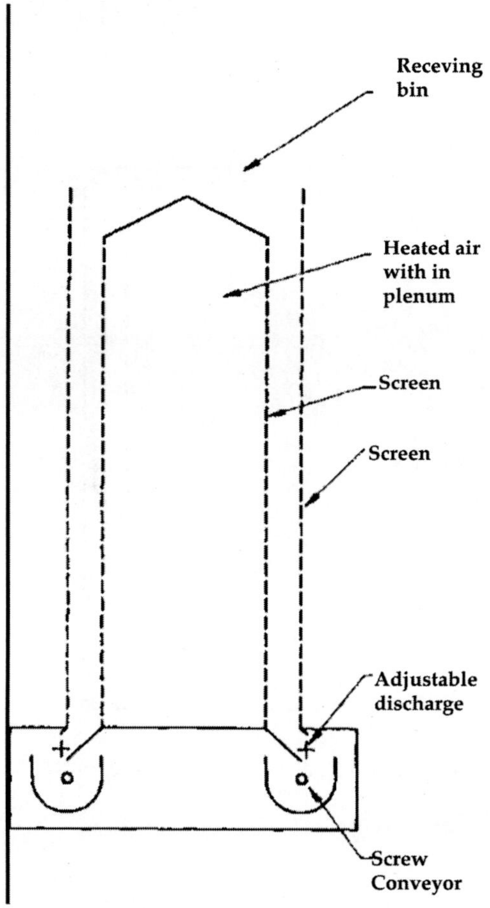

Figure.: 3.9 Mixing type baffle dryer

- Feed hopper
- Plenum chamber
- Exit air
- Dry grain outlet
- Screened grain column

CONTINUOUS FLOW DRYER (NON-MIXING)

Recirculatory Batch Dryer

- Continuous flow non mixing type
- Consists of 2 concentric circular cylinders, set 15-20 cm apart

Bucket elevator is utilized to feed &recirculated the grain Centrifugal blower blows the hot air into the inner cylinder, acts as a plenum Grain is fed at the top of the inside cylinder; comes in contact with a cross flow of hot air The exhaust air comes out through perforations of the outer cylinder Grain is recirculated till it is dried to desired moisture content Drying is not uniform as compared to mixing type

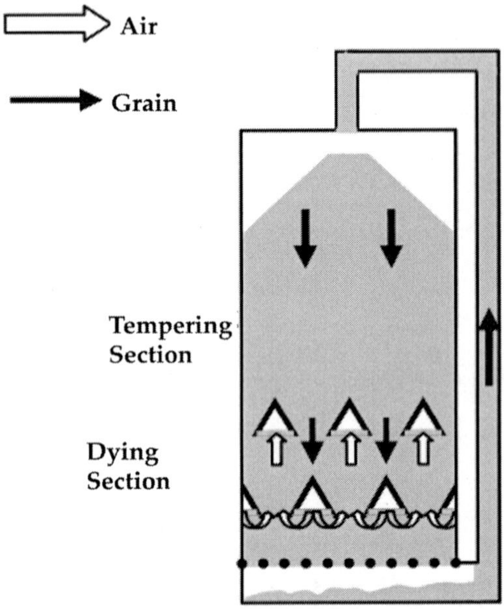

Figure.: 3.10 Recirculatory Batch dryer

Recirculating Batch Dryer

LSU dryer

- Developed at Louisiana state university (LSU)
- Continuous mixing type dryer
- Developed specifically for rice to ensure gentle treatment, good mixing & good air to grain contact
- Consists of rectangular chamber, holding bin, blower with duct, grain discharging mechanism and air heating system
- Layers of inverted V shaped channels are installed in the drying chamber; heated air is introduced through these channels at many points

- Alternate layers are air inlet & outlet channels; arranged one below the other in an offset pattern
- Air temp. are 60 &85°C for raw & parboiled paddy
- Ribbed rollers are provided at the bottom of drying chamber for the discharge of grain
- Capacity varies from 2-12 tonnes
- Recommended air flow rate is 60-70 m3/min/tonne
- Inlet port consists of few full size ports & two half size ports; all ports are of same size arranged in equal spacing
- Uniformly dried product can be obtained
- It Can be used for different types of grain
- It requires high capital investment

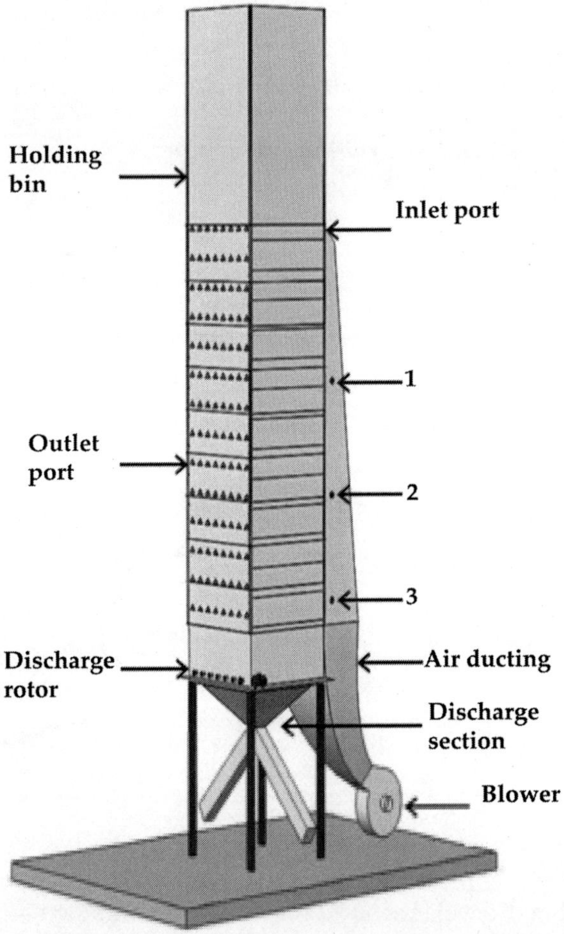

Figure.: 3.11 LSU Dryer

- Garner
- Duct
- Dry material outlet
- Hopper
- Continuous flow
- Door
- Roof

LSU Dryer

Tray driers

- In tray dryers, the food is spread out, Usually quite thinly, on trays in which the drying takes place.
- Heating may be by an air current sweeping across the trays, or heated shelves on which the trays lie, or by radiation from heated surfaces.
- Most tray dryers are heated by air, which also removes the moist vapours.

Working of Tray Dryer

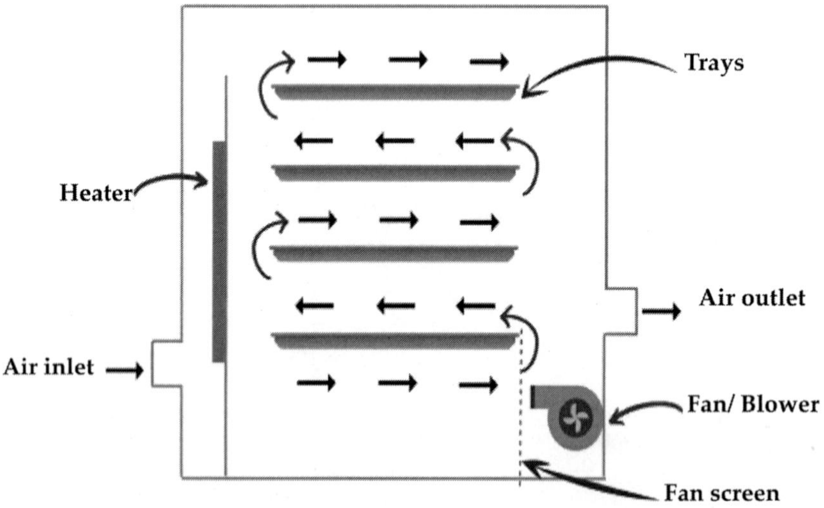

Figure: 3.12. Tray dryer

Fluidized Bed Dryers

In a fluidized bed dryer, the food material is maintained suspended against gravity in an upward-flowing air stream. Heat is transferred from the air to the food material, mostly by convection.

Figure.: 3.13 Fluidized Bed Dryers

Pneumatic Dryers

In a pneumatic dryer, the solid food particles are conveyed rapidly in an air stream, the velocity and turbulence of the stream maintaining the particles in suspension.

Heated air accomplishes the drying and often some form of classifying device is included in the equipment.

In the classifier, the dried material is separated, the dry material passes out as product and the moist remainder is recirculated for further drying

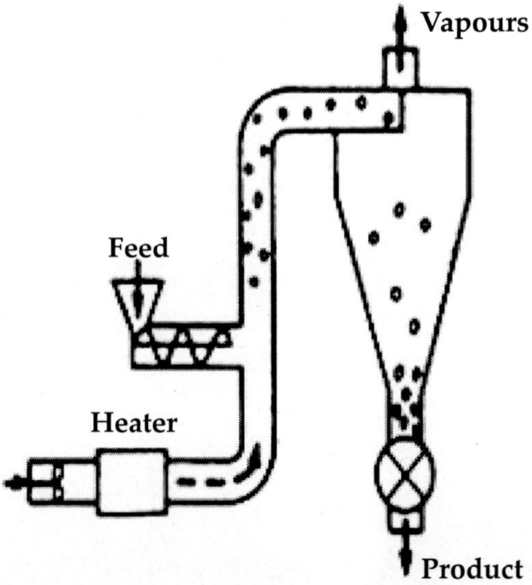

Figure.: 3.14 Pneumatic dryer

Rotary Dryers

The food product moves through a horizontally inclined cylinder, where it is heated either by airflow passing through the cylinder or by heat conduction from the cylinder walls.

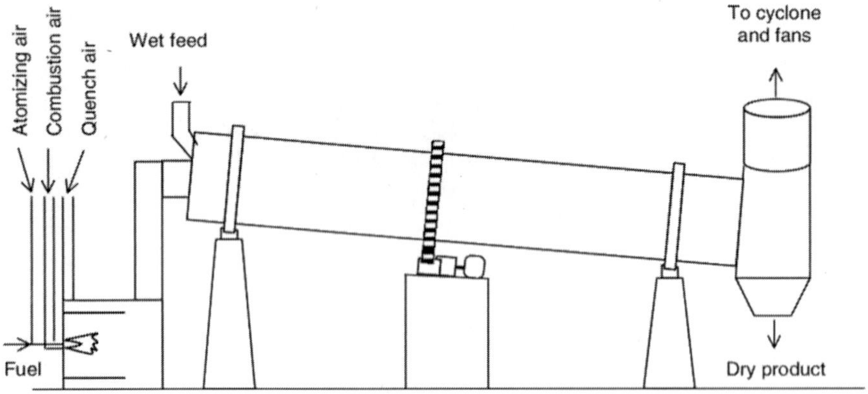

Figure.: 3.16 Rotary dryers

In some cases, the cylinder rotates and in others the cylinder is Stagnant and a paddle or screw rotates within the cylinder conveying the material through.

4

Operation and Maintenance of Rice Milling Machineries

Rice milling machines are crucial in the rice production industry, as they are used to remove the husk and bran layers from paddy, resulting in polished white rice. Various types of rice milling machines, such as hullers, whitening machines, polishers, and graders, are available, each designed for a specific function in the milling process.

When selecting a rice milling machine, it's essential to consider factors such as capacity, efficiency, power consumption, and maintenance requirements. Additionally, the machine's size should be aligned with the scale of rice production operations.

By investing in the right machinery, producers can enhance overall efficiency and product quality, while reducing manual labor and processing time.

OVERVIEW OF RICE MILL MACHINERY

Rice mills are food-processing facilities where raw paddy is converted into rice. These mills use modern machinery to process the paddy harvested from fields, transforming it into the final product, rice. Various types of rice mill machines are utilized throughout the milling process to ensure efficient and effective production.

Applications of Rice Mill Machinery

Milling is one of the key steps in the production of rice. It is generally performed post the production of rice. The paddy produced industrially cannot be consumed in its natural forms.

This is why paddy is processed post its production, by the process of milling. It removed in order to make it fit for human consumption.

Variants of Rice Mills

There are many types of rice mills, each tailored to specific processing needs and production capacities. Below is a list of machines used in rice mills:

- **Single-Pass Rice Mills:** These machines are designed for simpler rice milling operations. They typically perform the essential tasks of husking and whitening in a single pass.
- **Multi-Pass Rice Mills:** Ideal for large-scale operations, multi-pass mills carry out multiple milling stages. These stages include cleaning, husking,

whitening, polishing, and sorting in separate passes, resulting in highly refined rice.

- **Compact Rice Milling Machines:** Designed for small to medium-sized operations, compact rice mills are versatile and often incorporate several functions. These machines are space-efficient and easy to operate.
- **Commercial Rice Milling Machines:** Engineered for large-scale rice processing, commercial rice mills offer high production capacities and advanced features, capable of handling substantial rice volumes while maintaining efficiency.
- **Mini Rice Mills:** Compact and portable, mini rice mills are designed for small-scale milling. They are ideal for local rice growers or small businesses seeking to process rice on-site.
- **Modern Automated Rice Mills:** Equipped with cutting-edge technology, modern automated rice mills perform various tasks, such as cleaning, dehusking, whitening, polishing, and sorting, with minimal manual intervention. These machines are highly efficient and boost production rates.
- **Parboiling Plants:** Parboiling is a pre-milling procedure involving soaking, steaming, and drying rice. Parboiling plants contain the necessary equipment for these steps, improving the rice's nutritional value and quality.
- **Paddy Separator Machines:** Paddy separator machines are crucial for separating unhusked paddy from brown rice after husking, enhancing the efficiency of the milling process.
- **Rice Graders:** Rice graders are used to sort milled rice into different categories based on size or other traits, ensuring a uniform and consistent final product.
- **Rice Polishers:** Rice polishers complete the milling process by removing the outer bran layer, giving the rice its polished, finished appearance.
- **Rice Whitening Machines:** These machines are specifically designed to whiten rice by using friction or abrasive methods to remove the bran layer from brown rice, resulting in white rice.
- **Color Sorters:** Color sorters use advanced technology to identify and eliminate discolored or defective grains from the rice, ensuring a high-quality product.
- **Bucket Elevators:** Bucket elevators are used to move rice vertically during the milling process. These machines feature buckets attached to a belt that transport rice to different stages of processing.

RICE MILL & RICE WHITENING STONE

Milling is primarily described as a material removal process used to eliminate unwanted parts of rice. This process involves rice milling machinery, a workpiece, a fixture, and a cutter.

The workpiece, a key component of the milling machine, is fixed securely onto the fixture before being placed on the platform inside the milling machine.

The cutter, equipped with sharp teeth, spins at high speeds and is also secured within the machine. Both the workpiece and the cutter operate together during the milling process.

The material is first fed into the workpiece, which is then introduced to the rotating cutter. As the cutter rotates, it removes material in the form of small chips, shaping the rice as required. Milling enables the creation of three-dimensional rice that may not be symmetrically aligned along the axis.

Components of Rice Mill Machinery

Rice Mill machines are available in different sizes and shapes depending on the type of operation and the end product that has to be performed. The two most important things, the workpiece, the cutter practically remain the same in every milling process. The following are the components in the modern rice milling operations:

- **Base and column:** This is the milling machine rests on the ground and is required to support the machine. It has a large column that is attached to the base and is connected to other components.
- **Table:** When the workpiece is mounted on the platform, it is called a table. It sits in a T form and is attached along its surface. It is secured with the vise and can be clamped on the three slots directly.
- **Saddle:** It is also a part of the table that allows the milling machine to move in the longitudinal motion. It can also move in the horizontal section of the workpiece in the Y direction along with other platform known as the knee.
- **Knee:** It supports the saddle and the table in all the milling operations. It can also be referred to as the column and helps in the vertical motion of the workpiece. It can move vertically when the cutter is stagnant. When the cutter is moving in the vertical direction, then the cutter is stationary. This aids in cutting the workpiece and effective milling operation.

Rice Processing and Milling Techniques

Before starting the milling process, it is crucial to understand what milling entails. The total time required for rice production involves two components: the initial setup time and the cycle time for each part.The setup time of a milling machine includes the duration needed to prepare the machine for operation, plan tool movements, and install fixtures. The cycle time, on the other hand, depends on four factors:

- **The load and unload time:** This refers to the time required to load the workpiece into the machine and secure it with the fixture, as well as the time needed to unload the finished product. The load time can vary based on the size, weight, complexity of the workpiece, and the type of fixture used.
- **The cut time:** This is the time taken to perform all necessary cuts on the workpiece during each operation using the cutter. To calculate the cut time, divide the total cut length by the feed rate, which gives the operation speed of the cutter relative to the workpiece.

- **The ideal time:** Also known as non-productive time, this is when neither the workpiece nor the cutter is involved in the milling process. It includes tasks such as tool approach and retraction, tool movement between features, machine setting adjustments, and tool changes.
- **The tool replacement time:** This is the time required to replace a tool that has worn out and exceeded its operational lifespan. This time is not included in every operation but must be accounted for when a tool reaches the end of its useful life and must be replaced during the milling process.

Operation Cost of Rice Milling

There are three key cost drivers in the rice mill operation:

- **Material cost:** This is determined by the quantity of stock and its unit price, which affects the workpiece size, stock size, cutting method, and production quantity.
- **Production cost:** This arises from the total production time and hourly rate. It includes setup time, load time, cut time, idle time, and tool replacement time. The overall production cost is influenced by the operator's skill level.
- **Tooling cost:** This is determined by the number of cutting tools required and the unit price of each tool. Since various unique tools are needed for different operations, the lifetime of each tool decreases with daily use, adding to the tooling cost.

Rice milling is a critical process, and modern rice mill machines are essential for achieving the correct dimensions for the rice being processed.

5

Operation and Maintenance of Dal Mills and Oil Mills

The operation and maintenance of Dal Mills and Oil Mills are crucial components in ensuring the efficient processing of pulses and oilseeds. These mills play a significant role in the food processing industry, where the transformation of raw pulses and seeds into consumable products is vital for meeting the needs of consumers worldwide. The proper functioning of these mills requires a well-structured operation strategy, which includes careful planning and execution of each process from raw material intake to the final product output. For Dal Mills, the primary operation involves cleaning, de-hulling, splitting, and polishing pulses, while for Oil Mills, the process revolves around seed cleaning, pressing, and extraction of oil from oilseeds like sunflower, soybean, and groundnut.

Maintenance is a critical aspect of ensuring the smooth operation of these mills. Regular maintenance schedules, including inspection of machinery, replacement of worn-out parts, and calibration of equipment, help prevent costly breakdowns and extend the life of the machines. Preventive maintenance practices also contribute to the overall efficiency of the mill by minimizing downtime and optimizing energy consumption. Furthermore, the quality of the final product is closely tied to the condition of the milling machines. Proper maintenance ensures the production of high-quality dal and oil that meet industry standards and consumer expectations.

The effective management of both operational processes and maintenance procedures is essential for the profitability and sustainability of Dal and Oil Mills. Skilled personnel, adherence to safety guidelines, and a proactive approach to troubleshooting and repairing equipment are key to achieving consistent output and high product quality. This chapter will delve into the specifics of the operation and maintenance practices required to run Dal Mills and Oil Mills efficiently, providing insights into best practices, challenges, and solutions that contribute to the overall success of these milling operations.

SELECTION OF IDEAL DAL MILL EQUIPMENT

Selecting the appropriate dal mill machinery is essential for ensuring both efficiency and quality in pulse processing. Dal, an integral part of Indian cuisine, requires careful processing to meet consumer expectations. This Selection delves into various types of dal mill equipment, such as cleaners, polishers, and graders, providing valuable insights to help you choose the best options for your requirements. Additionally, there are many images to visually demonstrate different equipment used in the dal milling process.

Figure.: 5.1 Dal mill machine

Understanding Dal Mill Equipment

- **Cleaners:** The initial step in dal milling involves cleaning the pulses to eliminate dust, dirt, and other contaminants. Cleaners come in various forms, such as pre-cleaners and fine cleaners, each designed for different phases of the cleaning process.
- **De-huskers and Splitters:** De-huskers remove the outer covering of the pulses, while splitters cut the de-husked pulses into two halves. These machines are crucial for improving the dal's appearance and making it easier to digest.
- **Graders:** Grading equipment sorts the dal based on size, ensuring consistency in the final product. This step is important for meeting consumer expectations and securing better market prices.
- **Polishers:** Polishers give the dal a shiny finish, enhancing its visual appeal. They use water or oil and can significantly influence the marketability of the product.

Selection of Right Equipment

- **Assess Your Needs:** Evaluate the scale of your operation, the types of pulses you will process, and the quality you aim to achieve. This assessment will guide your choice of equipment, ensuring it aligns with your production objectives.
- **Efficiency and Capacity:** Select equipment that meets your desired output while maintaining efficiency. High-capacity machines are ideal for large-scale operations but should be energy-efficient to keep operational expenses manageable.

- **Durability and Maintenance:** Choose machines known for their robustness and ease of upkeep. Reliable equipment reduces downtime and extends the life of your dal mill.
- **Cost-Effectiveness:** While initial cost is important, consider the long-term advantages of the equipment, such as energy savings, reduced operational costs, and the possibility of future upgrades.
- **Vendor Reputation:** Opt for equipment from well-established vendors who provide after-sales support, including installation, training, and maintenance services. Strong vendor support can greatly simplify the integration of new machinery into your operations.

Recent Advances in Dal Mill Equipment

Innovation in dal mill technology has led our way to the development of advanced machines that gives us better efficiency, quality, and safety. For example, some modern polishers use less amount of water or oil, reducing the product's moisture content and increasing its shelf life. Similarly, advanced graders and sorters use optical sensors to ensure precise grading and sorting, improving the overall quality of the dal.

Practical Tips for Effective Implementation

- **Training:** Ensure that your staff is sufficiently trained to operate the new equipment. Proper operation is vital for achieving the desired efficiency and product quality.
- **Maintenance Schedule:** Establish a regular maintenance schedule to keep the equipment in optimal condition. Preventive upkeep can help avoid costly repairs and downtime.
- **Quality Control:** Implement quality control measures at different stages of the milling process. Regularly check the output to ensure it meets your quality standards.

STRUCTURAL DESIGN AND SETUP OF DAL MILLING UNITS

The mini dal mill is designed for simplicity in construction and ease of operation and maintenance. It is specifically developed for de-husking and splitting food legumes such as pigeon pea, gram, and black gram. The mill features a horizontal tapered roller coated with emery, surrounded by a screen that discharges husk powder.

The processed dals pass through an aspirating fan and an oscillating sieve unit, where they are appropriately graded. The vibratory sieves are equipped with varying hole sizes to meet the specific needs of the dal being processed. The vibration is driven by a cam-operated link mounted on a counter shaft, powered by the motor-driven shaft. Additionally, this mini dal mill from Jas Enterprise includes a paddle-type screw mixer, constructed entirely of mild steel, with a worm shaft for enhanced functionality.

Dal Milling Process and Techniques

The fundamental processes involved in dal milling include cleaning, grading, conditioning, de-husking, splitting, separation, polishing, and bagging. The primary variation in the process occurs during the de-husking stage. In some cases, linseed oil is applied during dry milling to enhance the shine or visual appeal of the milled dal. Milling pulses involves removing the outer husk and splitting the grain into two equal halves. To make the de-husking and splitting processes more efficient, an alternating wetting and drying method is often employed.

Pulses

↓

Cleaning, chaffs, dirt, etc.

↓

Pitting

↓

Pretreatment with Linseed Oil

↓

Conditioning

↓

De husking and splitting mixture of husk, small broken and powder

↓

Grading

↓

Polishing

↓

Grade I pulse

Figure.: 5.2 Flow diagram for milling of pulses

Pre milling of dals

To achieve optimal results during the de-husking and splitting of pulses in Jas brand mini dal mills, it is essential to perform pre-milling, including grading the pulses based on size. Initially, raw pulses are cleaned to remove dust, chaff, stones, and other unwanted materials. After cleaning, sieves are used to grade the pulses. These graded pulses are then soaked in cement tanks with a depth of 6 inches, ensuring the water level is 1 inch above the pulses, and the height of the soaked pulses is around 5 inches.

After soaking for a specific duration, the pulses are placed on a sieve. The swollen pulses that do not pass through the sieve are set aside for heaping in the shade, while the pulses that pass through are also kept for the same purpose. The degree of heaping for swollen pulses should be between 30 to 40 percent, and this process continues until the pulses are soaked to the desired level. Subsequently, the pulses are dried in thin layers under the open sun, with the drying duration depending on the prevailing weather conditions.

Once sun-dried, the pulses are heaped in the shade again to ensure uniform moisture content before de-husking. Finally, the pulses are re-graded and fed into the pulse de-husking machine in Jas mini dal mills in graded lots to achieve the best results with minimal breakage. For the convenience of entrepreneurs, the details of the pre-milling process, following proper cleaning, are provided in a tabulated chart.

IARI Dehusking CUIITT Splitting Machine

This machine is a small-capacity, low-cost, and portable device designed for de-husking and splitting pulses. It features a cylinder concave set, a feed hopper, and a blower, all mounted on a sturdy angle-iron frame. The clearance between the cylinder and concave is adjustable to accommodate different pulses. The blower, with its duct, helps separate the husk from the mixture of dal, unhusked pulses, and husk. Powered by a 1hp, 3-phase electric motor, the machine operates efficiently through the rubbing action between the rough surfaces of the rotating cylinder and the stationary concave. The de-husking and splitting process is further facilitated by impact forces.

The mixture of husk, unhusked grains, and splits is expelled from the bottom outlet of the machine. An air blast is applied to the mixture, which removes the husk and other lighter materials. The de-husked dal and splits are then collected at the main outlet. The machine claims to achieve de-husking efficiencies of 94% for soybean, 97% for chickpea, and 98% for peas. It also boasts a splitting efficiency of 98%, with only 10% breakage.

CIAE Dehusking and Splitting Machine

CIAE Bhopal has developed a low cost dehusking and splitting dal mill for the use in overall areas. The machine has an abrasive carborundum roller dehusker and has a capacity of 100 kg/hr. This machine can be owned, operated and manned by less skilled people of rural and semi-urban areas. The mill operates with a 1.5 KW, 3 phase electric motor. The cost of milling was estimated to be 14 Rupees/ Quintal. The average recovery in case of pigeonpea, mungbean and urdbean was claimed to be 75% and 74% each, respectively. As water treatment is recommended with the mill, the Utilization of edible oil in the process of dehusking has been completely removed in this process.

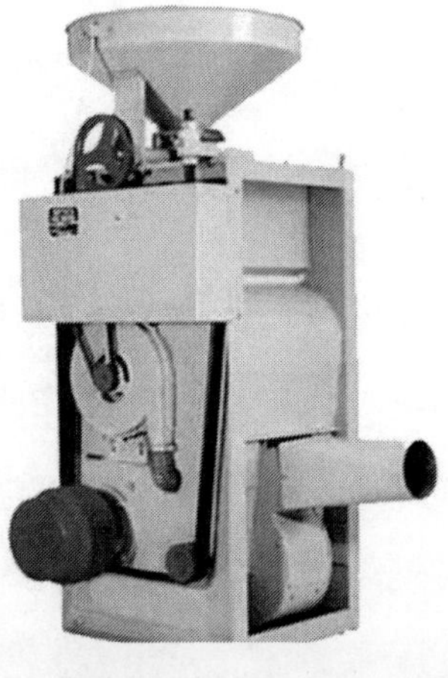

Figure.: 5.3 CIAE Mini Dal Mill

PKV Mini Dal Mill

The mill is composed of four main units: the splitting unit, sieve, aspirator, and polisher. A pre-milling treatment involves soaking difficult-to-mill pulse grains in a sodium bicarbonate solution.The splitting unit consists of two emery discs powered by a 1.0 hp single-phase electric motor. One disc is stationary, while the other rotates. The gap between the discs is adjustable using a screw mechanism operated by a hand wheel. This unit has a processing capacity of 40-45 kg per hour for pigeonpea and around 60 kg per hour for mungbean and urdbean.The sieve unit features two reciprocating sieves that are easily removable. Different sieve sizes are used to accommodate various grain sizes. The sieves separate the milled mixture into three parts: broken dal, dal, and a mixture of husked and dehusked grains. These parts are directed to individual outlets.The aspiration unit includes two blowers (aspirators) and a cyclone separator. The first aspirator is placed near the splitting unit's outlet to separate husk and powder from the milled mixture, ensuring a dust-free operation. The second aspirator removes husk from the dal as it moves through the polisher unit. Both aspirators are connected to a cyclone separator, which collects the powder from the husk and powder mixture, preventing it from dispersing into the air.In the polisher, polishing is achieved with two screw conveyors covered in leather and housed in a casing. The friction between the dal and the leather, as well as the casing's inner surface, helps polish the dal and removes any husk that remains adhered to it.

Figure.: 5.4 PKV Mini Dal Mill

It is essential to give pre-treatment to pigeonpea grains before milling. Grains are soaked in 6% solution of Sodium bi-carbonate for 40 minutes and dried. The grains of mungbean and urdbean do not require any premilling treatment. In case of pigeonpea, the maximum efficiency over 72% can be obtained. This machine is recommended to be use at cottage industries level.

CFTRI Hand Operated Pulse Dehusking Machine

The CFTRI in Mysore has developed a hand-operated abrasion-type machine for processing pulses at the household level. This machine performs both dehusking and splitting operations with minimal breakage and powdering. It is capable of dehusking 40-60 kg of pre-conditioned pulses per hour. The machine is suitable for dehusking pulses such as pigeonpea, chickpea, soybean, and peas that have been properly pre-treated. Husk and broken pulses are separated through winnowing and sieving. The machine is claimed to achieve 95-98% dehusking efficiency, with a yield of head dal around 75-80%. A motorized version is also available. This machine is simple to operate and can be maintained and repaired at the rural level. It was designed to replace traditional chakkis.

CFTRI Mini Dal Mill

The CFTRI mini dal mill is designed to dehusk 100-150 kg of pre-treated pulses per hour and is recommended for small-scale operations. This mill consists of a dehusking and splitting unit, an aspirator, and a separator unit, all powered by a 1 hp single-phase motor. The machine is capable of dehusking bold pulses like pigeonpea, chickpea, peas, and soybean.

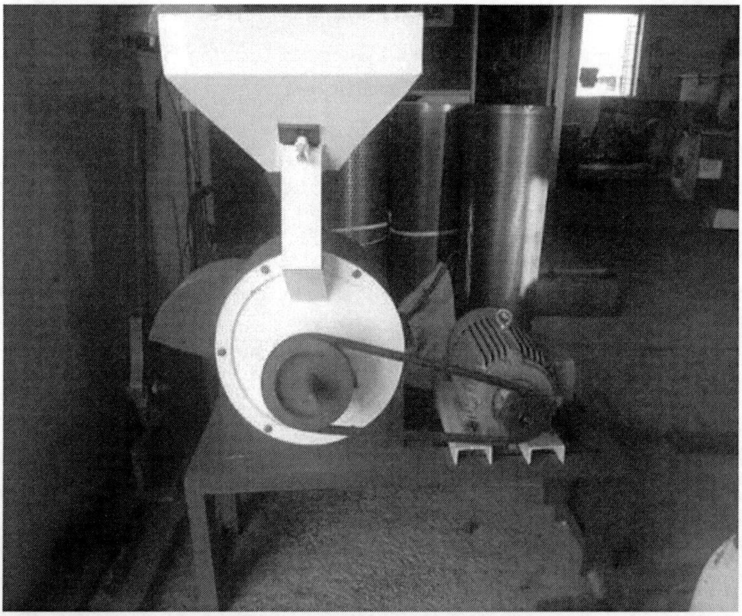

Figure.: 5.5 CFTRI Mini Dal Mill

For mungbean and urdbean, the mill can also achieve splitting of unhusked grains. It is claimed that this mill provides a yield of 77–80% with dehusking efficiency ranging from 97-99%. This integrated unit includes a grader powered by a 1/2 hp single-phase motor, capable of grading 200-250 kg of soaked (wet) pulses per hour. The machine dehusks and splits grains simultaneously. Dehusking occurs through the abrasion of grains between the rotating emery-coated cone and the wire mesh cage. The aspirator separates the husk, while the broken grains are segregated by the reciprocating sieve assembly. The dehusked and unhusked grains are collected at separate outlets. The machine offers a higher yield and good quality dal at lower processing costs. This technology promotes a pollution-free environment while minimizing power consumption. The mini dal mill is straightforward in design, easy to operate, and can be repaired and maintained at the rural level.

A Brief Overview of Pantnagar Manually Operated Dal Mill

This mill is designed to be used by farmers at cottage scale with a view to enable them to market their produce after primary processing so as to augment their income. It consists of hopper, screw conveyor, emery rollers and cylindrical separators. The mill has a capacity of 50 kg/hr. The mill can be operated with the help of paddles. The dal is treated with 10% sodium bi-carbonate solution followed by tempering and drying to 10% moisture content. It gives 75% dehusking for pigeonpea grains. The mill was found effective for urdbean, chickpea, soybean etc. The yield of head dal is 50 kg/hr and broken amount to 5-6%. Only one labour is required to operate this mill.

Pantnagar Mini Dal Mill

The machine consists of emery rollers, a hopper, conveyors, and separators, and operates with the help of a 1.0 hp motor, offering a processing capacity of 100 kg per hour. It is specifically designed for processing pigeonpea, requiring five hours for complete milling. The pre-treatment process utilizes a 10% NaHCO3 solution. The milling yield is 50 kg per hour of dehusked dal, with an 80% dehusking efficiency.

The first prototype of the IIPR Mini Dal Mill was developed in 1992, and since then, several upgraded models have been created and commercialized, with around 175 units established across the country. The mill comprises a feeding unit, milling unit, and cleaning unit. The feeding unit includes a feed hopper and auger-type mechanism that ensures a steady flow of treated pulse grains to the milling unit. The milling unit is a vertical attrition system, featuring stationary rubber and rotating corrugated steel disks. The gap between the disks can be adjusted to accommodate different pulse crops and grain sizes. After milling, air suction via a blower separates the husk and powder through a cyclone separator. The use of rubber disks in the milling unit results in a 5-10% higher dal recovery compared to emery roller mills.

The latest version of the IIPR Mini Dal Mill includes provisions for grading both raw materials and finished products, ensuring uniformity during milling.

Grading of the finished product separates various fractions of the milled material. Additionally, an emery roller (3810 x 1524 mm) is added to perform pitting operations, which speeds up the pre-milling treatment and significantly reduces residence time. The new model also produces 'gota' (dehusked whole) lentils, known as "MalkaMasoor," a product difficult to achieve with earlier models due to splitting in vertical attrition mills. Improvements have also been made to the disk holding mechanism and the quality of rubber disks. Pitting, milling, cleaning, and grading can now be done simultaneously.

The machine can also be used to make 'dalia' or grits for animal feed by replacing the rubber disk with a steel disk. This mini dal mill has the potential to generate a monthly profit of Rs. 5,000 while providing employment for three individuals. It holds great promise as a cottage-scale industry, benefiting rural entrepreneurs, unemployed youth, and progressive farmers.

Figure.: 5.6 IIPR Dal Chakki

Figure.: 5.7 IIPR Dal Mill

Table.: 5.1 Relative Performance of Three Most Popular Mini Dal Mills

Category	Parameter	IIPR Dal Mill	CIAE Dal Mill	CFTRI Dal Mill
Chickpea	Raw Grain			
	Dehusking Efficiency	61.86%	58.26%	60.10%
	Dal Recovery	53.20%	49.20%	54.00%
	Soaked			
	Dehusking Efficiency	90.23%	88.00%	89.00%
	Dal Recovery	77.60%	68.70%	76.50%
Pigeonpea	Raw Grain			
	Dehusking Efficiency	49.53%	40.35%	45.35%
	Dal Recovery	42.60%	38.00%	40.60%
	Soaked (11h)			
	Dehusking Efficiency	87.90%	77.09%	88.10%
	Dal Recovery	75.60%	68.00%	76.60%
Oil & Water Treated Pigeonpea	Dehusking Efficiency	98.90%	79.86%	98.20%
	Dal Recovery	77.20%	51.40%	75.80%
$NaHCO_3$ Treatment	Dehusking Efficiency	95.20%	85.48%	94.75%
	Dal Recovery	75.38%	50.70%	72.20%

Upkeep of Dal Mill

Proper upkeep of a dal mill ensures smooth operation, enhances efficiency, and prolongs the life of the equipment. Maintenance can be categorized into routine (preventive) and corrective maintenance.

Preventive Maintenance

- Daily Maintenance:
  - **Cleaning**: Ensure that all parts, especially the feeding mechanism, sieves, and air ducts, are free of accumulated dust and pulse husks.
  - **Lubrication:** Lubricate bearings, rollers, and moving parts as per the manufacturer's specifications to reduce wear.
  - **Check Belts and Chains:** Inspect the belts and chains for wear, and adjust or replace them if necessary.
- Weekly Maintenance:
  - **Inspect Dehulling and Splitting Units:** Check the dehulling and splitting machines for wear and tear. Ensure that the screens and rollers are functioning properly.
  - **Monitor Air Pressure**: Inspect the air blower system for proper air pressure and functioning. Clean the air filters regularly.
  - **Check Electrical Components:** Inspect the electrical panel for any loose connections or signs of overheating.
- Monthly Maintenance:
  - **Clean and Inspect Motors:** Check the motors for overheating and cleanliness. Ensure they are properly ventilated and clean the dust from motor vents.
  - **Inspect Grading and Sifting Units:** Ensure that the grading and sifting screens are clean and free of blockages.
  - **Test Moisture Levels:** Test the moisture content in the pulses. Proper moisture content is critical for effective dehulling and splitting.
  - **Check Condition of Polishing Unit:** If polishing is done, check the condition of polishing drums and surfaces.

Corrective Maintenance and Preventive Strategies

- Motor or Electrical Failure:
  - Check the electrical components for issues like damaged wiring or faulty connections.
  - Replace any worn-out parts, such as fuses, relays, or contactors.
- Clogging or Jamming:
  - If the mill gets clogged or jams, check the feeding mechanism, sieves, and air ducts for blockages.
  - Clear out any material stuck in the system and ensure smooth flow during operation.
- Excessive Vibration or Noise:
  - If unusual vibrations or noises are heard, inspect the bearings, rollers, and other moving parts.
  - Ensure that all components are properly aligned and that there are no loose parts.

- Dehulling or Splitting Issues:
  - If the husks are not being removed properly or the pulses are not splitting well, check the condition of the abrasive or impact dehuller.
  - Adjust the machine settings and replace any worn-out rollers, discs, or blades.

Resolving Common Issues in Dal Mill

- Low Dehulling Efficiency:
  - **Possible Cause:** Incorrect moisture levels, poor conditioning, or damaged dehulling units.
  - **Solution:** Adjust the moisture content of pulses, inspect and clean the dehulling equipment, and replace any worn-out components.
- Splitting Problems (Incomplete Splitting):
  - **Possible Cau**se: Worn-out roller mills, incorrect pressure, or feeding speed.
  - **Solution:** Check the roller mills for wear, adjust the feeding speed, and ensure proper alignment.
- Broken Dal (High Percentage of Broken Dal):
  - **Possible Cause:** Over-drying of pulses, excessive moisture, or poor quality of raw pulses.
  - **Solution**: Ensure proper conditioning, check for any cracked pulses, and adjust the machine settings.
- Poor Polishing:
  - **Possible Cause:** Worn-out polishing drums, incorrect polishing time, or inadequate polishing material.
  - **Solution:** Clean and inspect the polishing drums, adjust the polishing settings, and replace worn-out polishing material.
- Safety Considerations
  - **Electrical Safety:** Ensure that all electrical components are properly insulated and grounded. Use appropriate safety switches and breakers to prevent accidents.
  - **Dust Control:** Ensure proper dust collection systems are in place to prevent dust accumulation, which can be a fire hazard.
  - **Protective Guards:** Install safety guards around moving parts like the rollers, motors, and blades to prevent accidental injuries.
  - **Personal Protective Equipment (PPE):** Operators should wear appropriate PPE, including gloves, ear protection, and dust masks, especially when operating or cleaning machinery.

OIL MILL

An oil mill is a facility used to extract oil from various seeds, such as sunflower, soybean, mustard, groundnut, and cotton. The mill processes seeds through mechanical or hydraulic pressing methods, followed by refining to produce edible oils. Proper operation and maintenance are crucial for maximizing output, ensuring oil quality, and prolonging the life of the equipment.

Main Components of an Oil Mill

- **Seed Cleaning Section:** Machines like air blowers and sieves to remove impurities like dust, stones, and other foreign materials.
- **Crushing or Pressing Units:** Mechanical or hydraulic presses to extract oil from seeds.
- **Expeller or Press:** The machine used for extracting oil from seeds.
- **Oil Filter:** A filtering system to remove any solid particles from the extracted oil.
- **Refining Section:** In some mills, a refining section is included to purify the oil by removing unwanted compounds like free fatty acids, moisture, and color.
- **Solvent Extraction Unit:** If applicable, a solvent extraction system for additional oil recovery.
- **Packaging Unit:** To pack the final refined oil into containers.

Preparation of Raw Materials

Oilseeds and nuts must be thoroughly dried before storage and cleaned to eliminate contaminants such as sand, dust, leaves, and other debris. It is crucial to sort the raw materials to remove stones and moldy nuts, as some molds, particularly in groundnuts, can cause aflatoxin contamination, which is harmful. When storage is necessary, it should take place in weatherproof, well-ventilated rooms, protected from birds, insects, and rodents. Certain raw materials, like groundnuts and sunflower seeds, require dehusking or decorticating. This process is essential for maximizing oil yields and reducing the volume of material to be processed. However, expellers typically need a portion of fibrous material to operate effectively, and for groundnuts, adding some husk helps facilitate the release of oil from the press. Coconuts are manually dehusked and split by skilled workers. Most oilseeds, including copra, palm kernels, and groundnuts, need to be ground in mills before oil extraction to enhance yields. Maintaining the proper moisture content in all oil-bearing materials is critical for optimizing oil production.

Methods of Oil Extraction

1. Mechanical expression

During the process of mechanical expression, the oil seeds are compressed in various types of compression devices/equipment. Expression is the process of mechanically pressing liquid out of liquid containing solids. Screw press, roll presses, collapsible plate are some examples of wide range of equipment used for expression of liquid.

- **Hydraulic press:** The hydraulic press is considered of a series of horizontal corrugated iron plates. These plates are separated by 4 – 14 premoulded oil seed cakes. Pressing is completed in two stages. In first stage, the oil seeds are pressed at about 5 MPa for 15-20 min and then pressure of 28 MPa is applied for 5-10 min to complete the expression process. The recovery of the oil varied depending upon the sizes and seed being pressed. But, the at commercial level, the hydraulic press is replaced by screw type presses.
- **Screw press:** A screw press features a horizontal main shaft with an integrally formed screw assembly. The screw rotates inside a cage or barrel, which is constructed from case-hardened, tool steel bars or rings to allow oil drainage as pressure builds on the feed material. At the discharge end, a movable choke or cone regulates the operating pressure by adjusting the width of the annular space through which the oil cake passes. This adjustment is made via a hand wheel located at the opposite end of the screw. The screw's design ensures that the volume displacement at the feed end is significantly larger than at the discharge end, leading to increasing pressure as the material moves from the feed end to the discharge end. This rising pressure compresses the material, causing the oil to be expelled through the gaps between the cage lining bars.
- **Ram press:** A long pivoted lever moves a piston backwards and forewords inside a cylindrical cage constructed from a metal bars spaced to allow the passage of oil. At one end of the piston's stroke, it opens an entry port from the seed hopper so that seed enters the press cage. When the piston is moved forward, the entry post is closed and the oilseed is compressed in the cage. As a result, oil is expelled from the oilseed the emerges through the gaps in the cage. Compressed seed is pushed out through the gaps in the cage. Compressed seed is pushed out through circular gap at the end of the cage.

2. Oil Extraction

Extraction is a process that separates a liquid from a solid system using a solvent. It relies on diffusion, often utilizing a solvent with a low boiling point, which results in a higher oil recovery and a drier cake compared to expression methods. Solvent extraction can extract nearly all of the available oil from oilseed meal and produces meal with better preservation and higher protein quality.

In this process, the solvent is introduced to the well-prepared material, followed by the diffusion of the oil-solvent mixture to the surface of the solid for oil recovery. N-hexane, with a boiling point of 65.5°C, is the most commonly used solvent in India. The oil is separated from the oil-hexane mixture, known as miscella, through distillation and stripping under vacuum. The extracted meal, containing hexane, is then de-solventized by heating it with live steam in a de-solventizer, producing deoiled cake with less than 1% residual oil. The solvent from the distillation and stripping processes, as well as from the de-solventizer, is condensed, recovered, and stored in a solvent storage tank. After cooling, the separated oil is transferred to the storage tank.

Solvent extraction plant use hexane as a solvent to extract oil from oilseed cake. These plants are expensive and only suitable for large volumes which justify the capital cost of equipment. Where large amounts of oilseed cake are available, solvent extraction becomes a commercially- viable option to extract residual oil left in the cake and leave an almost oil-free powder known as oilseed meal. Both cake and meal are incorporated in animal feeds.

Oil Refining Process

In many local markets, further refining may not be necessary as unrefined oils are preferred. However, international markets often favor lighter, less intense oils for cooking, which require additional processing. Several refining processes can be conducted after the oil has been filtered.

- **De-odorizing:** Volatile compounds that cause unpleasant odors are eliminated by sparging, which involves bubbling steam through the oil under a vacuum.
- **Wintering:** The oil is allowed to stand at low temperatures for a period, during which glycerides with higher melting points solidify. These can then be filtered out. Over time, glycerides can break down and release fatty acids, increasing acidity and reducing oil quality.
- **Neutralization:** Fatty acids can be neutralized by adding a sodium hydroxide solution (caustic soda) or by stripping, a process similar to de-odorizing.
- **Bleaching:** Oils with dark colors, which may be unappealing to consumers, can be lightened through a bleaching process.
- **De-gumming:** For seeds with high phosphatide content, de-gumming involves mixing the oil with 2 to 3% water. The hydrated phosphatides, which cause gum formation, can then be removed by settling, filtering, or centrifuging.

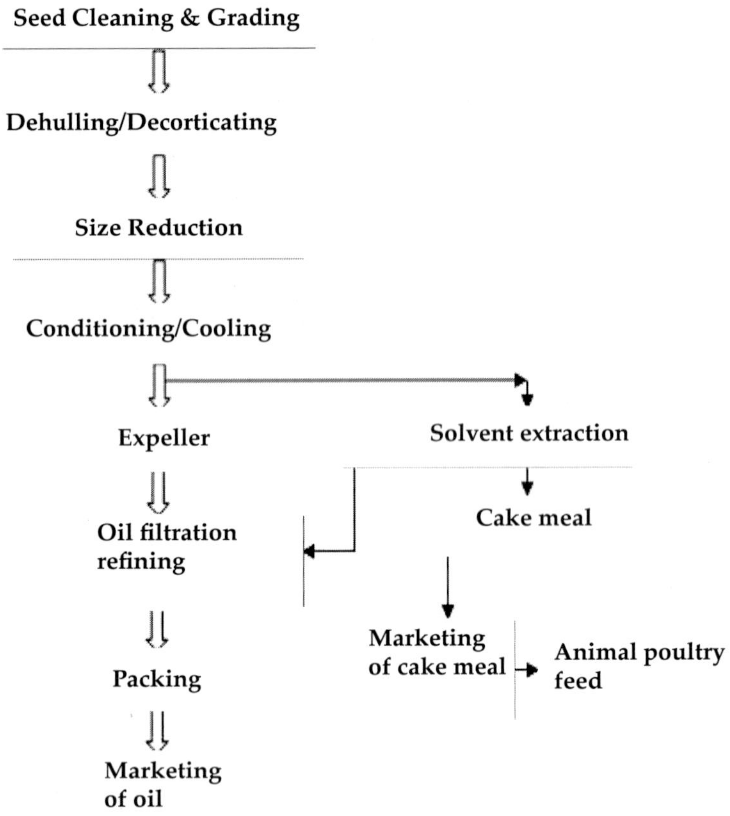

Figure.: 5.8 Flow chart of oil seed processing

KEY OPERATIONS AND PROCESSES IN OIL MILL

Some of the oil seeds are crushed in oil expellers directly while some are not crushed. This decision is taken based on the oil percentage in the oil seed. In general if the oil percentage is more than 20% the seed is treated in expellers, otherwise. It is not economical to expel the seed.

Sourcing and Acquistion of Raw Materials

At the time of purchase the purchaser should consider moisture content, percentage of damaged seed, maturity of seeds, oil percentage and other foreign matter, The rates are decided based on market price considering the above factors. There are guidelines available in various markets and specifications are followed accordingly. Raw material procurement is an important factor affecting productivity along with profitability.

Oilseed Storage and Preservation

- Usually the oil seeds are stored in godowns packed in gunney bags. Care should be taken of proper moisture content in seed and proper aeration should be ensured. Sometimes the seeds get damaged due to self combustion, if they are not dry. The most modern method of storing of oil seeds is to stock them in ling vertical well ventilated bins or "silos" which may be constructed either with concrete, steel or wood.

Oilseed Processing

- Before actual crushing of the seed for obtaining oil, following important steps should be observed.

Pre-Cleaning of the Seed

Seeds generally contain impurities like sand, stone, stems of plant, earth sutli, leaf, grass etc. Sometimes they contain iron and metallic pieces too. These impurities should be removed in order to obtain high quality of the oil. These impurities inspite of injuring the quality of the cake, lower the oil yield by absorption of certain amount oil and tends to wear out of the machinery.

Pre-cleaning of the seed increases the life of expellers and minimises unwarranted breakdowns and keeps the better quality of finished products.

Various types of seed cleansing machines are utilized in the oil mill industry.

- Hand cleaning machines
- Stationary seed cleaning machines
- Vibration seed cleaning machines
- Rotary seed cleaning machines
- Brushing machines

Process of Decortication

Before seeds are sent to decortication machines, they must first pass through de-stoner machines to remove stones that are similar in size to the seeds, which may have been missed during pre-cleaning.

Certain seeds, such as groundnuts, castor, and cotton seeds, have an outer covering called shell or husk. This husk contains almost no oil and makes up about 30% of the seed's total weight. Removing it before crushing is important for the following reasons:

- It enhances the mill's pressing capacity.
- If the husk is not removed, it will be pressed into the cake, absorbing oil and leading to a lower oil yield.
- The husk also affects the oil's color.
- Being siliceous in nature, the husk can harm the expellers.

It is necessary to frequently check the decorticator machine settings to ensure that husk does not carry small kernel pieces, which would result in a direct loss.

In these machines, seeds are passed through special rollers equipped with cutting edges and ridges that break the shells while leaving the seed intact. Various types of decorticator machines are used depending on the size and nature of the seed, including groundnut decorticators, castor seed shellers, and cotton seed hullers available in the market. After the husk is broken, the seeds are cleaned by blowing off the husk.

Seed Conditioning

In order to extract better quality of oil most efficiently, using minimum pressure and electricity, proper conditioning of the seeds is very important.

Seed Cracking

Before crushing the seeds, it is advisable to pass them through a seed cracker machine, where they are fed between two rotating chilled steel rollers. In some cases, the rolling operation is performed by passing the seed through a set of five heavy rollers stacked vertically. Various types of machines, such as disintegrators, edge-runners, and reduction rolls, are used for the preliminary reduction of Various seeds like mahua, copra, rapeseed, sesame, and groundnuts. For copra, specialized cutters and breaking machines are employed. Cracking the seeds beforehand helps in enhancing the efficiency of subsequent cooking and drying processes in the expeller kettles.

Cooking and Drying

This is a key step in the extant step in the extraction of oil by expeller method. The cracked seeds are properly cooked with open steam. Given below are the main objects of cooking:-

- To regulate the moisture content of the seed meal.
- To coagulate the proteins in the walls of the fat containing cells.
- To make the cell walls permeable to the flow to oil.

The oil droplets in seeds are almost ultramicroscopic and distributed throughout the seed. One key effect of cooking is the merging of these tiny droplets into larger drops that can flow out of the seed. Another effect is the drying of the seed to achieve the necessary plasticity for efficient pressing. Cooking also reduces the oil's affinity for the solid surface of the seed, ensuring the best possible oil yield when pressed. Additionally, cooking causes the insolubilization of phosphatides and other impurities, destroys molds and bacteria, increases cotton seed fluidity, and detoxifies substances like gossypol. Seeds that are too dry cannot be efficiently extraction, and the cooking process aids in regulating the moisture content. The optimal moisture level varies depending on the seed variety and the extraction method used.

During cooking, the cracked seeds are placed in steam kettles located over the expeller machine. The seed temperature is raised, and the moisture content is reduced to about 5% by drying in a steam-jacketed kettle. Typically, cooking and drying in the expeller kettle takes around 40-45 minutes for groundnuts, though this duration can vary depending on the seed. There are no strict guidelines for seed treatment, and the process relies heavily on experience.

The theory behind cooking is that the combination of heat and moisture breaks down the oil cells, softens their gelatinous coatings, increases the clarity of the oil, and coagulates the alumina sediment in the seed, making it easier for the oil to flow out when pressure is applied.

Crushing the Oil Seeds & Nuts

The expeller consists of a pressing box or cage that encircles a horizontal shaft fitted with a series of worms. The feeding end of the cage has an opening where the seed meal is introduced into the expeller, while at the discharge end, a cone restricts the passage. As the horizontal shaft rotates, the meal is pushed forward by the screw action of the worms, which increases the internal pressure, thereby squeezing out the oil. The pressure inside the expeller is controlled by adjusting the cone. The extracted oil flows through the perforated box, while the cake exits through the opening around the cone.

The expeller is a self-contained unit, equipped with its own heating kettle and an automatic feeding mechanism. Once set up, the expeller requires no further attention, as long as the temperature and moisture content of the seed meal are properly regulated. As the meal moves through the expeller, it becomes hotter due to frictional heat.

The design of the worms is crucial for the efficient extraction of oil from different seeds. High-grade steel worms are highly resistant to pressure and abrasion, ensuring a longer lifespan. Expellers are available in two pressure designs: low and high. Low pressure expellers remove only a portion of the oil from the seed meal and typically have high capacities, ranging from 30-80 metric tons of seed per day. These are often used in combination with high pressure expellers, solvent extraction plants, or to extract oil from seeds with a high oil content, where complete extraction in one go is not feasible. High pressure expellers, on the other hand, extract all the oil that can be removed from the seed meal in one pass and operate at pressures of 2.5-3.0 tons per square inch. However, they have lower capacities.

Filtration of Oil

The oil extracted from the expeller contains impurities such as foots, suspended particles of seed, and cake remnants. Before the oil can be stored in tanks, it must undergo filtration. This process involves pumping the oil to a filter press, where it passes through a layer of filter cloth. The liquid oil filters through the cloth, while the solid particles are deposited on it.

There are two key types of filter presses usually used in the oil mill industry:

- Recessed Plate or Chamber Type Filter Press
- Plate and Frame Type Filter Press

Recessed Plate Type Filter Press

This press consists of a series of cast iron plates, each with a recessed center and a raised rim around the periphery. When the plates are brought together, the recessed centers form a chamber between them. When the press is open, a filter cloth is laid over each plate, hanging down on both sides and extending beyond the edges. Each plate has a circular feed hole in the center, with corresponding holes in the filter cloth. The cloths are secured around the central feed hole using special tightening nuts.

Once all the plates and cloths are assembled and tightened, the cloth creates a tight seal between the machined edges of the plates. The tightening process is achieved using a rack and pinion system, with the pinion being rotated by a tommy bar inserted into holes around its flange.

Plate and Frame type Filter Press

In this type of filter press, the edges of the plates are finely machined and nearly level with the filtering surface. An independent frame is positioned between the plates to form a chamber. The plates and frames are arranged alternately, and the filter cloth is simply hung over them. When the plates are closed, the cloth is nipped between the edges of the plates and frames. The plates are designed with special recesses to provide a fitting surface and facilitate drainage. The filtered oil is discharged through bib spouts or cocks.

This filter press type offers an advantage over the recessed plate type in terms of capacity. It can accommodate a larger amount of sediment, allowing more oil to be filtered at once without the need to open the press. The foots separated during the filtration process are typically mixed with the oilseed before feeding it into the expeller.

Storage Management of Oil and Cake

Storage of Oil

The filtered oil from the filter press is usually pumped on to the storage tanks. The capacity of oil storage necessary for a mill generally depends on its capacity and commercial considerations. Greater storage capacity is always considered better since it enables the crusher to continue its operations even when the oil market is unfavourable.

Storage of Cake

The storage of oil cake is just as important as the storage of oilseeds. Freshly produced cake is hot and contains surface moisture. To cool it down, the cake is spread on well-ventilated floors for 24-36 hours, allowing the moisture and temperature to adjust according to the atmospheric conditions. Once cooled, the cake can be packed into gunny bags and stacked properly. Special care should be taken to ensure that the cake storage areas are well-ventilated to prevent moisture buildup and ensure proper preservation.

Quality Control

The oil mill managers should always be conscious about the quality. They should purchase the raw material of good quality for getting best profits and enhanced yields. This rule applies to oilseeds as well as other inputs like gunney bags, fuel, spare parts etc. They should always have an eye of the oil content of the oil seeds purchased. Similarly they should check regularly the quality of the oil and cake produced in their mills.

OIL MILL MAINTENANCE AND UPKEEP

The operation of an oil mill involves complex machinery that requires regular maintenance for smooth functioning, efficiency, and safety. Regular preventive maintenance and addressing issues promptly can prolong equipment life and minimize downtime.

- Daily Maintenance:
  - **Cleaning:** Ensure that machines, conveyors, and pipelines are cleaned regularly to avoid build-up of residual oil or seed debris.
  - **Lubrication:** Lubricate the moving parts like bearings, gears, and motors to avoid friction and wear. Follow the manufacturer's guidelines for the type and frequency of lubrication.
  - **Check Oil Filter:** Inspect the oil filter for blockages and clean it as necessary to ensure efficient filtration of the oil.
- Weekly Maintenance:
  - **Inspect Pressing Units:** Check for wear and tear in the pressing units. Clean the expeller and other pressing machines, and check the oil press cage and screw for any damages.
  - **Examine Seed Cleaning System:** Inspect sieves, air blowers, and conveyors used in the cleaning process. Ensure they are functioning optimally.
  - **Check Oil Extraction Unit**: Inspect the solvent extraction system for leaks, and ensure that all seals and gaskets are intact.
- Monthly Maintenance:
  - **Check Hydraulic Systems:** In case of hydraulic presses, inspect the hydraulic system for any leaks or signs of low pressure.
  - **Inspect Refining Units:** If refining is part of the process, check the equipment for proper functioning, including degumming, decolorization, and deodorization units.
  - **Monitor Oil Storage:** Check the storage tanks for any leaks or signs of contamination.
- Quarterly Maintenance
  - **Examine Motors and Electrical Components:** Inspect the motors for overheating, excessive vibration, or unusual noises. Clean dust from electrical components to prevent malfunctions.
  - **Inspect Solvent Extraction Equipment:** For mills that use solvent extraction, check for any issues related to solvent leakage and ensure proper ventilation in the extraction area.

Diagnosing and Resolving Common Issues

- Low Oil Yield:
  - **Possible Cause**: Insufficient seed crushing, improper moisture content in seeds, or issues with the press.

- **Solution:** Adjust the pressing settings, ensure proper seed moisture content, and maintain the expeller in good condition.

- Excessive Heat in Press:
    - **Possible Cause:** Overloading of the pressing machine or improper lubrication.
    - **Solution:** Check the load on the machine, lubricate moving parts regularly, and ensure proper cooling.
- Clogged Oil Filter:
    - **Possible Cause:** Build-up of solid impurities or improper filtration.
    - **Solution:** Clean the oil filter or replace it, depending on the condition.
- Solvent Leaks (Solvent Extraction Systems):
    - **Possible Cause:** Worn-out seals or damaged pipes.
    - **Solution:** Inspect all seals, valves, and pipelines for leaks and replace faulty components. Ensure proper ventilation to avoid fire hazards.
- Electrical Failures:
    - **Possible Cause:** Loose connections, overheating, or faulty components.
    - **Solution:** Check the wiring for damage, clean electrical components, and replace any worn-out parts.

Safety Measures and Best Practices

Safety is paramount in the operation of an oil mill due to the high-pressure Equipment, solvent use, and risk of fire or explosion.

- **Electrical Safety**: Ensure proper grounding of electrical equipment and conduct regular checks for damaged wiring or overheating.
- **Fire Prevention:** Install fire extinguishers, flame arresters, and proper ventilation in the solvent extraction areas to prevent fire hazards.
- **Personal Protective Equipment (PPE):** Operators should wear gloves, helmets, safety glasses, ear protection, and other necessary PPE to prevent injuries from moving parts and equipment.
- **First Aid:** Ensure that first aid kits are easily accessible and that staff are trained in basic first aid, especially in case of burns or electrical shocks.
- **Proper Training:** Operators should be adequately trained on the safe operation of machinery, handling chemicals (such as solvents), and responding to emergency situations.

The working and upkeep of an oil mill require a systematic approach to ensure efficient oil extraction and a high-quality product. Routine preventive maintenance, proper handling of machinery, and safety precautions are essential to ensure long-term operation and prevent costly breakdowns. Regular troubleshooting and addressing operational issues promptly will enhance the efficiency of the mill, reduce downtime, and maximize oil yield.

6

Operation and Maintenance of Flour Mills and Pulverisers

OPERATING MECHANISM OF A FLOUR MACHINE

The flour grinding machine operates using blade cutting, high-speed air impact, and a two-layer destruction function that integrates collision and particle sorting. The principle of operation involves the rotor generating high-speed airflow during blade cutting. As the material accelerates within the airflow, repeated impacts cause it to be destroyed in two layers simultaneously, enhancing the destruction rate.

As airflow enters the classification chamber, the destruction process rotates at high speed, and the classification rotor generates centrifugal force. The viscous effect of the airflow creates centripetal force. When the centrifugal force on the particles exceeds the centripetal force, the coarse particles return to the destruction chamber, while fine particles are carried with the airflow to the powder collector for collection.

There are three primary operating characteristics of the flour mill. First, the main shaft in the power system is sequentially equipped with bearing caps, radial ball bearings, bearing pads, and thrust ball bearings from top to bottom. Second, the grinding system consists of a spring, spring pad, inner grinding head, adjusting nut, and outer grinding head mounted on the spindle. Lastly, the separation system features a brush mounted on the spindle, with a tension spring above and an adjusting nut below the brush.

The core principle of the flour grinding process is to reduce grains like wheat, corn, or rice into flour particles. Raw grains are introduced into the mill's hopper and then conveyed to the grinding chamber containing the grinding stones or rollers. As the grains pass through the chamber, the high-speed rotation of the stones or rollers generates friction that crushes, grinds, and pulverizes the grains into a coarse powder, which gradually becomes fine flour.

Flour mills are equipped with adjustable settings to regulate the gap between the grinding stones or rollers, allowing for varying flour fineness. This ensures the production of flour suitable for different culinary needs, from coarse flours for rustic bread to fine flours for delicate pastries. The ground flour particles are then sifted to separate any bran or impurities, ensuring a refined final product. Flour mills use advanced sieving mechanisms to ensure only the finest particles pass through, while larger particles are recycled for further grinding.

Flour mills incorporate advanced technologies to optimize performance, including powerful motors, precise control systems, and safety features to ensure smooth and efficient operation.

FLOUR MILLING MACHINERY: CORE OF PRODUCTION EFFICIENTY

Cleaning Equipment

The initial step in the milling process involves thorough cleaning of raw grains. Cleaning equipment, such as vibratory sieves and magnetic separators, removes impurities, ensuring the purity of the final product.

Aspiration Separator

One of the initial steps in the flour milling process is cleaning the raw grains. An aspiration separator is a key machine for this purpose. It helps remove impurities, dust, and other foreign materials from the grains, ensuring a clean and high-quality end product.

Destoner

A destoner is another vital cleaning machine that separates stones and heavier particles from the grains. This ensures that the subsequent milling stages are not hindered by unwanted materials, contributing to the overall efficiency of the flour mill.

Different Types of Flour Mills

As home flour milling gains popularity, various types of flour mills are now available. These range from manual to electric models and include different grinding technologies, such as burr and impact mechanisms, used in both home and commercial flour mills.

Electric Grain Mills

Electric flour mills provide fast, automated milling at the push of a button. Many feature dual stainless steel or stone burr grinding systems for efficient milling and a cool grind that helps preserve nutrients. Popular electric mills include the Silence by Waldner and Mockmill 100.

Waldner Grain Mills

These iconic Austrian-made mills feature high-quality stone burrs that produce super-fine, velvety flours perfect for delicate pastries and cakes. The burrs turn slowly to reduce heat buildup. Waldner mills are treasured for their exceptional craftsmanship and performance.

Mockmill Grain Mills

This brand of electric mills has engineered its stone burrs to grind more coolly than traditional mills, preserving nutrients better. Mockmill burrs are designed not to touch, reducing friction and heat. These are available in different models, which includes the Mockmill 100 and 200.

Manual Grain Mills

For trad itionalists, manual and hand-crank flour mills provide old-fashioned milling experience. Units like the Farina or Flocker attach to a counter or tabletop and are powered by turning a hand crank.

The flour mill types we make are roller mill, disc mill and stone mill. There are three types of milling techniques that produce different flour qualities and are usually used in different processing and eating scenarios.

Disc Mill

The working principle involves placing the material into the hopper, where it enters the crushing chamber and is crushed by the continuous cutting action of round and flat teeth, along with the friction from the tooth plate. Once the material becomes fine powder or slurry, it is discharged through a screen outlet, aided by centrifugal force and airflow. Based on this principle, the disc mill machine is usually used for milling whole grains or beans, where the required fineness is not very high. It is suitable for both human and animal food production, offering a low-cost solution that requires minimum amount of space, making it ideal for markets with less stringent flour quality demands.

Stone Mill

The interior of both the upper and lower layers of the stone mill, as well as both sides of the middle layer, feature regular grooves with the middle being deeper and the outer sections shallower, creating a gap in the center. As the grain enters, it first moves through the gap in the middle, guided by the engraved chute channel. With the rotation of the middle stone, the gap slowly becomes narrower , ultimately turning the grain into powder. Stone mill machines have a long history spanning thousands of years and are associated with nutrition, environmental sustainability, and healthy eating. They are particularly effective for milling grains with smaller particles, and when combined with modern sieving methods, they can produce very fine powder suitable for human consumption. While they require a large footprint and significant investment, stone mills are recognized for producing the highest quality flour, typically sold in the premium segment of the market.

Roller Mill

The working principle involves a pair of cylindrical grinding rollers of equal diameter that rotate at different speeds, generating an even extrusion and shearing force on the material entering the milling area. The variation in rotational speeds of the rollers causes the material to be crushed under the combined effects of extrusion, shearing, friction, and tearing as it passes through the milling zone. The roller mill is ideal for milling small grains or beans (which can be crushed into smaller pieces), producing flour with high fineness, suitable for human consumption. This type of mill requires a high standard of workshop conditions, occupies a large area, and demands a significant investment. However, the resulting product is of superior quality, targeting the high-end market.

MAINTENANCE GUIDELINES OF AUTOMATIC ROLLER MILL

- Ensure the transmission components, belts, and other devices are properly balanced, with fasteners tightened correctly.
- Lubricating parts should be regularly filled with oil, kept clean, and maintained hygienic. Routinely check for overheating or abnormal sounds in bearings and motors.
- After opening the mic door, make adjustments starting with the first skin milling according to process requirements. Avoid any changes after the first skin mill adjustment.
- The rollers should be round and properly ground; any rollers that do not meet technical specifications must not be used. Ensure both fast and slow rollers are balanced, and the diameter difference between them should not be excessive.
- There should be no radial runout or axial movement during the operation of the grinding roller.
- Ensure uniform feeding and proper distribution of material along the entire length of the roller. If feeding is uneven or blockage occurs, check for foreign objects in the baffle or irregularities in the baffle, and address the issue.
- The rolling distance between rollers should be consistent. When adjusting the distance, loosen the tight end first to ensure uniformity before making adjustments.
- Before starting the machine, check for any remaining material. If present, manually turn the transmission wheel to discharge it, and start the machine without load.
- If material supply is interrupted or stopped suddenly, immediately loosen the rolling distance. In case of blockages in the grinding chamber, loosen the rolling distance, stop milling, and clear the milling pipes.
- After inspecting or replacing the roller, carefully check for foreign objects in the feeding barrel or roller to prevent metal impurities from entering. If any are found, stop the machine for processing.
- In the event of a dust explosion, remove the air duct, stop the machine, notify relevant authorities immediately, and take fire-fighting measures to prevent further spread.

Flour Plansifter

- Transmission parts should be properly lubricated, fasteners must be secure, the hoisting should be balanced, and the lubricating oil should not spill during the bearing operation. If any abnormal noise occurs, stop and inspect immediately.
- The sifter must start fully in one attempt and should not be restarted. The sieve operates anti-clockwise and must begin from a complete stop. Ensure a latching device relay is installed in the electrical connection to prevent the motor from restarting within 3 minutes of a power failure.

- When disassembling or assembling the flat sifter, pay attention to the order and direction of the sifter grids and avoid damaging the sieve surface or material blocks.
- Each flat sifter in the same system should have an evenly distributed inlet flow. The load capacity of each sifter bin should be similar, and the unscreened rate should be minimized while maintaining quality.
- Ensure the cleaning block remains flexible and supports the sifter flat.
- The sifter grid should be tightly pressed, with consistency on both sides and uniform pressure.

Purifier

- The transmission parts should operate normally, be flexible, and the fasteners should be secure.
- The feeding device should operate sensitively to ensure the material is evenly distributed across the sieve surface.
- The sieve surface must be properly tensioned, and the distance between the cleaning brush and the sieve should be appropriate with consistent spacing.
- Ensure the suction channel is clear, and the damper is correctly adjusted to provide adequate suction volume.
- Regularly check the quality of the material at each outlet to ensure that the cleaning effect meets the required standards.

Plane Rotary Sifter, High-Efficiency Vibrating Sifter

- The feeding hopper should maintain an appropriate amount of material, and the feeding mechanism should be flexible, allowing flow adjustment to ensure even distribution of material across the sieve surface.
- Avoid striking the sieve surface to prevent unevenness, and ensure the sieve is placed horizontally to avoid material shifting to one side.
- Frequently check and adjust the suction to ensure it doesn't carry whole grains.
- Select the appropriate screen mesh size based on the physical properties of the wheat and impurities.
- Keep the sieve holes clear. Under normal conditions, more than 80% of the sieves should not be blocked. The cleaning ball should beat continuously and be flexible. When cleaning, use a brush to clean the sieve surface or tap the sieve frame with a rubber hammer. Clean at least twice an hour.
- Always inspect the screen surface for any wheat overflow or leakage.

KEY COMPONENTS OF MILLING MACHINES

Machines utilized in milling industry are composed of individual components or components groups. They all have their particular function and could be classified by their functional purposes. Briefly, we can classify them following:

- Casings, machine inserts, protection, safety and control equipment
- Bearings

- Movable parts; vibrating (separators, destoners etc.), rotating (scourers, bran dusters etc.), or oscillating (plansifters)
- Connecting, fixing elements
- Shut-off and control elements
- Seals
- Upkeep and Service of machines and components

Casing, Machine Inserts, Protection, Safety and Control Equipment

The casing is composed of supporting structures such as stands, traverses, and frames. Functional parts like sieves and channels are installed within the casing and are referred to as 'machine inserts. To reduce accident risks, operating elements must be protected from rotating or hazardous machine parts (e.g., gear wheel covers, belt covers, rotor casings, and electrical insulation). Certain machine parts, like electronic components, may also require protection against dust, moisture, and ambient temperatures. Items like doors, control windows, covers, rpm monitors, and measuring devices fall into this category.

Materials used for machine parts include cast iron, sectional steel, pipes, cast aluminum, and wooden beams for supporting parts; sheet steel, plastic materials, wood, and aluminum for machine inserts; and steel or aluminum sheet and plastic material for protection and control equipment.

Bearings

Bearings support the rotation of shafts or rotors in machines and are vital components for machine performance. Proper maintenance is crucial for the machine's longevity and safety. Bearings are designed based on their usage, considering factors like stress (axial and radial loads), construction (ball bearings, roller bearings, sleeve bearings), and function (pedestal and flange bearings for protection and fastening). Ball or roller bearings are commonly used in milling equipment, with roller bearings requiring that the inner race ring be tightly fixed to the shaft, while the outer race ring is mounted in the bearing casing for easy assembly and disassembly. Sleeve bearings are typically replaced by roller bearings but are used in specific cases, such as intermediate bearings in screw conveyors or air locks, where low rpm allows for simple lubrication.

Bearings are installed in protective bearing bodies or casings (pedestal or flange bearings). Proper lubrication is crucial to avoid metal-to-metal contact, ensuring a lubrication film between the rolling body and bearing shaft. Incorrect lubrication, such as using low or high viscosity lubricants, can cause bearing issues, including excessive temperature rise. Only pure lubricants ensure proper lubrication, extending the service life. Regular bearing cleaning helps extend their longevity by removing old grease and oil residue. Always follow the manufacturer's operational manuals for inserting and replacing bearings.

Movable Parts (Rotation, Vibration, and Oscillation)

Movable parts in milling engineering can be categorized as follows:

- **Rotating parts:** Shafts and rotors, with many milling machines using rotors and rollers supported on shafts.

- Backward and forward moving parts
  - **Oscillating parts:** Some milling machines operate with oscillating movements, generated by an eccentric shaft and connecting rod, such as in plansifters.
  - **Power transmitting equipment:** Includes couplings, belt drives (e.g., for belt conveyors, bucket elevators, V-belts for roller mills), and chain drives (e.g., chain conveyors, drag conveyors, wheel drives).
  - **Vibration (free swinging drives):** Used in various milling machines like separators, destoners, and vibro feeders.

Connecting, Fixing Elements

Components can be categorized as follows

- **Detachable connections:** Screwed connections and taper-lock
- **Permanent connections:** Rivets, welding, soldering, and gluing/pasting
- **Other connections:** Dowels, anchor rails, cotter pins, axial securing parts, and springs

Shut-off and Control Elements

In the milling industry, regulating, shutting, setting, and metering devices are widely used for applications such as water, air, and bulk loading/unloading. Common components include valves, slide valves, flap valves, and airlocks.

Seals

Seals are critical in milling due to the presence of dust and airborne particles, which may escape through pipes as materials like grain, flour, bran, and screenings move. Elastic or easily formable materials such as rubber, felt, malleable metals (copper, aluminum), plastic, leather, and paper are commonly used for sealing. The primary purposes of seals are:

- Preventing dust or foreign materials from entering sensitive components like bearings
- Preventing lubricants or viscous materials from leaking from bearings, pipes, etc.
- Containing dust within machines or pipes
- Sealing spaces with varying pressures, including pipes, mill sections, and pistons

Upkeep and Service of Machines and Components

Upkeep is important for the machine's performance and includes three main categories which are :

- **Cleaning:** While neglecting cleaning may not immediately damage machines, pests or mold can harm the equipment over time due to food processing. Factors such as ambient temperature, air moisture content, and material being processed, along with regular plant cleaning, directly impact machine performance.

- **Lubrication:** Refer to operation manuals for lubrication procedures, which should include details on the type of lubricant, amount, periodic oil changes, lubrication points, and bearing cleaning procedures.
- **Control:** Regular inspection by the miller, emergency alarms, and prompt response to troubleshooting are essential.

Replace worn or defective parts such as sieve cleaners, sieves, seals, rolls, filter bags, and hammers on rotors, as well as any other rotating or stressed components that require immediate replacement.

FLOUR MILLING PROCESS: KEY STAGES AND OPERATIONS

The flour milling process is comprised of six key steps: cleaning, tempering and conditioning, gristing, separating, milling, and blending. Each step is vital and should not be disregarded. Let us have a close look at the importance of each stage in the process.

Cleaning

The first step involves cleaning, where foreign materials are eliminated from the grains to ensure the final flour quality is high. The grains are carefully inspected and sorted to eliminate stones, dirt, and other impurities.

Following the initial cleaning, the grains undergo a second cleaning known as scouring, where they are rubbed together to remove any remaining contaminants from the surface. This step ensures the grains are thoroughly cleaned before moving to the next stage.

Modern cleaning techniques utilize advanced equipment such as vibrating screens, magnetic separators, and air aspirators to achieve optimal purity. By removing impurities, the cleaning process guarantees the flour will be safe for consumption and free from harmful contaminants.

Tempering and Conditioning

After cleaning, the grains are ready for tempering and conditioning. Tempering involves adding moisture to the grains, making them more flexible and easier to mill. This step is vital for achieving the desired quality and consistency of the flour. Conditioning follows tempering, allowing the grains to rest and absorb moisture evenly, ensuring uniform milling.

Modern systems control moisture levels and resting time precisely, ensuring predictable and consistent results, leading to high-quality flour with the right characteristics, such as texture, color, and baking performance.

Gristing

Once tempering and conditioning are complete, the grains proceed to the gristing stage. Gristing involves breaking the grains into smaller particles called grist, which are then further refined into flour. This process typically uses roller mills to crush the grains and separate the bran from the endosperm and germ.

The gristing stage plays a critical role in flour quality, as it affects particle size and distribution, which in turn influence the flour's performance in various uses.

Modern roller mills feature advanced technologies that allow for precise control during grinding, ensuring a consistent grist. This results in flour with the desired particle size and properties, suitable for a range of applications.

Separating

The next stage, separating, involves dividing the components of the grist—endosperm, bran, and germ. Separation is essential for producing different types of flour with varying levels of bran and germ content. It also facilitates the extraction of valuable by-products, like wheat germ oil, which has both nutritional and industrial uses.

Milling

Following separation, milling further grinds and refines the endosperm to produce fine flour particles. This is done using a series of reduction rolls that progressively decrease the particle size of the endosperm.

Milling is crucial for determining the quality and functionality of the flour, influencing factors like gluten development, baking performance, and shelf life.

Blending

The final stage of the flour milling process is blending. In this stage, different flours and other ingredients are mixed to create customized blends that meet specific needs.

Blending enables flour millers to produce a wide range of flours with varying characteristics such as protein content, gluten strength, and color. It also allows for fortifying flours with vitamins, minerals, and other additives to enhance nutritional value and functional properties.

Modern blending systems automate the process, ensuring precise control over ingredient proportions and thorough mixing, which guarantees the consistency and uniformity of the final product, catering to diverse customer requirements.

Ensuring Quality: Essential Control Measures

Ensuring the quality of your flour involves implementing stringent control measures throughout the production process.

Moisture Testing Equipment

Maintaining optimal moisture levels is improtant for the longevity and quality of flour. Moisture testing equipment, like hygrometers, aids in precise moisture content assessment.

Color Sorting Machines

To guarantee a uniform product, color sorting machines eliminate discolored grains, ensuring the final flour has a consistent appearance.

Packaging Machinery

Efficient packaging machine is the final touch to a successful flour mill operation.

Bagging Machines

Investing in automated bagging machines streamlines the packaging process, enhancing efficiency and reducing human error.

Once the flour is processed and purified, it needs to be packaged efficiently. Bagging machines are utlized to fill and seal bags with the final product. These machines come in various designs, including automatic and semi-automatic options, allowing mill operators to choose the most suitable packaging solution for their production scale.

Quality Assurance Systems

Implementing quality assurance systems guarantees that every packaged product meets the highest standards. This includes metal detectors to ensure no contaminants make their way into the final product.

Flour Mill Maintenance

Flour mills are essential machines for small and medium-sized flour production businesses. They are used frequently in daily operations, and any malfunction can significantly impact production efficiency, leading to substantial losses. Therefore, regular maintenance is crucial to extend the machine's lifespan, reduce aging, and ensure maximum efficiency.

Frequent Fueling for Upkeep

Regular fueling of the flour mill is essential to keep it running smoothly and minimize issues caused by machine wear and tear.

Routine Inspection of Components

Frequent inspections should be conducted on the flour mill components, checking for any unusual noises or overheating parts. This helps identify potential issues early, preventing more significant problems that could disrupt operations.

Regular Tightening and Replacement of Screws

It's important to check the flour mill regularly for loose screws and tighten them promptly. Old and worn-out screws should be replaced to maintain the machine's stability and proper functioning.

Clean Surroundings and Machine

Timely cleaning of wood shavings and debris around the flour mill is necessary. If foreign objects get inside the machine, they can damage the motor, affecting its performance and longevity.

In daily operations, maintenance should focus on prevention rather than waiting for major faults to arise. Addressing small issues before they turn into larger problems ensures the flour mill operates smoothly, supporting consistent production without interruptions.

A high-quality flour mill benefits from advanced technological research and development. By incorporating new technologies in design and manufacturing, it becomes easier to operate and maintain, offering better control and enhanced reliability and stability. Technologies such as electromechanical integration, computer-aided design, pneumatic systems, and green and reliability design principles are adopted to improve efficiency.

A strong management team is crucial for the rapid development of a flour machinery company. To become recognized in the industry and achieve high efficiency, having a top-tier management and after-sales team is essential. KMEC prides itself on having an advanced management team and a first-class service system, making significant contributions to the flour machinery industry and society.

MAINTAINING THE ROLLER FLOUR MILL

- Always refuel and maintain the roller flour mill, keep the machine running smoothly, and minimize machine damage caused due to machine operation problems.
- Frequently inspect all parts of the roller flour mill, such as checking whether there are noises in the running parts or whether overheating will occur, avoiding bigger problems and affecting the use of the roller flour mill.
- Regularly inspect the screws in each part of the roller flour mill for looseness, and tighten the screws on the roller flour mill in time. Replace the screws that are aging because of age and maintain the stability of the roller flour mill.
- Remove wood chips and other debris around the flour mill in a timely manner to prevent the debris from entering the inside of the roller flour mill, affecting the rotation of the engine, causing damage to the engine and affecting the use of the engine.
- Do not wait until the roller flour mill has a major fault affecting the use of the product before repairing it. This would waste time and affect the service life of the roller flour mill. Enterprises should pay attention to the roller flour mill in their normal work. The maintenance, to prevent the emergence of major problems, affect the use of flour mills and the smooth progress of the company's work.
- The roller flour mill is promoted to life and production by us. It brings us huge number of economic benefits and satisfaction of all kinds of living food. Therefore, when we treat the roller flour mill, we must regularly maintain and repair it. This is important.

PULVARISERS

Pulvarisers machines are designed to break down materials into fine particles. These machines can crush a wide variety of materials, including food grains, spices, concrete, coal, rocks, resin, tires, and medical waste. Pulvarizer machines come in various types, such as impact pulvarizers, hammer mills, ring mills, double roll crushers, granulators, impactors, and shredders.

Agriculture plays a critical role in India's economy, and technology has become a key factor in its advancement. Traditionally, after harvesting, farmers burn a significant amount of agricultural waste. This practice is repeated annually, contributing to environmental pollution. To address this, there has been a push to find practical ways of utilizing agricultural waste for economic benefits, such as in power plants and industries. This has led to the development of machines designed to shred agricultural waste efficiently, without using electricity. These machines help reduce the negative environmental and health impacts caused by conventional methods of waste disposal. Key components of these machines include an agitator, hopper, collector tank, bevel gear pairs, pulleys, flat belt drive, and a paddling mechanism, which work together to enhance the efficiency of waste processing.

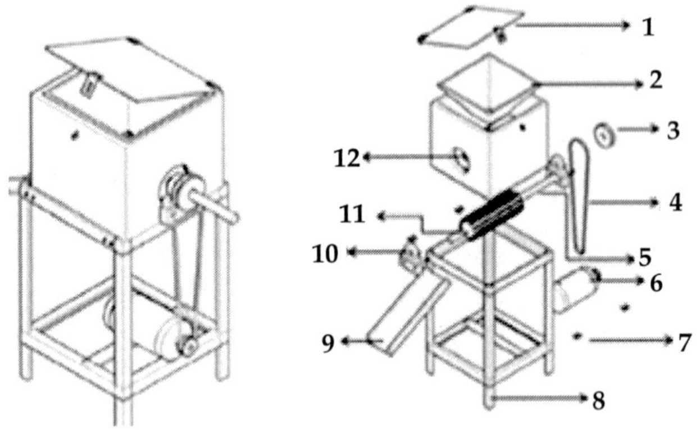

S/N	Description	QTY	S/N	Description	QTY
1	COVER	1	7	SCREW	4
2	HOPPER	1	8	FRAME	1
3	PULLEY	1	9	SPROUT	1
4	BELT	1	10	BEARING AND HOLDER	1
5	SHAFT	1	11	ROLLER	1
6	ELECTRIC MOTOR	1	12	PULVERIZING CHAMBER	1

Figure.: 6.1 Key Components of Machine

Design, Fabrication a nd Performance Evaluation of Moringa (Oleifera) Dried Leaves Pulverizer

Moringa oliefera *Moringa pterygosperm Gaertner* leaves popularly honored as'eweigiiyanu'in Nigeria. The current study is to develop a from locally sourced paraphernalia. The proposed machine works with the shearing medium. The main features of the machine are creek frame, belt, pulley, compartments and electric motor. The machine was designed, fabricated and tested fulfilling the all scientific morals D used for drying moringaoleifera leaves at average temperature of 40 – 50 C for 3 days,

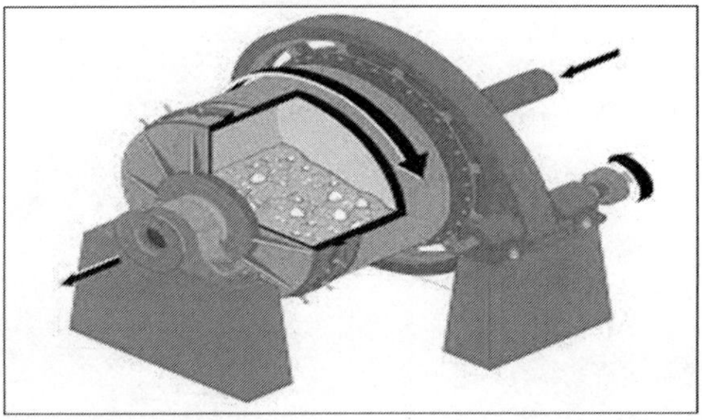

Figure.: 6.2 Diagram of rotary blade glass pulvarizing

Rotary Blade Glass Pulvarizing Machine

Glass waste can be recycled and repurposed, serving as a key ingredient in the production of new glass and various other products such as abrasives, astroturf, and ceramics. The process of recycling glass often involves crushing it into small particles using specialized pounding machines. This study focuses on the design of a glass pounding machine, which includes a drop-loading hopper that facilitates the glass's entry into the crushing chamber. The machine features a horizontally oriented shaft, with three blades positioned at 120-degree intervals along the shaft. These blades work together to effectively crush and break down the glass into smaller fragments, making it suitable for reuse in various applications.

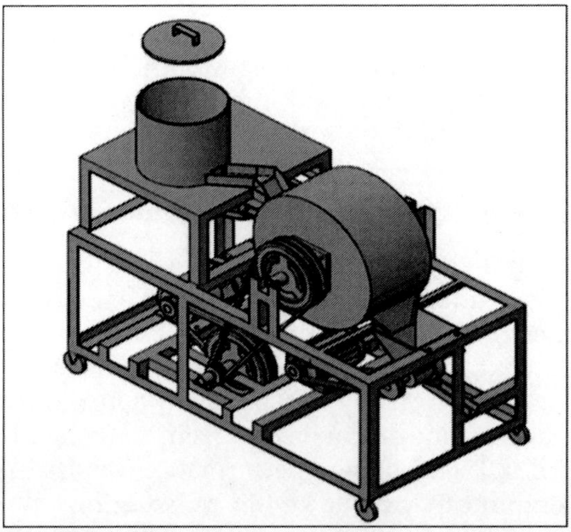

Figure.: 6.3 Design of a plantain machine

Development and Contruction of an Enhanced Plantain Processing Machine

Nigeria is the largest patron of plantain in West Africa with large chance of it attained in the southern part of the country. Plantains are of great nutritional significance, and the proximate analysis reported for plantain shows that per 100g eatable portion, plantains contain 67.30 g water, 116 kcal of energy, and 31.15 of carbohydrate. Although there are various machines that can exercise plantain but a complete machine that does pulverization, milling, drying, etc. is not readily available in Nigeria.

Figure.: 6.4 Design and optimization of pulverizer for non-Ferric alum production

A Pulvarizer is a mechanical device for the grinding of different types of paraphernalia. Under pulvarizer generally we have to handpick one of types of capper. Crushers are one of the major size reduction outfit that is used in mechanical, and other different aspect of that type of industries. A capper is a device that is designed to reduce large solid raw material into lower chunks. They live in various sizes and capacities which range from 0.1 ton/ hour to 50 ton/ hour.

Diabetes, arbitrated a threat factor for coronavirus contagious complaint 2019 (COVID-19), can be managed through consumption of plantainand its associated products. Plantain is usually processed into flourand other ready-made/ value-added productsdue to its veritably short shelf- life. To reuse callow plantain pulps into flour, there's a need for size reduction after drying

Design Of A Medium Scale Ginger Pulvarizing Machine For Rural Dwellers

The concept behind the design of medium-scale machines is to optimize energy efficiency. These machines are particularly effective in rural or pastoral areas, as they offer better energy conservation compared to large-scale commercial equipment. In this context, a 120 kg/hr medium-scale gusto pulvarizer was designed and fabricated, using approximately 80% of locally sourced materials. The design process was empirical, drawing on knowledge from textbooks, practical experience, and scientific principles. The machine's performance was assessed based on several metrics, including output capacity (96 kg/hr), pulvarizing efficiency (80%), energy consumption (0.032 ton/hp-hr), energy losses (24.63%), and the size reduction rate (211), all of which indicate its effectiveness and practicality for local applications.

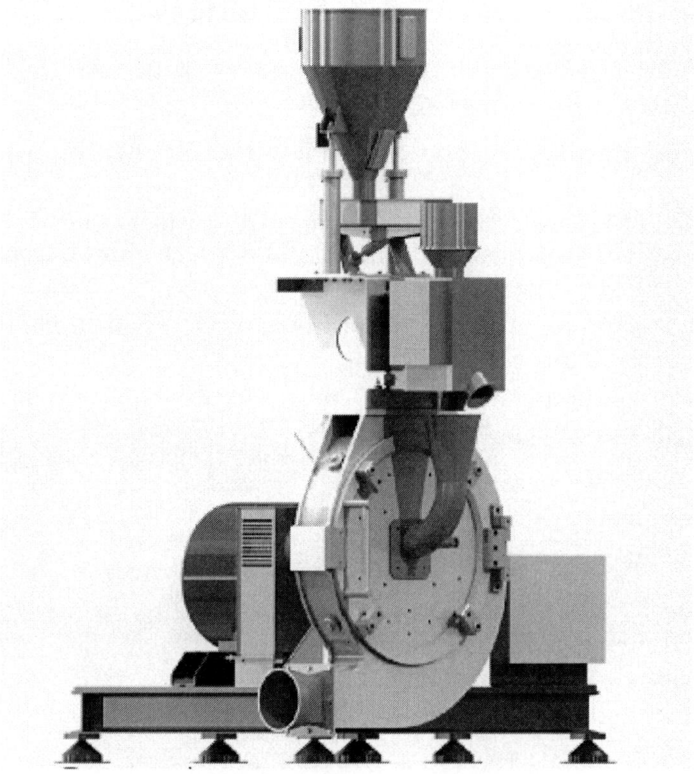

Figure.: 6.5 Structure of pulvarizer Machine

Design And Fabrication of Pulverizer Machine

Pulvariser is a hay or straw cutting machine which is used in uniform chopping of the chaff for livestock or raw material to agro industries. The various types of fodder can be processed in this machine are forage grass, green grass, dry corn straw, and wheat stalk etc. The final products can be used to feed cattle, goats, deer, and horses. It can also process cotton stalk, bark, and small branches. Chaff cutters have developed gradually.

Production of Turmeric Powder Using a Hammer Mill-Type Pulvarizer

The effect of humidity content, rotor blade tip speed and grinding screen perforation periphery on the performance of a hammer shop- type pulverizer was studied. One hundred sixty five kilograms of turmeric rhizomes were washed, sliced, dried to different humidity contents and ground by the pulverizer. The trial used the Box-Behnken design and the parameters were optimized using the Surface Response Methodology approach.

Problem Identification

- Vibration during pulvarization
- High power consumption

- Pulverize stones during working and damaged blade
- Exprensive machine

Salient Features of Pulvarizer

- By utilizing this machine you can manufacture 300-400 Kgs master batches p/h.
- Available in M.S. Materials with Casting parts for longer life of machine. We use good quality bearings and pedestal Pillow blocks with Bitters for cutting/ Grinding, Blower type.
- Stainless Steel Material's made pulvarizers are also available in the market for special purposes like herbals etc.
- The power consumption is minimal compare to other pulverizing machines.
- Production cost will be cheaper.
- Cutting size :- 0.75 inch to 1 inch.
- Eassy installation
- Very Low maintenance.
- Higher production capacity.
- Minimum man-power for operating the machine.
- High Quality and lower wastage
- Economical and cost effective
- Produces fine micro Powder
- Gives high output rates

7

Operation and Maintenance of Boiler, Pasteurizer and Sterilizer

A boiler is a sealed vessel designed to heat water or other liquids, producing steam or vapor for various applications, including heating, power generation, cooking, and industrial processes. The operation of a boiler is similar to that of a pressure cooker but on a larger scale. The steam or vapor generated is used for domestic or industrial purposes, with the system usually involves involving combustion products that heat the water.

Boilers come in various types, tailored for specific uses. While domestic boilers are compact and suited for household needs, industrial boilers play an important role in production processes, often operating on a much larger scale. These industrial boilers can be environmentally friendly when powered by natural gas or other low-emission fuels, helping industries reduce harmful emissions while maintaining performance.

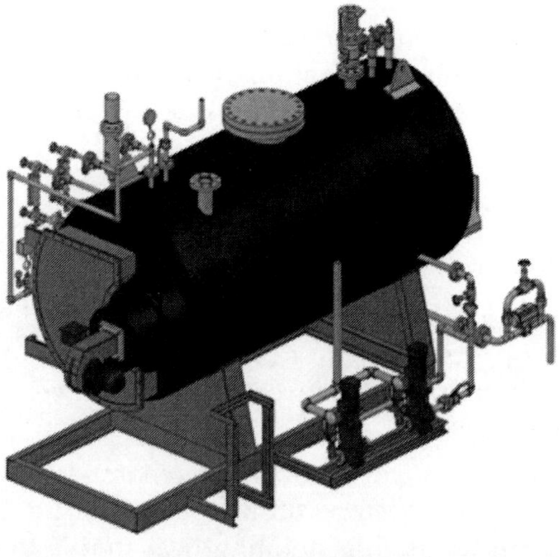

Figure.: 7.1 A diagram of industrial boiler

Industrial boilers have been a part of various sectors for centuries, with applications ranging from steam-powered locomotives to power plants. Their primary benefit lies in their energy efficiency and capacity to generate significant heat, supporting industrial operations. Whether in cooking or running manufacturing plants, heat plays a central role in daily life, and boilers provide a reliable means of delivering it efficiently.

In industries, the use of industrial boilers helps reduce dependency on costly electric energy. As electricity can be expensive on a large scale, boilers allow manufacturers to lower operational costs. Additionally, industrial boilers require less management and minimize dependence on electricity, making them an economical and efficient option for industries.

FUNDAMENTALS OF INDUSTRIAL STEAM BOILER

In today's world, the importance of efficient boiler technology has grown significantly. Heat energy is now playing a crucial role in improving the efficiency of industrial equipment. Many industries rely on pressurized steam to power machines, which not only boosts production efficiency but also offers environmental benefits in several ways.

One of the main advantages of using steam-powered systems is the reduction in electricity consumption, which is both costly and harmful. According to a 2015 article, industries wasted a staggering three billion units of power. Imagine how much energy was consumed overall—quite alarming, right? Fast forward to 2020, and the energy consumption statistics remain similarly concerning.

The fuel typically used in boilers includes natural gas, various fossil fuels, and coal. Therefore, selecting the right boiler is essential to prevent heat wastage and ensure more efficient energy delivery compared to other sources. For instance, top boiler manufacturers such as Thermax offer waste heat recovery solutions. These systems capture and utilize the heat that would normally be lost as exhaust gas, ensuring that the maximum amount of heat is put to productive use. With advanced designs and ongoing innovations, companies like Thermax are working to extract the most value from their boilers, offering enhanced performance and efficiency.

Essential Components of an Industrial Boiler

Parts of Industrial Boiler

- **Burner:** The burner initiates the combustion reaction within the boiler. It has a mechanism that triggers the process of heat production. A nozzle in the burner sprays the fuel, which is pumped from the fuel source, and ignites it, starting the combustion process.
- **Combustion Chamber:** The combustion chambers, typically constructed from cast iron, can reach temperatures of several hundred degrees within minutes. They burn the fuel, generating heat that is then transferred to the heat exchanger.
- **Heat Exchanger:** Also known as the economiser, it is responsible for increasing the efficiency of the boiler. The heat exchanger is placed before the air heater in the fuel gas path.

- **Steam Drum and Mud Drum:** The steam drum collects the steam while the mud drum is placed beneath the steam drum and collects the solid which is removed periodically.

Fuel Sources Used in Boilers

- Coal
- kerosene
- Natural gases

OPERATION OF INDUSTRIAL BOILER

Industrial boilers are vessels that contain water and generate heat through a fuel source. This heat is transferred to a series of tubes connected to industrial equipment. The steam produced is used to power machinery, offering industries a cost-effective method to drive their production processes.

Operating Principles of an Industrial Boiler

The functioning of boilers is simpler than it might seem, combining fundamental scientific principles with modern innovations. The system is composed of separate components placed strategically at different points. The heat source and water vessels are housed in distinct compartments, and metal rods connect the water vessel to the heat source, facilitating steam production. This steam is collected in a dome where it is condensed before being released from the boiler. This process increases pressure, generating energy to power production processes. For safety, boilers are equipped with a safety valve to prevent accidents caused by excessive pressure. Various types of boilers exist, each designed for specific purposes, which will be explored further in the section.

Maintenance Practices for Enhanced Longevity and Performance

To enhance the lifespan of boilers, it is essential to follow a few key maintenance practices:

- Conduct general safety inspections regularly to ensure optimal boiler performance.
- Maintain the appropriate boiler temperature, as overheating can lead to breakdowns.
- Monitor fuel levels, circulation, and pressure to avoid inefficiencies in operation.
- Equip the boiler with smoke detectors and alarms for low fuel and pressure to ensure safer functioning.
- Clean chimneys, vents, and outlets routinely to improve the productivity and efficiency of the boiler.

Classification of Boilers

The type of boiler you need will depend on your production requirements. Various types of boilers serve different purposes. The classifications are based on the amount of pressure it can create, the capacity to hold the fuel and water and the type of fuel one will be using.

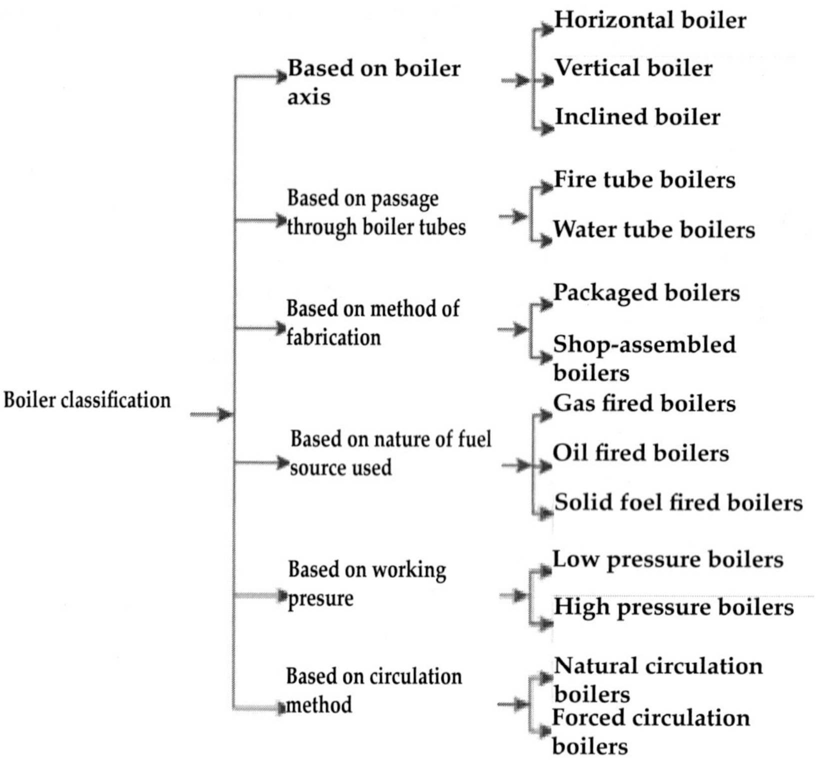

Figure.: 7.2 Boiler Classification

Fire Tube Boiler

Fire Tube Boilers are extensively utilized in small to medium-sized industries due to their convenience and efficiency. These factory-made units, often referred to as packaged boilers, come equipped with pumps and control systems, enabling immediate operation upon connection to fuel and water supplies. Designed for low to medium-pressure steam needs, they operate by allowing combustion gases to flow outside the water pipes.

With the capability to generate steam up to 2200 horsepower pressure, they are highly effective but carry a significant risk of explosion. Additionally, their cost may pose a challenge for businesses that do not require continuous steam energy.

Water Tube Boiler

The Water Tube Boiler stands out for its versatility and functionality, differing significantly from Fire Tube Boilers in design and operation. These boilers are typically employed in large manufacturing facilities where high-pressure steam is essential. They operate by circulating water between the mud drum and the steam drum, with density differences providing better control over the circulation.

Ideal for applications requiring frequent adjustments in steam quantity, Water Tube Boilers have a lower water content, allowing for quicker response times. Unlike Fire Tube Boilers, they are generally constructed on-site and are not commonly available as packaged units.

Electric Boiler

The electric boiler is among the most popular boiler types due to its remarkable efficiency and eco-friendly nature. Unlike traditional boilers, it operates without fossil fuels, resulting in a significantly smaller carbon footprint and no exhaust emissions. Its low installation cost, minimal noise, and compact size make it particularly favored by rural users.

Despite these advantages, electric boilers have drawbacks. They rely solely on electricity, leading to substantial energy consumption, which can make them less cost-effective compared to other boiler types.

Condensing Boiler

Condensing boilers operate uniquely compared to other boiler types. They utilize natural gas and feature two heat exchangers, making them highly efficient. By extracting heat from exhaust or waste gases, they significantly reduce energy wastage, achieving up to 98% thermal efficiency. This exceptional efficiency has made them a preferred choice for central heating, gradually replacing traditional boilers.

Many HVAC experts consider condensing boilers to be the most sustainable option, as their dual heat exchangers not only minimize wastage but also lower operational costs, enhancing both environmental and economic benefits.

Oil Boiler

The efficiency of oil-fired boilers is usually 86% while oil condensing boilers are 90% or more efficient. The fuel used here is not natural gas but oil. The oil is ignited in the combustion chamber, and then the heat exchanger heats the cold water. It is usually used in the household to get warm water in showers, taps or radiators.

Natural Gas Boiler

Natural Gas Boilers, as the name implies, rely on natural gas as their primary fuel. They operate with the assistance of a temperature gauge for regulation and a thermoelectric device to minimize fuel wastage. The gas ignites the pilot, which subsequently heats the coils within the boiler. In rural areas, propane gas is often used as an alternative fuel source.

Understanding your specific requirements is crucial when selecting a boiler, and this classification can serve as a useful guide. Consulting with experts from manufacturers like Thermax or similar companies is highly recommended. Such discussions will help you make an informed decision, ensuring the boiler meets your needs without being too small or too large, while also considering factors such as fuel type and efficiency.

Utilization of Steam in the Food Industry

Steam boilers are an integral part of the food processing industry. They rely heavily on steam for the different processes in the plant. Here are some of the typical applications of steam in food processing plants:

- **Sterilization and Disinfection:** Food safety is paramount in any food processing plant to ensure the food produced is fit for human consumption. Food processing plants in India are regulated by the Food Safety and Standard Authority of India and the State Food Safety Authority. They ensure the plant follows stringent standards to clean, sterilize, and disinfection of all the tools/utensils/surfaces used for food processing. Safety has become even more paramount after the current Covid-19 pandemic as processing units need to follow protocols for their workers and equipment to ensure product safety. Utensils and surfaces need to be sterilized before preparing food.
- **Reducing Microbiological Risks:** There is an inherent risk of food getting contaminated by parasites or bacteria or microbes that can cause food-borne diseases. Steam pasteurization is one of the popular methods to control microbiological risks.
- **Cooking, Curing, and Drying:** Tertiary food processing units cook the food before it is packed. Steam and hot water are used to ensure the food produced is smooth, soft, and easy to digest. Complex cooking processes such as curing or drying also require steam. These plants require large quantities of steam for processing.

Categorization of Steam Utilized in Processing Plants

- Plant Steam or utility steam is produced in the boiler and can be used for application where the steam is not in direct contact with the food product or the surfaces that are in contact with cooked food. Utility steam is used for indirect heating applications.
- Culinary steam is directly injected into the product. It also sterilizes and disinfects plant surfaces. Culinary steam contains additives to prevent corrosion and scaling within the boiler. The steam is usually filtered before it comes in contact with the food.
- Pure steam (hygienic steam) does not contain any additives. Pure steam is created by heating untreated water that is stored separately.

The steam that comes in contact with food is either pure steam or culinary steam. Most food processing plants use culinary steam, though pure steam may be used for some specific applications.

Boilers in Food Processing Plants

Packaged boilers are generally used in food processing plants due to their compact design and ease of operation. These boilers come as a single unit and only require connections for steam, water piping, and electricity to function. Boilers optimize heat transfer through radiation and convection which ensures efficiency. Typically used for heating applications, it is important that the steam produced is food-grade.

Key features of the thermal units in these boilers include

- **Fuel Combustion:** Thermal energy is generated in the furnace by burning fuels such as solid fuels (coal, biomass), natural gas, or fuel oil.
- **Tank/Evaporator:** Water is heated in this component by the burner until it reaches evaporating temperature.

- **Superheater**: Converts saturated steam to dry steam, enhancing boiler efficiency. Superheating raises steam temperature without increasing pressure, producing superheated steam.
- **Economizer:** Captures residual heat to preheat feed water, improving overall efficiency.

Tips for Selecting a Steam Boiler for Food Processing Plants

- **Adaptability to Fluctuating Demand:** The boiler should handle the plant's varying steam requirements efficiently.
- **Ease of Maintenance:** With extensive steam use in food processing, the boiler should be low maintenance to avoid breakdowns that disrupt daily operations.
- **Fuel and Water Efficiency:** Choose an energy-efficient boiler to manage rising utility costs without compromising productivity. The boiler must also comply with strict emission norms in food processing plants.

Role of industrial Steam Boilers do in Food Processing

Steam boilers power essential tasks across food plants by generating high-pressure steam.

Their Functions Include

- **Consistent Cooking and Heating:** Boilers provide the even heat essential for cooking large batches of food, pasteurizing, and boiling. In high-stakes operations like sauce production or dairy pasteurization, consistent heat is key to maintaining texture, flavor, and safety.
- **Dehydration and Drying:** Removing moisture in products like grains and fruits preserves quality and shelf life. Steam helps control moisture efficiently, keeping food fresher longer.
- **Food Sanitation:** To kill bacteria, viruses, and contaminants, food facilities rely on the high temperatures boilers generate, ensuring food safety and regulatory compliance.
- **Cleaning and Equipment Sanitation:** Steam is invaluable for cleaning equipment and surfaces, preventing contamination and supporting food safety standards.

Operational Process of Boiler

The boiler's operation can be broadly categorized into two simultaneous processes: the furnace process and the boiler process. The furnace process involves fuel combustion and heat transfer on the flue gas side of the heating surface. On the other hand, the boiler process encompasses various activities on the working fluid side, including the heat transfer between the metal and the working fluid, as well as the heating, evaporation, and superheating of the working fluid. Moreover, it involves the working fluid's flow process and various thermochemical processes, such as maintaining steam quality, managing salt precipitation, addressing heating surface fouling, and preventing corrosion.

In-furnace process

The process of coal combustion in a boiler begins with coal being fed from the coal storage to the coal bin and then into the coal pipe via gravity through a slide hopper. The coal enters the combustion room after moving forward along the chain grate. The required combustion air is forced into the air preheater by a blower, where it is heated before being directed to the segmented air supply bin under the grate. This air mixes thoroughly with the coal on the grate, ensuring a vigorous combustion reaction.

The high-temperature flue gas generated transfers heat to the water or steam-water mixture within the water-cooled walls around the combustion chamber through radiation heat exchange. As the flue gas exits the combustion chamber via the smoke window, it flows through the slag condensing tube and superheater, transferring heat to the steam. It then passes laterally through the boiler tube bundles along the fire wall, utilizing convective heat transfer to warm the working fluid, which includes steam, water, and soda-water mixtures.

The flue gas, now at a reduced temperature, reaches the tail-end heating surfaces and flushes the economizer, transferring additional heat to the water in the economizer tubes via convective heat exchange. Simultaneously, preheated air in the air preheater tubes absorbs heat from the flue gas, which strengthens the furnace combustion and raises the furnace temperature, thereby improving the boiler's thermal efficiency.

Once the flue gas reaches an optimal low temperature, it exits the boiler and is discharged into the atmosphere via the dust collector, induced draft fan, flue, and chimney. The ash and slag generated during combustion are collected and transported to the slag yard through an ash removal system, completing the process.

Process in the pot

The feedwater that has been processed by the water treatment system and meets the boiler water quality requirements is sent to the economizer by the feedwater pump through the water supply pipeline. The water absorbs the heat of the flue gas in the tail flue in the economizer, and the preheated feedwater enters the upper drum. The downcomer flows into the radiant heating surface (water wall) through the header at the lower part of the water wall. The water in the water wall absorbs the high-temperature radiant heat in the furnace to form a steam-water mixture and flows into the upper boiler tube;

The same process is also carried out in the boiler tube bundle. The boiler water in the upper drum flows down the lower drum along the weakly heated tube bundle, and the lower drum undergoes the stronger heated tube bundle to form a steam-water mixture and then flows back to the upper drum.

The steam-water mixture is separated in the upper drum through the steam-water separator. The saturated steam is sent to the steam superheater from the upper part of the drum. The steam exchanges heat in the steam superheater with the high-temperature flue gas outside the tube to absorb the heat of the high-temperature flue gas. After that, superheated steam is formed, and reaches the rated superheated steam temperature through the steam temperature regulating device.

The qualified steam is merged into the superheater outlet header, enters the sub-cylinder through the main steam valve, and then is distributed to the heat users.

ESSENTIAL FEATURES TO CONSIDER IN A FOOD PROCESSING BOILER

When selecting a boiler, consider features that impact efficiency, reliability, and operational cost. Here are the essentials features:

Figure.: 7.3 Food Processing Boiler

- **High Thermal Efficiency:** Look for boilers with efficiency rates above 85%. Condensing boilers and those with economizers capture excess heat, pushing efficiency higher and reducing fuel costs.
- **Advanced Combustion Control:** Automated controls, like Oxygen Trim, continuously adjust the air-to-fuel ratio for optimal combustion. This maximizes fuel efficiency and reduces emissions, aligning with environmental standards.
- **PLC-Based Automation:** PLCs (Programmable Logic Controllers) automate the control of temperature, pressure, and water levels, ensuring safe and reliable operations. Systems with HMI (Human-Machine Interface) screens offer real-time monitoring, giving operators full visibility over boiler performance.
- **Safety Systems:** Critical safety features include low-water cutoffs, pressure relief valves, and flame safeguard systems, which automatically shut down the boiler under unsafe conditions.
- **Durability and Maintenance Access:** Look for boilers with corrosion-resistant materials like stainless steel and modular designs that simplify inspection, cleaning, and repair.

- **Steam Output and Pressure:** Ensure the boiler's steam output (measured in pounds per hour, or PPH) meets the demands of your facility. Large-scale operations typically benefit from water-tube or modular boilers, which offer flexible and scalable output options.
- **Fuel Type:** Evaluate the fuel availability and costs in your area. Natural gas is commonly chosen for its affordability and low emissions, whereas biomass is increasingly favored by facilities focused on sustainable energy sources.
- **Water Quality and Treatment:** Poor water quality can cause scaling, corrosion, and blockages within the system. To maintain high efficiency and prevent damage, incorporate water treatment systems such as reverse osmosis, demineralization, or chemical dosing.
- **Compliance with Emission Standards:** Modern environmental regulations require boilers to meet low emissions standards. Ensure the boiler is equipped with low-NOx burners and flue gas recirculation systems to comply with guidelines set by authorities like the U.S. Environmental Protection Agency (EPA) or the EU.
- **Installation Space and Maintenance Access:** For facilities with limited space, consider compact or modular boiler designs. Ensure that there is easy access to key components, such as blowdown valves and control panels, to simplify maintenance and reduce operational costs.

Key components of Boiler

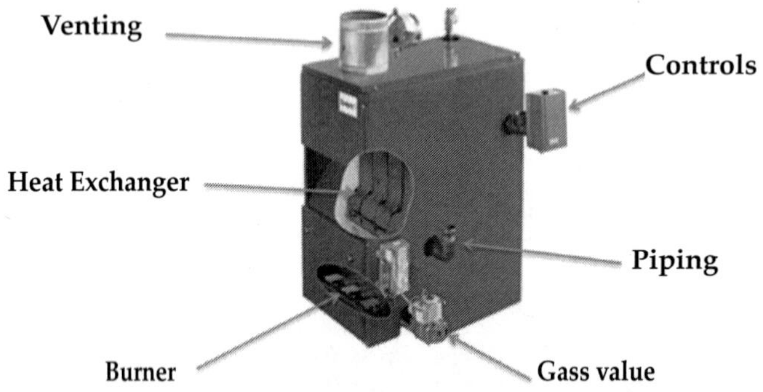

Figure.: 7.4 Boiler work

The parts of a boiler can be classified into following divisions:

- **Boiler Mounting:** These are the essential parts that defines the performance of the boiler.
- **Water Level Indicator:** This is used to check the water level inside the boiler which is fitted in the front of the boiler consisting of three cocks and a glass tube.
- **Pressure gauge:** This is utilized to measure the pressure inside the boiler which is fitted in the front of the boiler.

- **Safety valve:** This is fitted on the drum and is used to prevent the explosion of the boiler due to high pressure which blows off when the pressure inside exceeds the limit. These are always present two.
- **Stop valve:** This is used to control the flow of steam from the boiler to the steam pipe.
- **Blow off cock:** This is fitted at the bottom of the drum and is used to blow off mud and water and is used to empty the boiler.
- **Feed check valve:** This is used as a Non-Return Valve which is fitted slightly below the normal water level on the drum. It is used to regulate the supply of water.
- **Grate:** It is the space in the furnace used to burn the fuel.
- **Boiler accessories:** These are the parts that are responsible for the efficiency of the boiler.
- **Feed pump:** It is used to pump the water into the boiler for continuous working. Either electricity or steam turbine is used for the running of the feed pump.
- **Super heater:** This is used to superheat the steam before it is passed in the turbine as saturated steam causes corrosion.
- **Economizer:** It is used to increase the efficiency of the boiler as the flue gases from the boiler is made to flow through the economizer before releasing it to the atmosphere.
- **Air preheater:** It is also used to increase the efficiency of the boiler by preheating the air.

WORKING PRINCIPLE OF BOILER

The working principle of a boiler is quite straightforward. It is essentially a closed container where water is stored. Fuel is burned in the furnace to produce hot gases, which are directed to the water vessel. The heat from these gases is transferred to the water, converting it into steam. The core function of the boiler is to use heat energy to turn water into steam. Various types of boilers are used, each designed for specific applications.

Efficiency of Boiler

The efficiency of the boiler is defined as the percentage of total heat exported by the outlet steam to the total supplied fuel.

Boiler efficiency (%)=(heat exported by outlet steam/heat supplied by the fuel)×100

Tips for Safety & upkeep

While reliability and asset lifespan are important, they are not the main concerns when it comes to boiler failures. A malfunction in a boiler can pose significant hazards to nearby workers, making proper maintenance not only essential but also a legal requirement. Regular inspections of components such as the drum, headers, and piping help ensure that the boiler operates according to national and state regulations, while also ensuring the safety of workers.

The safety of operators is important, but so too is that of your maintenance crew. When they're performing boiler maintenance, make sure your technicians adhere to all necessary safety protocols and best practices, such as following LOTO procedures and wearing PPE.

Maintenance Program

The first place to start is owner's manual. This will provide you with the manufacturer's recommended maintenance plan and upkeep suggestions.

Daily Maintenance

- Check water level gauge glass, record the pressure gauge and temperature gauges
- Check LWCO and ALWCO operation and ensure the burner shuts down
- Blowdown the water column and gauge glass
- Turn off burner control switch, observe the response to flame failure
- Observe operating control and high limit control
- Perform bottom blowdown to remove sludge and sediment.
- Observer burner refractory cone, looking for broken chunks or hot spots

Weekly Maintenance

- Check all linkages on burner controls and the automatic draft controllers
- Check air damper on the burner
- Test valve operation in gas train
- Check pilot and igniter, look at the condition of the flame
- Check process of LWCO – blowdown boiler water level through the drain. Watch gauge glass to see burner cut off before losing sight of water.

Monthly Maintenance

- Test limit controls on boiler.
- Test flame detection controls.
- Check blowdown for sludging at bottom of boiler.
- Verify blowdown separator and cooler operation.
- Check floor drains for proper function.
- Check boiler fresh air inlet screens.

Annual Maintenance

- Disassemble and check LWCO and ALWCO for sludge, corrosion or electrical switch defects.
- Verify and tune up burners and settings.

- Inspect fire side for soot or damage and water side for scale or corrosion &Clean the boiler inside and out.
- Hydro test boiler for leaks (tube joints and piping).
- Inspect all refractory for fallen broken chunks.
- Check gas regulator pressure settings.
- Replace or re-certify safety valves.
- Bubble test fuel train safety shut-off valves.

PASTEURIZER

The performance of the pasteurizer is an important factor for the overall efficiency of the dairy plant, as it is considered the heart of the operation. Its ability to pasteurize milk effectively while requiring minimal service helps reduce the plant's operational costs. One key parameter for evaluating pasteurizer efficiency is Regeneration Efficiency.

Methods of Pasteurization

There are two basic methods, batch and continuous.

Batch method

Batch pasteurizers are designed with specific features and auxiliary equipment to ensure thorough pasteurization of every particle of milk. The milk is heated to the desired temperature in the vat using hot water, either sprayed on the sides of the vat, circulated around a double jacket, or through heating coils surrounding the inner jacket. The heating and cooling process typically takes place in one or more tanks. The milk is heated to at least 63°C for 30 minutes and then rapidly cooled to below 10°C to ensure safety and quality.

The parts of a typical batch pasteurizer are following

- Insulated outer casing
- Insulated hinged cover
- Stainless steel inner vessel
- Agitator and its motor
- Outlet cock and heating water distribution pipe.

This system is ideal for small-scale operations, where less than 3000 to 5000 liters of milk are available. While the vat can be rectangular, a vertical, cylindrical design is preferred for practical reasons. The vat typically consists of an inner vessel surrounded by an insulated outer casing, forming a jacket through which hot water or steam circulates. Once the milk reaches the required temperature of 63.0°C, it is held at that temperature for a fixed period, typically 30 minutes. Afterward, it is rapidly cooled, often using refrigerant or chilled water, or through a plate/surface chiller. Cooling the milk with circulating refrigerant or cold water through the vat or jacket can be time-consuming, so a separate surface, tubular, or plate cooler may be used for faster cooling. This also allows the vat to be ready sooner for another batch. Batch pasteurizers have a relatively small heating surface area compared to their contents, so heat transfer is significantly improved by agitating the milk. Different agitator designs are used, such as double-walled paddles or devices with internal steam or water circulation. Care must be taken to avoid foam formation during filling, as it can prevent uniform heating and allow microorganisms in the foam to survive pasteurization. Preventing foam formation is easier when the inlet valve is positioned at the bottom of the vat. Alid or cover helps maintain a consistent temperature and prevents skin formation on the milk.

Figure.: 7.5 Batch Pasteurizer

Continuous Method

The continuous method offers several advantages over the batch method, with the most notable being time and energy efficiency. For continuous processing, a high-temperature short-time (HTST) pasteurizer is employed. The pasteurization process is carried out using a plate heat exchanger, which consists of a series of corrugated stainless steel plates clamped together in a frame. Various flow patterns can be used, and gaskets are employed to define the boundaries of the channels and prevent leakage. The heating medium can either be vacuum steam or hot water.

Cold raw milk, initially at 4°C, is drawn from a constant level tank into the regenerator section of the pasteurizer. In this section, the milk is warmed to approximately 57°C - 68°C by heat transferred from hot pasteurized milk flowing in the opposite direction through thin stainless steel plates. The raw milk, still under suction, then passes through a positive displacement timing pump, which delivers it under positive pressure through the rest of the HTST system.

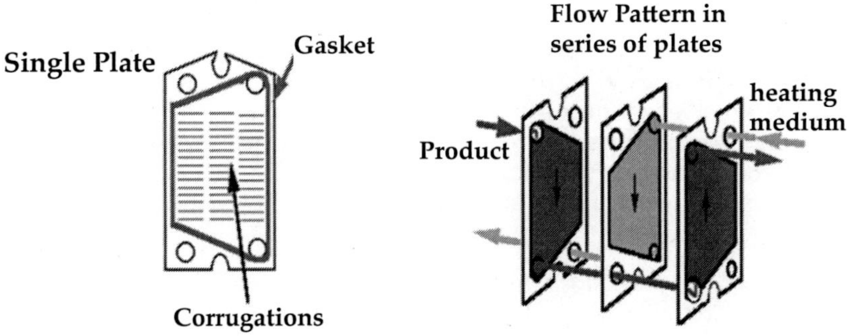

Figure.: 7.6 HTST milk flow overview

The raw milk is pumped through the heater section, where hot water on the opposite sides of the plates raises the milk temperature to at least 72°C. Once the milk reaches pasteurization temperature and is under pressure, it flows through the holding tube, where it is maintained for at least 16 seconds. The velocity is determined by the timing pump speed, the diameter and length of the holding tube, and surface friction. After passing through temperature sensors, including an indicating thermometer and a recorder-controller at the end of the holding tube, the milk enters the flow diversion valve (FDV).

If the milk has reached the preset cut-in temperature (>72°C), the FDV moves to the forward-flow position. If the milk has not reached the required temperature, the FDV stays in diverted-flow, and the inadequately heated milk returns to the raw milk constant level tank. Properly heated milk flows into the forward flow of the FDV, then into the pasteurized milk regenerator, where it transfers heat to the raw milk and is cooled to approximately 32°C - 9°C. The milk then moves through the cooling section, where it is cooled to 4°C or below by coolant passing through the opposite sides of the stainless steel plates. Finally, the cooled, pasteurized milk passes through a vacuum breaker positioned at least 12 inches above the highest point of the raw milk in the HTST system and proceeds to the storage tank filler for packaging.

Figure.: 7.7 Basic flow- HTST Pasteurization

Holding Time

When fluids move through a pipe, either of two distinct types of flow can be observed. The first is known as turbulent flow which occurs at high velocity and in which eddies are present moving in all directions and at all angles to the normal line of flow. The second type is streamline, or laminar flow which occurs at low velocities and shows no eddy currents. The Reynolds number, is used to predict whether laminar or turbulent flow will exist in a pipe:

- Re < 2100 laminar
- Re > 4000 fully developed turbulent flow

There is an impact of these flow patterns on holding time calculations and the assessment of proper holding tube lengths. The holding time is determined by timing the interval for an added trace substance (salt) to pass through the holder. The time interval of the fastest particle of milk is desired. Thus the results found with water are converted to the milk flow time by formulation since a pump may not deliver the same amount of milk as it does water.

Pressure Differential

For continuous pasteurization, it is crucial to maintain a higher pressure on the pasteurized side of the heat exchanger. By ensuring that the pasteurized milk is at least 1 psi higher than the raw milk in the regenerator, contamination of pasteurized milk with raw milk is prevented in case a pinhole leak occurs in the thin stainless steel plates. This pressure differential is maintained in simpler systems using a timing pump, while more complex systems use differential pressure controllers and back pressure flow regulators at the chilled pasteurization outlet. The position of the timing pump is critical to ensure suction on the raw regenerator side and that milk is pushed under pressure through the pasteurized regenerator. Additional factors that contribute to maintaining the pressure differential include:

- The overflow level of the balance tank must be lower than the lowest milk passage level in the regenerator.
- A properly installed booster pump is the only pump allowed between the balance tank and raw regenerator.
- No pump should be placed after the pasteurized milk outlet leading to the vacuum breaker.
- There should be a vertical rise of at least 12 inches to the vacuum breaker.
- The raw regenerator should drain freely to the balance tank during shut-down.

Regeneration in HTST Pasteurizer

Thermal regeneration is a method designed to reduce service loads and enhance energy efficiency. Regeneration efficiency can be defined in various ways, and because of these differing approaches, heat exchangers with the same thermal performance might appear to have different regeneration efficiencies.

One way to define regeneration efficiency is as "the temperature range over which the product is heated by regeneration, expressed as a percentage of the total heating range."

Consider a simple heat exchanger in which a product is heated from 5°C to 85°C using 80% regeneration, with the remaining heat applied in a heating section.

Once the product reaches 85°C, it is held in holding tubes and returned to the regeneration section at that temperature.

The total heating range is (85 - 5)°C = 80°C. The portion of the heating range covered by regeneration is 80% of 80°C, which equals 64°C. This means the product's temperature will rise from 5°C to 69°C through regeneration, and then from 69°C to 85°C in the heating section. Afterward, the heated product is returned to the regeneration section at 85°C, where it is cooled by the incoming cold product at 5°C. This process can be illustrated as follows:

Considering now the heating loads involved and assuming a flow rate of Q then:

- Steam load in heating section = Q (85 – 69) = 16Q
- Total heating load = Q (85 – 5) = 80Q

The heat load in the heating section is 20% of the total heating load. Therefore the regeneration percentage (or efficiency) of 80% truly represents 80% of the total heating load.

Key Equipments of HTST Pasteurizer

Balance Tank

The balance or constant level tank ensures a steady supply of milk and is fitted with a float valve assembly to maintain a nearly constant liquid level, thereby providing uniform head pressure on the product leaving the tank. The overflow level must remain below the lowest milk passage level in the regenerator, which aids to maintain higher pressure on the pasteurized side of the heat exchanger. Additionally, the balance tank prevents air from entering the pasteurizer by positioning the top of the outlet pipe lower than the lowest point in the tank and ensuring downward slopes of at least 2%. The balance tank also facilitates the recirculation of diverted or pasteurized milk.

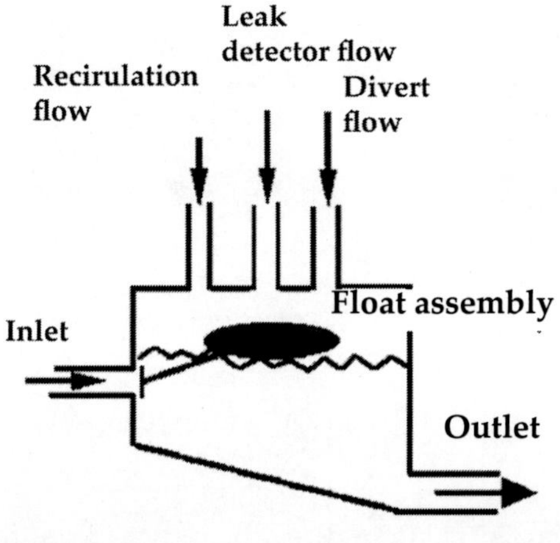

Figure.: 7.8 Milk balance tank/flow control unit

Regenerator

Heating and cooling energy can be saved by using a regenerator which utilizes the heat content of the pasteurized milk to warm the incoming cold milk. Its efficiency may be calculated as follows:

% regeneration = temp. increase due to regenerator/total temp. increase

For example, Cold milk entering system at 4° C, after regeneration at 65° C, and final temperature of 72° C would have an 89.7% regeneration:

$$\frac{65-4}{72-4}=\frac{61}{68}=0.879=89.7\%$$

Timing Pump

The timing pump draws the product through the raw regenerator and forces the milk under pressure through the pasteurized regenerator, controlling the flow rate through the holding tube. It must be a positive displacement pump with a variable speed drive that can be sealed at the maximum rate to ensure the minimum holding time in the holding tubes. Additionally, it must be wired to operate only when the FDV is fully in the forward or diverted position, and it must have a fail-safe mechanism. Alternatively, a centrifugal pump equipped with a magnetic flow meter and controller can also be used.

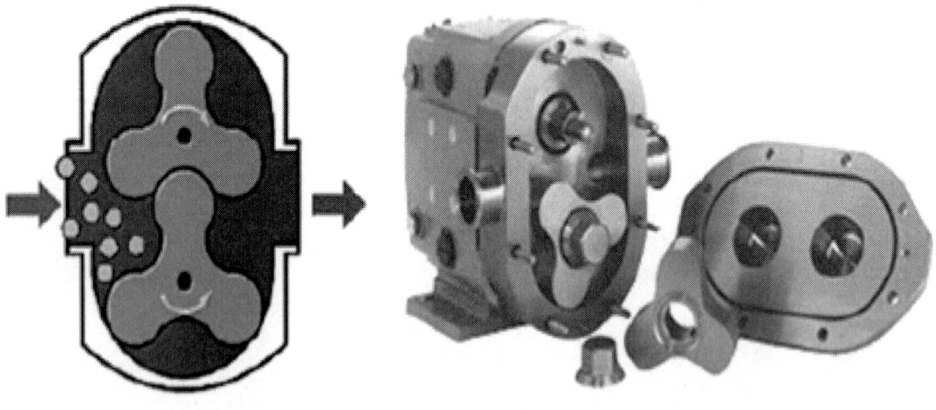

Figure.: 7.9 Timing pump

Holding Tube

Must slope upwards 1/4"/ft. in direction of flow to eliminate air entrapment so nothing flows faster at air pocket restrictions.

Figure.: 7.10 Holding tubes

Indicating Thermometer

The indicating thermometer is considered the most accurate temperature measurement. It is the official temperature to which the safety thermal limit recorder (STLR) is adjusted. The probe should sit as close as possible to STLR probe and be located not greater than 18 inches upstream of the flow diversion device.

Safety Thermal Limit Recorder-Controller (STLR)

The STLR tracks the milk temperature and time of day, monitors, controls, and records the position of the flow diversion valve (FDV), and supplies power to the FDV during forward flow. Controllers can be pneumatic or electronic. The operator is responsible for recording various details such as the date, shift, equipment ID, product type, quantity, indicating thermometer temperature, cleansing cycles, cut-in and cut-out temperatures, any anomalies, and their signature.

Indicating themomter **STLR**

Figure.: 7.11 Safety Thermal limit recorder-Controller

Flow Diversion Valve (FDV)

It is also known as the flow diversion device (FDD), it is positioned at the downstream end of the upward-sloping holding tube. The FDD is essentially a 3-way valve that opens to forward flow when the temperature exceeds 72°C, requiring power. If the temperature is below 72°C, the valve closes to its normal position and diverts the milk back to the balance tank. It is crucial to note that the FDV operates based on temperature, not time, at the end of the holding period.

There are two types of FDV

- **Single stem:** An older valve system, which cannot be cleaned in place.
- **Dual stem:** Consists of two valves in series for added fail-safe protection. This type can be cleaned in place and is better suited for automation.

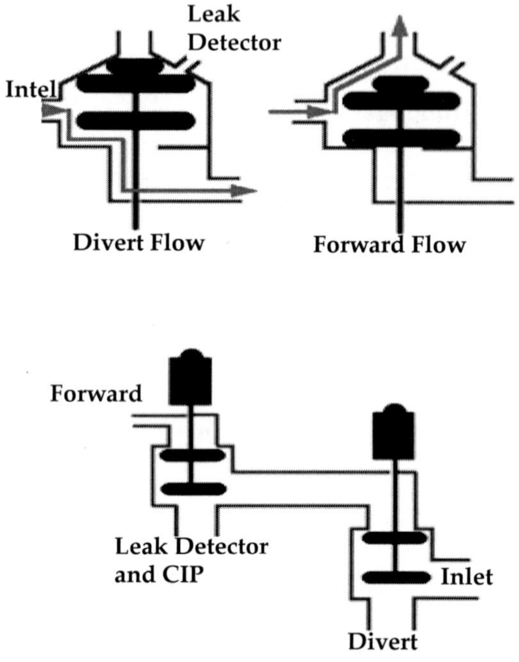

Figure 7.12 Single-Stem FDD (Top), Dual-Stem FDD (bottom)

Vacuum Breaker

At the pasteurized product discharge is a vacuum breaker which breaks to atmospheric pressure. It must be located greater than 12 inches above the highest point of raw product in system. It ensures that nothing downstream is creating suction on the pasteurized side.

Auxiliary Equipment

Booster Pump

It is centrifugal "stuffing" pump that supplies raw milk to the raw regenerator for the balance tank. It must be used in conjunction with pressure differential controlling device and shall operate only when timing pump is operating, proper pressures are achieved in regenerator, and system is in forward flow.

Upkeep of HTST Pasteurizer

The plant should be inspected externally for leakage of all kinds. It should be monitored continuously throughout the process and any abnormalities noted be investigated and rectified. The flow rate of milk and media should be checked by measuring the time to process a known quantity of milk.

Plates

- The Pasteurizer must be CIP cleaned regularly after day's operations.
- The plates should be cleaned manually periodically. It should be done with nylon or fiber brush or coir. It should never be cleaned with metal wire brushes.
- The proper tightening and dismantling procedures have to be followed. Care should be taken not to tighten beyond the mark, provided by the manufacturer. The tightening has to be done such a way that plates move parallel to each other and the measurement of length at the top of the plate pack should be same as at the bottom.

Gaskets

Gaskets should be made of nitrile rubber, capable of withstanding temperatures up to 120°C. The use of harsh acid solutions during CIP cleaning may damage the gaskets. It's advisable to replace gaskets as a complete set to avoid misalignment of the plates. New gaskets should be tightened minimally, and as they age, tightening should be increased to prevent leakage. When replacing old gaskets, carefully remove any remnants from the gasket groove. Old adhesive, grease, dirt, and other residues should be cleaned with acetone, and the groove should be thoroughly dried. The replacement gaskets should be lightly sanded on the back, cleaned, and dried. Apply a thin, even coat of adhesive to both the gasket groove and the back of the gasket using a small brush. While the adhesive remains sticky, fit the gasket into the groove. Apply slight pressure for a few minutes to help secure the gasket in place. Any excess adhesive should be removed.

Frame

The frame having threads and spindle should be lightly coated with grease, to help easy movement of the plates.

Filter

Filter cloth should be checked from time to time for any tear or worn out patches. It should be washed after dismantling. Cloth should be replaced if any damage is observed. So is the case with wire gauge filter screen protecting the filter cloth.

Instruments

All thermometers should be checked periodically for accuracy. All air operated instruments should be supplied with clear dry air. The air filters should be inspected periodically, cleaned or changed when required. The components of controlling instruments should be replaced when ever damaged or functioning inaccurately. Leakages in the control instruments of steam supply should be checked, as they are susceptible for corrosion because of higher temperatures.

Pumps and motors

The pumps and motors should be thoroughly overhauled once in a year. The shaft seals if leaking should be replaced immediately. Motors if noisy should be checked for damaged bearings. Misalignment is one of the most common sources of pump troubles. Scales in hot water pump should be removed.

STERILIZATION

Sterilization is commonly used to eliminate all forms of living microorganisms in a substance. The primary goal of sterilization is to preserve the substance for extended periods. It involves applying heat or chemicals to products such as food, drugs, surgical equipment, and nutraceuticals. If food materials are not properly sterilized, they may contain harmful bacteria that can cause severe infections upon consumption. Since disease-causing bacteria are often invisible to the naked eye, various sterilization methods are employed in microbiology.

Sterilized milk is a product achieved by heating milk in a commercial cooker or retort to temperatures ranging from 110-130°C for 10-30 minutes. This process is also known as in-container sterilization. Sterilized milk is typically intended for long-term storage at room temperature for up to 6 months. The primary objective of heat sterilization is to eliminate microbial and enzymatic activity. The processing time and temperature depend on factors like the type of product, the number and heat resistance of microorganisms, and enzymes in the milk. The heat resistance of microorganisms and enzymes is often measured using the D-value or Z-value, while the sterilization load is expressed in terms of the F0 value.

Theoretical Basis

Clostridium botulinum is regarded as the standard organism for determining thermal sterility in foods. In anaerobic conditions, within a sealed container, it can produce botulinum toxin, which is highly toxic and can be fatal to humans in 65% of cases. Therefore, eliminating this organism is a fundamental requirement of heat sterilization. Since milk is a low-acid food (with a pH greater than 4.5), it is recommended to achieve 12 decimal reductions for C. botulinum. This can be accomplished by heating the milk at 121°C for 3 minutes. However, while this treatment ensures the milk is safe, it may not be commercially sterile, as more heat-resistant spores, such as B. stearothermophilus or B. sporothermodurans, may still be present. These spores are non-pathogenic but may require a higher level of heat treatment, equivalent to two or more decimal reductions, which corresponds to an F0 value of 8. To ensure commercial sterility, spoilage rates should be limited to fewer than one survivor in every 10,000 containers.

Different methods of Sterilization

Although there are many techniques of sterilization available out there, heat and chemical method is widely employed to sterile metals and food substances.

Apart from that, there are numerous techniques out there. In this section the most commonly used sterilization techniques are discussed:

Gaseous sterilization method

Despite heat sterilization is unstable for thermolabile equipment like delicate, plastic and rubber items, it has become popular due to its capital cost. This method applies a chemical in a gaseous state to destroy micro bacteria. Ethylene oxide is widely used in this method for medical and pharmaceutical fields.

Filtration Method

Filtration includes removing microbes from a solution using a filter. When a liquid passes through the mechanical filter, microorganisms are trapped in the small pores of that filter. The fluid that a container receives has no bacteria as it is sterilized. The fluid is decontaminated by just using a filter. Since the filtration method is user-friendly, it is widely employed in beverages, bacteriological media, pharmaceuticals etc. There are several types of mechanical filters available for this method such as Chamberland Filters, Berkefeld Filters, Mandler Filters, Fritted-Glass Filters, Asbestos Filters, Jenkins Filter, Ultrafilter, Membrane Filter, Cleaning Filters

Preservation

Preservation involves the use of salt on various substance like fish, cereals. Metals and other food materials. Drying is an essential technique that preservation requires. Most of the food can be preserved in our kitchen through this amazing method. When a food substance is salted, it undergoes diffusion, which increases the salt concentration and reduces the water molecules, then it undergoes the osmosis process where microbes in it shrivel and die. The same technique is used in highly sugared foods such as jams, jellies, syrups etc.

Radiation

Ultraviolet (UV) light is an effective method for controlling microbial contamination in food substances. It operates within a wavelength range of 100 nm to 400 nm, with the most effective energy at around 265 nm, which is potent enough to destroy microbes. When microorganisms are exposed to UV radiation, the light penetrates their DNA, specifically targeting the thymine molecules. This causes the thymine molecules to become linked in a way that prevents proper alignment with adenine in RNA molecules during transcription, leading to a disruption in the microorganism's molecular structure. This results in impaired chromosome replication, rendering the microorganism unable to produce proteins and causing it to die. UV light, naturally emitted by the sun, plays a crucial role in controlling microorganisms in the air and soil, and this principle is applied in various settings to reduce microbial populations. UV light is commonly used to sanitize surfaces in environments such as morgues, restrooms, pharmacies, hospital rooms, and food processing areas.

Infrared Radiation

When a substance is exposed to infrared radiation of 0.3 to 0.4 Mrads, it can cause tenfold reduction in the microbes endospores. Ionizing radiation is widely employed to sterilize substance. Mostly, plastic substances that contain microbes are subjected to sterilization by using gamma radiation. Most of the sterilization procedures involve exposure to radiation of cesium 137. When microorganisms are subjected to sterilization by exposing them to infrared or microwave radiation of higher temperature, microbes can be killed indirectly. However, microwaves don't kill the microbes directly, hence food items that are baked in the micro ovens may not kill these microbes.

Ultrasonic waves

Ultrasonic frequencies are not audible to human ear. Ultrasonic vibrations are used for research and study parts of tissues. The dentist uses the Cavitron device to clean teeth and destroy bacteria. The ultrasonic machines are used for cleaning dental plaques, coins, metals, jewelry etc.

Heat Method

Heat method is the most common method of sterilization that kills the microbes directly. Depending on the duration of heating and the temperature of heat, the effect of sterilization varies. When a substance is exposed to the direct flame for a long time, the microbe molecules shrink and die. The two types of heat methods are dry heat methods and moist heat methods. Heat method is the easiest way to kill harmful bacteria that survive on the food particles.

Moist heat Method

Here, the substance is subjected to sterilization by applying heat flame directly. Some of the most common moist heat methods are boiling, pasteurization and autoclave method.

- **Boiling technique:**It is mostly used for sterilization of metallic devices like scalpels, surgical scissors, needles etc. These substances are boiled to high temperatures to kill the disease-causing bacteria.
- **Pasteurization:** It is the simple process of heating milk at high temperatures. Once the milk is boiled, it is again subjected to cooling. In this way, microbes in the milk get killed automatically.
- **Autoclaving:** It is a type of sterilization that uses steam sterilization equipment. Here, any substance is exposed to a temperature of 115 degrees for an hour. It is a powerful method for killing bacterial spores.

Dry Heat Method

Dry heat method involves flaming, incineration and hot air oven techniques.

- **Flaming:** The substance is exposed to the flame for just a few minutes. The flame burn out the microbes directly.
- **Incineration :** It is an effective method of sterilization in microbe cultures. The end of the microbe loop is exposed to red hot flame;thus, it kills microorganism. It is the easiest way to destroy microbes in metals.

- **Hot Air oven :** The application of hot air oven is dry materials like glassware, heavy metals, thermostable materials etc. Here, hot air is allowed to circulate at a certain time and temperature. This way hot air oven works.

VARIANTS OF STERILIZATION PLANTS

Sterilizing retorts can be either batch-type or continuous in operation. Batch-type sterilizers are available in vertical or horizontal configurations. Horizontal retorts are more convenient for loading and unloading and come with features for agitating containers or cages. However, they require more floor space. Typically, these horizontal retorts feature concentric cages, where cans are loaded horizontally into the annular space between the cages. Once the cages are filled, the retort is sealed, and the cages are supported by guide rails that slowly rotate them. This agitation helps ensure even heating of the contents. Continuous retorts, on the other hand, are typically equipped with more advanced controls and gradually change the pressure inside the cans, leading to more uniform heating. The gradual pressure change also reduces strain on the can seams compared to the batch process.

Continuous Sterilizers

Sterilizers are usually classified into three main types:

Cooker-coolers,

Hydrostatic sterilizers, and

Rotary sterilizers.

Cooker-coolers

Cooker-coolers operate by carrying cans on a conveyor that passes through three sections of a tunnel, each maintained at different pressures for preheating, sterilization, and cooling.

Hydrostatic sterilizers

Hydrostatic sterilizers consist of a chamber with steam injection capability, and the chamber is partially filled with water connected to two tall water columns (12 to 18 meters) that adjust the pressure inside. By varying the height of the columns, steam pressure changes, affecting the maximum achievable temperature. For instance, to reach 116°C, the height difference between the columns must be 10.7 meters, while 121°C requires a 13.7-meter difference. A conveyor that can accommodate various can sizes moves through the steam chamber, and the speed of the conveyor can regulate the heating time. Although hydrostatic sterilizers are highly flexible and suitable for large-scale operations, their large size and high capital costs are major drawbacks.

Rotary sterilizers

Continuous rotary sterilizers consist of multiple horizontally linked cylinders for preheating, heating, precooling, and cooling in up to four continuous stages. The vessel has a spiral track on its inner wall, and a reel or spoke at the center moves the cans along the spiral, ensuring even mixing and heat transfer. Rotary valves connect the cylinders and maintain pressure in the heating and cooling sections. Cans are introduced directly from the sealing machines, and their contents are mixed as they travel along the helix, minimizing heat damage. After the cooking process, cans are sent directly to labeling and palletizing machines. Rotary sterilizers are especially beneficial for heat-sensitive products like milk and milk-based items, which are prone to browning.

Description of the Canning Process

The conventional retorting or canning process involves several basic steps: preparing the raw material, filling the container, exhausting, sealing, sterilizing, cooling, labeling, and storage. Preparation of raw materials includes washing, peeling, cutting, blanching, precooking for fruits, vegetables, meats, etc., and preheating, mixing, homogenizing for milk. Containers are filled either manually or mechanically, with precise filling being crucial to avoid trapping excess air or gas, which could reduce heat treatment efficiency. Exhausting, a key operation, removes air/oxygen from the container before sealing. This step prevents strain on seams or seals from air expansion during heat processing, reduces the risk of internal corrosion, creates a vacuum during cooling, delays oxidative deterioration, and protects ascorbic acid from degradation.

Following exhaustion, the containers are sealed using appropriate sealing machines depending on the container type (metal cans, glass bottles, flexible pouches). Glass jars are vacuum-sealed, metal cans use double sealing and may also be vacuum-sealed, and flexible pouches are sealed by heat fusion. The sealed product is then heated in the sterilizer with saturated steam, hot water, or a steam-air mixture. Saturated steam is efficient because it condenses readily, transferring latent heat to sterilize the contents. A crucial step is venting, where all air in the retort is displaced by steam before the sterilizer reaches its operating temperature. This ensures uniform steam-air mixture and prevents underprocessing. The sterilization temperature and time typically range from 110°C to 130°C for 10-30 minutes. After sterilization, containers are cooled to room temperature for labeling and storage. To verify sterility, a turbidity test developed by Aschaffenburg is performed, which measures denatured whey proteins. Complete denaturation indicates proper sterilization of the product.

UHT (Ultra High Temperature) Processing

Definition

UHT milk can be defined as a product obtained by heating milk in a continuous flow to a temperature in excess of 125°C for not less than two seconds and immediately packaging in sterile packages under aseptic conditions. In India, UHT milk is generally processed at 140°C for 2 seconds.

Theoretical Basis

Heating milk kills microorganisms, but while pasteurization (71.7°C for 15 seconds) eliminates many bacteria, some, like *Bacillus subtilis* and *Bacillus stearothermophilus* spores, are highly heat-resistant. Of these, *Bacillus stearothermophilus* spores are the most heat-resistant, making them an ideal index organism for evaluating UHT (Ultra-High Temperature) processing. Heating milk at higher temperatures also causes undesirable chemical changes, with browning reactions being particularly significant. As the thermal load increases, so does browning, leading to a loss of flavor and quality. In the 100-120°C range, more time is required to kill most *B. stearothermophilus* spores, which can result in more browning. However, when milk is treated in the UHT range of 135-150°C for just a few seconds, nearly all spores are destroyed, and browning is minimized. This approach results in minimal loss of nutrients and overall quality, producing a product that is both microbiologically safe and superior in terms of quality.

VARIANTS OF UHT PLANTS

There are two main types of UHT (Ultra-High Temperature) plants: Direct and Indirect. In direct type plants, the product is heated by directly mixing it with steam. In contrast, in indirect type plants, the product is heated using steam or hot water, but without direct contact between the two. In direct type plants, heating occurs very quickly, particularly between 80-140°C, resulting in a lower total heat load and minimal changes in product quality. On the other hand, in indirect type plants, the temperature rise is gradual, leading to a higher heat load and comparatively more changes in the chemical quality of the product.

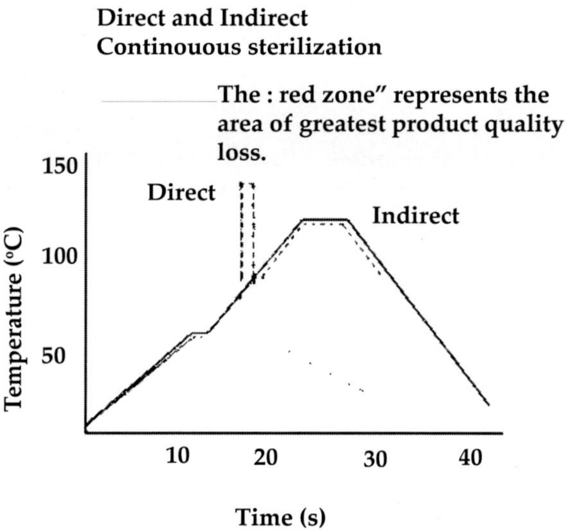

Figure.: 7.13 Direct and Indirect continuous sterilization

Direct Heating Plant

There are two types of direct heating plants

- Injection type
- Infusion type.

Injection type

The processing in this system is carried out through a steam-into-milk arrangement, where the steam injector plays a crucial role as the heart of the plant. Preheated milk, typically at 80-90°C, flows into the injector nozzles from one side, while steam at a slightly higher pressure enters from the other side. As the steam mixes with the milk, it rapidly condenses, heating the product quickly. This rapid condensation prevents air from entering the holding tube, which could otherwise lead to improper heating. Backpressure is maintained on the discharge side to ensure that the product does not boil within the holding tube, as boiling can cause fouling and improper heating of the milk. Various designs of injectors are available for this process.

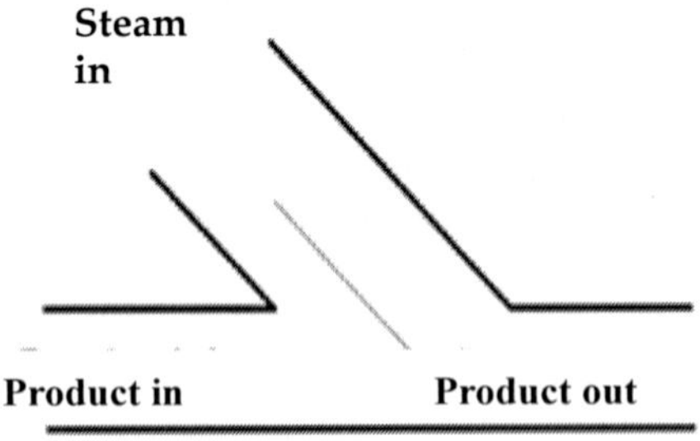

Figure.: 7.14 Injection Value

Infusion type

In this system, milk is heated using a milk-into-steam arrangement. The processing unit consists of a chamber filled with pressurized steam, and the milk enters the chamber from the top. There are two possible methods for distributing the milk. In the first, milk flows into a hemispherical bowl, with a loose circular disc covering the top. When the bowl fills, the milk overflows and falls in droplets through the steam environment. In the second arrangement, milk flows through a series of parallel horizontal distribution tubes, with slits along the bottom. The milk flows as a thin film through these tubes, and by the time it reaches the bottom of the chamber, it is heated to the desired temperature. This system is usually effective for thicker liquids or liquids with smaller solid particles suspended in them.

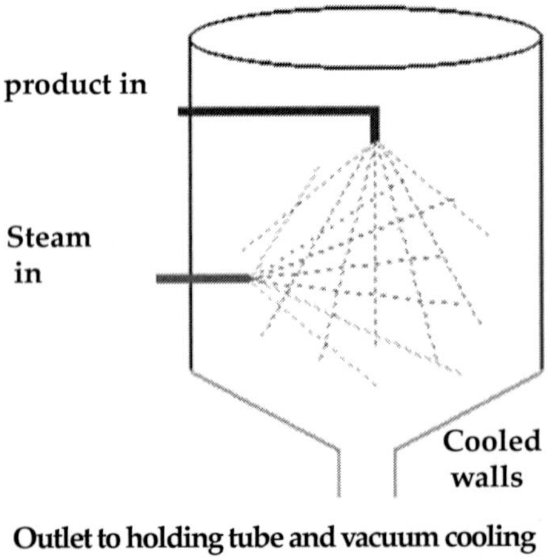

Figure.: 7.15 Infusion Chamber

Merits and Demerits Direct Heating System:

In direct heating systems, the condensation of steam that comes into contact with the product results in dilution, which necessitates the removal of excess water. This is achieved by cooling the product in an expansion cooling vessel. The expansion vessel removes not only evaporated water but also incondensable gases and undesirable volatile flavors produced during heating, improving the taste of the product. Steam injection causes casein aggregates to form, leading to a "chalky" or "astringent" mouthfeel. To address this issue, an aseptic homogenizer is often used after the final heating section to smooth the product. The rate of heating in direct systems is extremely fast, typically taking less than 1 second to reach sterilization temperature.

This system is suitable for processing thick or viscous liquids and minimizes deposit formation, allowing for longer operation times without cleaning. Flash cooling also removes undesirable flavors and reduces the risk of oxidized flavor defects during storage. However, the processing cost per unit volume of milk is high. The plant requires additional equipment, such as a vacuum expansion chamber and aseptic homogenizer, making it twice as costly as indirect systems. The heat energy requirements are substantial, and water and electricity consumption are 25-50% higher than for indirect systems. The system also requires culinary steam, necessitating a special boiler, and produces greater noise during operation.

Indirect Type Heating System

There are three variants of indirect heating systems.

- Plate heat exchangers
- Tubular heat exchanger
- Scraped surface heat exchanger.

Plate heat exchanger

This resembles plate heat exchanger of HTST plants. Several rectangular stainless steel plates with corrugations are arranged in sequence. These plates are then mechanically tightened to hold together. Corrugations on the plates induce turbulence and therefore result in high heat transfer. High temperature processing generates high internal pressure. The gaskets are therefore made of heat resistant materials such as medium nitrile rubber or resin cured butyl rubber. A major advantage of this plant is therefore simple design and comparatively less cost. If deposit formation is more, plates can be removed and manually cleaned.

Tubular heat exchanger

There are two main types of tubular heat exchangers: concentric tube and shell-and-tube type. Concentric tube heat exchangers consist of two or three stainless steel tubes placed one inside the other, with spacers to maintain their concentric arrangement. Multiple such tubes are grouped together and placed in an outer cylindrical housing. The two-tube design is typically used for basic cooling and heating processes. In the triple-tube version, the available heat transfer area is doubled, making it ideal for the final cooling stage. It is also suitable for processing thicker liquids, which tend to reduce heat transfer efficiency. In this setup, the product flows through the middle annular space, while the heating or cooling medium circulates through the inner tube and outer annular space.

In shell-and-tube heat exchangers, several straight tubes (with an internal diameter of 10-15 mm) are arranged within a larger outer tube. The smaller tubes are connected to the outer tube at both ends by a manifold. The product flows through the smaller tubes, while the heating or cooling medium passes through the shell surrounding the tubes. This design allows for efficient heat exchange, especially in larger-scale operations.

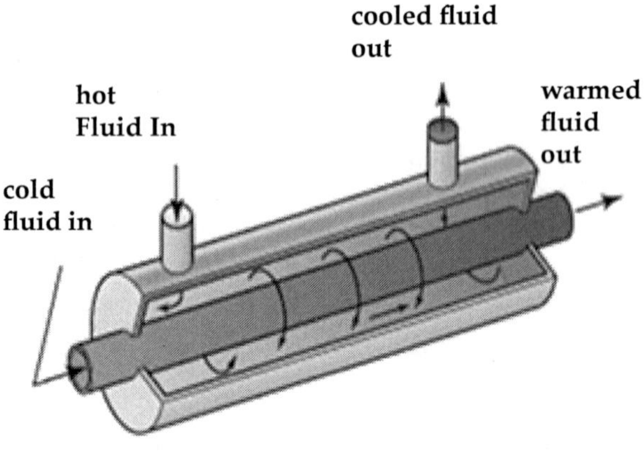

Figure.: 7.16 Concentric tube type heat exchanger

Heating or cooling medium passes through the space around them in a counter current flow. Tubular heat exchangers are mechanically very strong and can withstand even very high internal pressure generated during homogenization (200- 300 bar). Therefore the need for acquiring an aseptic homogenizer to be placed after heating section is totally eliminated. Instead, the high pressure reciprocating pump of an ordinary homogenizer can be placed before the sterile section. The homogenizing valve can be put at any point on the downstream side (even after final heating section). The problem of product contamination arises from the homogenization pump and not the valve. Therefore, with tubular heat exchangers, the product can be homogenized before sterilization, after sterilization or on both the occasions. Fat rich products like cream require homogenization after final heating to prevent re-association of fat globules due to high temperature processing after homogenization.

Scraped Surface Heat Exchanger (SSHE)

It is a very specialized type of heat exchanger. It consists of a jacketed cylinder. A shaft passes along the axis of the cylinder. The shaft is supported by bearings at both ends of the cylinder. The shaft also carries several scrapper blades. As shaft rotates, scrapper blades provide turbulence and physically remove the product from the surface of the wall. The colder product subsequently replaces the heated product and the cycle continues.

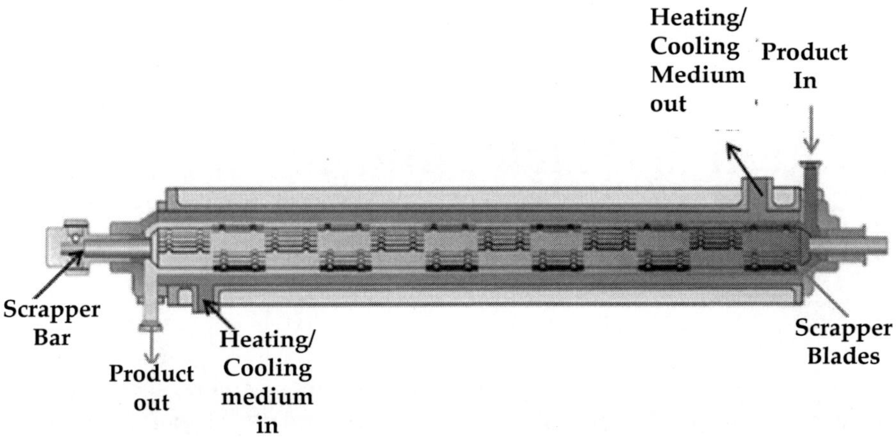

Figure.: 7.17 Scraped Surface heat exchanger

SSHE is used only for heating very thick liquids. SSHE units are very expensive and have poor energy conversion efficiency. The cost of processing is therefore very high.

Merits and Demerits of Indirect Heating System

The indirect type heat exchanger is simple in design and requires fewer pumps and controls, making it more cost-effective. It is capable of regenerating up to 90% of the thermal energy needed, which contributes to operational efficiency. Unlike direct type plants, it does not require an aseptic homogenizer, which is costly, nor does it require culinary steam or a specialized boiler. Additionally, the indirect type plant operates more quietly and has lower initial capital and operational costs. However, the rate of heat transfer in this system is lower, which leads to higher heat loads and potentially lower product quality. The increased heat load results in more deposit formation, meaning that the plant needs to be cleaned more frequently. Furthermore, to remove dissolved oxygen from milk, an additional piece of equipment, a deaerator, is necessary.

8

Operation and Maintenance of Peeler, Slicer, Pulper and Juicer

The upkeep of food processing equipment such as peelers, slicers, pulpers, and juicers are essential to ensure the smooth and efficient functioning of food production processes. These machines are commonly used in the food industry for preparing fruits, vegetables, and other raw materials by performing tasks such as peeling, slicing, pulping, and juicing. Proper operation of these machines enhances productivity, reduces processing time, and improves the consistency and quality of the end products. Efficient operation requires a comprehensive understanding of each equipment's mechanism and design, allowing operators to optimize the use of these machines while minimizing operational risks. For instance, peelers are designed to remove the skin of various fruits and vegetables without damaging the product, slicers are employed to cut products uniformly for further processing, pulpers are utilized to separate the pulp from seeds and skins, and juicers extract liquid from fruits and vegetables while retaining the flavor and nutritional content.

However, ensuring smooth operation also depends on regular upkeeping practices. This includes routine inspections, lubrication, and cleaning to prevent wear and tear, mechanical failures, or contamination. Maintenance tasks also involve checking for malfunctions or parts that need replacement to avoid costly downtime. In addition, proper calibration and adjustment are crucial to ensuring the machines operate at their optimum efficiency and meet safety standards. Failure to maintain these machines can lead to inefficiencies, product defects, and even safety hazards. Therefore, understanding both the operational and maintenance procedures for peelers, slicers, pulpers, and juicers is critical for sustaining production standards, minimizing operational disruptions, and prolonging the life of the equipment.

PEELER

Peeling machines are very important in the food processing sector, providing efficient and accurate skin removal from various fruits and vegetables. These machines simplify the peeling procedure, ensuring that products meet strict standards for subsequent processing or packaging. This detailed guide focuses on the use of blade peeling machines, examining their features and uses in the food industry.

Understanding Peeling Machines and Their Functions

Peeling machines are designed to automate the removal of skins or peels from fruits and vegetables using physical methods. This equipment is crucial in enhancing the efficiency and consistency of food processing operations. By automating peeling, these machines reduce labor costs, minimize waste, and improve the quality of the final product.

Varieties of Vegetable Peeling Machines

Various types of vegetable peeling machines are available, each designed for specific peeling tasks. Some machines utilize brushes, while others employ abrasive surfaces, particularly for peeling root vegetables. The peeling process differs based on the vegetable type and the machine's design, but the ultimate aim remains consistent: to produce clean, peeled vegetables that are ready for the next step in food preparation.

Brush Roller and Emery Roller Peeling Machine

This machine is designed for cleaning and peeling a variety of rhizome vegetables, such as potatoes, beetroots, cassava, radishes, carrots, and others. It utilizes food-grade brushes for transportation and cleaning purposes. The rotating brush, combined with a high-pressure spray, efficiently removes mud and stains from the surface of the vegetables.

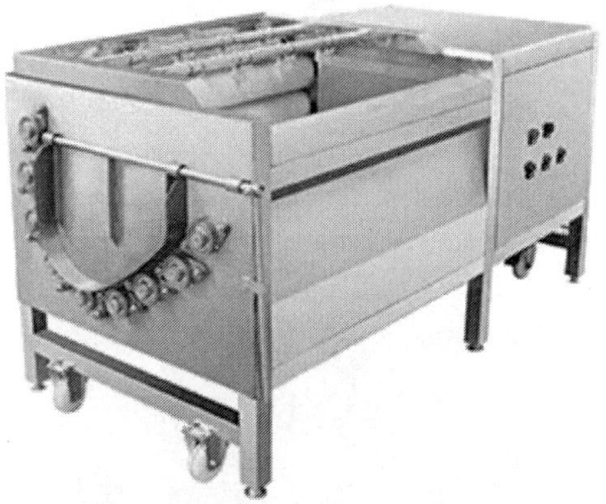

Figure.: 8.1 Potato beetroot peeling machine

The quantity and material of rollers are customizable. It is ideal for industrial, large and medium scaled food processing facilities.

This type of food peeling machine is always integrated with vegetable washing machine for thorough washing performance.

Small Batch Peeling Machine

This type of peeling machine is ideal for smaller capacities and is designed to peel root vegetables such as potatoes, sweet potatoes, and carrots. It utilizes an abrasive carborundum drum for peeling. The root vegetables are fed from the top and are processed inside a round drum with a carborundum-coated interior.

Figure.: 8.2 Small batch root vegetable peeling machine

It is great for enhancing potato processing and improving product yield.

Onion Peeling Machine

Onion peeling machines are designed for efficiently peeling various types of onions, including yellow onions, sweet onions, white onions, shallots, and red onions.

Figure.: 8.3 Industrial onion peeling machine

The peeling machine is entirely made of high-quality SUS304 stainless steel, ensuring durability and hygiene. It's user-friendly and easy to maintain. In addition to onions, it can also peel garlic.

Garlic Peeling Machine

Garlic peeling machines are specially designed to remove dry garlic skins efficiently. They provide fast peeling speeds and high peeling rates. Similar to onion peelers, these machines are made from durable SUS304 stainless steel. They allow for adjustable loading, peeling, and discharging times to suit specific operational needs

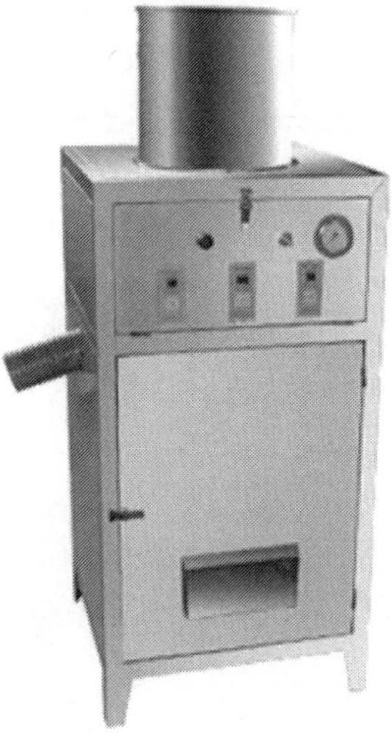

Figure.: 8.4 Industrial Garlic Peeling Machine

The garlic peeling machine is typically paired with a garlic clove separator, which efficiently divides garlic bulbs into individual cloves without causing damage. With a separation rate of over 95%, the machine ensures effective clove separation. It uses elastic rubber rollers and varying speeds to gently knead and separate the cloves. The distance between the rollers can be adjusted to accommodate different garlic sizes. Constructed from SUS304 stainless steel, the machine is both durable and easy to clean. For commercial or industrial garlic processing, these machines work together to simplify and enhance the production process.

Working of Peeling Machines

Blade peeling machines use sharp knives or blades to remove the skins from the produce. The method involves passing fruits or vegetables through the machine where the blades precisely slice off the skins, leaving the underlying product intact. This process is commonly used for root vegetables such as potatoes, carrots, and beets, as well as some fruits. Additionally, some peeling machines employ brush rollers to gently scrub away skins, suitable for products requiring a softer touch.

Merits of peeling machines

- **Efficiency:** Automating the peeling process significantly speeds up production and reduces manual labor.

- **Consistency:** Peeling machines provide uniform results, ensuring that each product is peeled to the same standard.
- **Waste Reduction:** Precise peeling minimizes product loss and waste, enhancing yield and profitability.
- **Safety and Hygiene:** Automated peeling reduces the need for manual handling, minimizing contamination risks and adhering to food safety standards.

Use in the Food Industry

Peeling machines are widely used across various sectors of the food industry:

- **Vegetable Processing:** Commonly used for peeling potatoes, carrots, and other root vegetables for frozen or fresh markets.
- **Fruit Processing:** Applied to certain fruits with tougher skins, enhancing preparation for further processing or packaging.
- **Snack Production:** Peeling is a crucial step in the production of chips, crisps, and other snack products, ensuring a clean and appealing final product.

SLICER

A multi-crop slicing machine has been designed, fabricated, and assessed for its performance. The key components of the machine consist of a hopper, mainframe, conveying disc, slicing unit, slicing shaft, idler shaft, pulley, bearing, electric motor base, and outlet. These components work together to ensure the efficient slicing of various crops, streamlining the food processing process. The design has been carefully evaluated to meet the required standards and performance expectations for commercial or industrial use.

Major Parts of Slicer equipment

In Agro processing, slicer equipment is used to cut or slice food items into specific shapes, sizes, or thicknesses for further processing, packaging, or cooking. These slicers can be manual or automated and are commonly used in the processing of vegetables, fruits, meat, cheese, and other food products. Below are some key components commonly found in slicer equipment:

Blades

- **Fixed Blade:** A stationary blade that remains in place while the food item is fed through the slicer.
- **Rotating Blade:** Often used in more advanced slicers, a rotating blade moves in a circular motion to slice food more efficiently.
- **Adjustable Blade:** Some slicers have blades that can be adjusted to change the thickness of the slices.
- **Material:** Blades are typically made from stainless steel or high-carbon steel for durability and resistance to corrosion.

Feeding Mechanism

- **Manual Feed**: In manual slicers, the operator feeds the product into the slicer, often by pushing it against the blade using a food pusher or guard.

- **Automatic Feed:** Automated slicers might use conveyor belts or rollers to feed food into the slicing mechanism.

Motor (in Electric Slicers)

A motor powers the slicer's blade and feeding mechanism. This allows for continuous operation without manual effort. The motor's power is usually measured in horsepower or watts, depending on the size and efficiency required for the specific application.

Cutting Plate or Table

A flat surface where the food item rests while being sliced. It can be designed with specific guides or tracks to ensure that the food is properly aligned before being sliced.

Adjustable Thickness Control

This feature allows the operator to set the desired thickness of the slices. It can be a manual knob or a digital control system, especially in more advanced slicers.

Food Pushers or Holders

Food pushers are used to safely and efficiently push the food toward the blade while protecting the user's hands from injury. These are often adjustable and can be designed for different shapes of food (e.g., for cylindrical vegetables like cucumbers or for large blocks of cheese).

Safety Features

- **Guards:** Shields to protect the user from coming into contact with the blade.
- **Emergency Stop Button:** In automated or electric slicers, a safety button allows the operator to stop the machine in case of an emergency.
- **Anti-Slip Feet**: Rubber feet or other mechanisms that prevent the slicer from sliding during use.

Conveyor Belt (in high-volume slicers)

In industrial-scale slicers, a conveyor belt moves food items through the slicer. The belt speed may be adjustable to ensure proper slicing speed for different types of food.

Discharge Tray or Collection Bin

After slicing, the food is usually discharged into a collection tray or bin. These bins can vary in size depending on the volume of product being processed.

Frame and Housing

The frame holds all the components of the slicer together. It's usually made of stainless steel for durability, ease of cleaning, and resistance to food acids or chemicals.

Cleaning Mechanisms

Some slicers include automatic or manual cleaning functions to maintain hygiene standards. This could include removable blades for easy cleaning or spray nozzles that clean the machine between uses.

Control Panel (for Automated/Advanced Slicers)

The control panel allows the operator to manage the slicer's functions, such as blade speed, thickness of slices, motor speed, and automatic feeding controls. In some cases, digital or touchscreen panels are used.

Drive Mechanism (in Automated Models)

- **Gearbox:** In some slicers, a gearbox or other drive mechanisms are used to transmit the motor's power to the blades.
- **Belt or Chain Drive:** Some slicers use belts or chains to transfer power to rotating components like blades or conveyor belts.

Variants of Slicer Equipment in Agro processing

- **Vegetable and Fruit Slicers:** Used for slicing produce like potatoes, cucumbers, tomatoes, or apples.
- **Meat Slicers:** Specifically designed for slicing meats, both for commercial and home use.
- **Cheese Slicers:** Often have specialized blades and features to slice through harder materials like cheese.
- **Bread Slicers:** Designed to slice bread into uniform pieces.
- **Multifunctional Slicers:** These may be adjustable and able to handle a variety of products, such as fruits, vegetables, meats, and cheeses.

Each type of slicer will have a slightly different set of components depending on the application, size, and complexity of the machinery.

Functions of Industrial Slicers in Food Processing

Industrial slicers play a key role in food production by contributing to several key processes, such as:

- **Precision Slicing:** Industrial slicers are designed to provide uniform cuts, ensuring each slice is consistently the same thickness. This is especially important in food processing, where consistency is crucial for meeting regulatory requirements and customer expectations. Whether slicing meats, cheeses, or vegetables, precision is essential for controlling portions and minimizing waste.
- **High Volume Production:** In large-scale food production environments, it's critical to manage high volumes efficiently. Industrial slicers, equipped with

powerful motors and durable components, can process hundreds of slices per hour. This ensures that production lines meet demand, reducing bottlenecks and boosting overall productivity.

- **Versatility Across Products:** Modern industrial slicers, such as those from Bizerba, offer the versatility to handle a variety of products, from delicate deli meats to tougher items like cheeses and frozen meats. Some models even come with interchangeable attachments that allow operators to switch between slicing and other tasks, such as using the machine to cut strips from larger cuts of meat.
- **Hygienic Design:** Food safety is a top concern in food processing, and industrial slicers are designed with hygiene in mind. Constructed from stainless steel, these machines resist rust and corrosion, even in environments with constant moisture exposure. Their smooth surfaces and removable parts make cleaning quick and efficient, helping to reduce the risk of contamination.

Advantages of Using Industrial Slicers

Incorporating industrial slicers into food processing offers many advantages:

- **Increased Productivity:** With their high-speed motors and cutting-edge technology, industrial slicers can significantly increase production speed, enabling businesses to meet rising demand without increasing labor costs or sacrificing quality.
- **Reduced Manual Labor:** By automating the slicing process, industrial slicers reduce the need for manual labor. This not only saves time but also minimizes workplace injuries and allows employees to focus on other critical tasks.
- **Consistent Quality:** One of the primary benefits of industrial slicers is their ability to produce consistent, uniform slices. Each slice is identical in thickness and size, ensuring professional-looking products that adhere to industry standards. This consistency is especially crucial for businesses that package
- **Customization Options:** Many modern slicers offer adjustable settings that allow operators to customize slice thickness. This flexibility makes it easy to switch between different products and slicing requirements, whether you need thin slices for deli meats or thicker cuts for steaks and roasts.

Salient Features of Industrial Slicers

Industrial slicers are built with a range of features that make them well-suited for the demanding needs of food processing:

- **Powerful Motors:** With high-performance motors, industrial slicers can handle large volumes of meat, cheese, and other products without overheating. This ensures uninterrupted operation, even during peak production hours.

- **Durable Construction:** Made from high-quality materials like stainless steel, industrial slicers are built to withstand heavy use and frequent cleaning, making them ideal for demanding environments.
- **Advanced Safety Features:** Safety is a key priority in food processing, and industrial slicers come with safety features such as blade guards, non-slip feet, and emergency stop buttons to help prevent accidents during operation.
- **Easy to Clean:** Designed for easy disassembly, industrial slicers allow for thorough cleaning of each part. This not only minimizes contamination risks but also helps businesses comply with hygiene standards more easily.

Uses of Industrial Slicers in Various Sectors

Industrial slicers are indispensable across various sectors of the food industry, including:

- **Supermarkets and Butcheries:** In retail environments, industrial slicers are used to prepare pre-packaged meats and cheeses, ensuring consistent slicing for customers. They are also essential for slicing on-demand at deli counters, where precision and freshness are critical to customer satisfaction.
- **Large-Scale Food Production:** In food processing plants, industrial slicers are essential for handling high volumes of meat, cheese, and other products. These machines help streamline production, ensuring that products are sliced quickly and uniformly, which is crucial for efficiency in large operations.
- **Catering Services:** Catering companies rely on industrial slicers to prepare large quantities of food for events. These machines allow chefs to slice meats, cheeses, and vegetables with precision, ensuring beautiful and consistent presentations.
- **Foodservice Industry:** Restaurants and foodservice providers use industrial slicers to prepare ingredients for a variety of dishes, from sandwiches to salads. The ability to adjust slice thickness enables chefs to create perfectly portioned meals, minimizing waste and enhancing overall presentation.

PULPER

A fruit pulper machine is a specialized piece of equipment used in commercial and industrial settings to extract fruit pulp or juice. It works by grinding, crushing, and separating the pulp from the juice using a fine mesh or screen. The resulting pulp can be utilized in producing various food products like sauces, jams, and juices, while the juice can either undergo further processing or be packaged for sale. The versatility of these machines allows them to process a wide range of fruits, such as apples, guavas, mangoes, and citrus fruits, making them valuable in juice production.

Fruit and vegetable processing is carried out in different ways depending on the type of product being created, with pulping being a key operation in the production of many processed foods. The methods used for pulping vary according to the size, shape, and texture of the fruits and vegetables. Commercial production of processed products often involves the use of specialized pulping machines designed to handle high capacities while maintaining hygienic standards in the production of processed foods.

Figure.: 8.5 Pulper

Equipment for Pulping

Pulping is process that is performed by the extraction or pulper equipment which crush the food products and separate the pulp, seed and skin of fruits and vegetable. Pulper may be either mechanicaly or electrically operated to forces that feed in the machine.

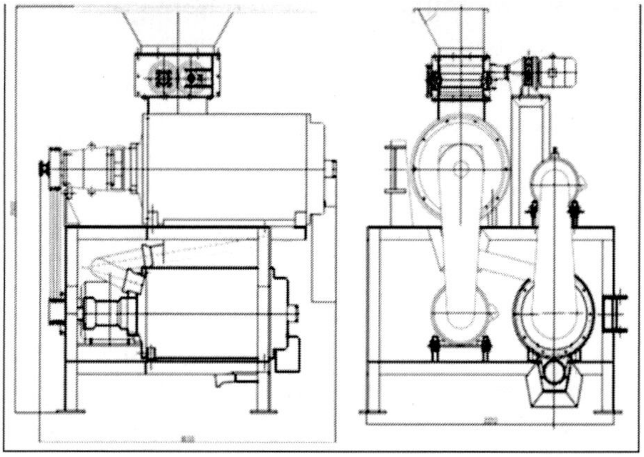

Figure.: 8.6 Pulper Machine

Fruit crusher

Powered machines designed to crush pineapples or other hard fruits feature a rotating screw inside a casing. This casing is equipped with a screen at the base, allowing the juice or pulp to drain out through an outlet while the skin is ejected from the end of the casing down a chute. To facilitate maintenance, the casing is typically fitted with wing nuts, allowing for easy removal.

During operation, pineapples are cut into large pieces and fed into the hopper. Regular maintenance includes weekly checks on the belt tension and electrical connections, as well as monthly greasing of bearings. It is advisable to keep a spare drive belt and fuse on hand to ensure smooth operation.

Fruit presses

Manual fruit presses feature a stainless steel cage in which a press plate is raised and lowered using a screw. To prolong the lifespan of the press, the screw should be made from a harder grade of steel than the bearing, as the bearing can be replaced more affordably compared to the screw. For larger presses, layer plates made of stainless steel, nylon, or painted mild steel may be added to improve pressing efficiency.

During operation, a muslin or cotton bag is placed inside the cage, and pulp is poured into the bag. The bag is then closed, and the press plate is lowered. After several minutes, additional turns of the screw increase the pressure, allowing the juice to be collected through a pipe. Once the pressing is complete, the screw is raised, and the bag is removed.

Fruit and Vegetable Pulper

The leading manufacturer of fruit & vegetable pulp based products. These fruit and vegetable pulper are used for the extraction of pulp from vegetables and fruits like mango, litchi, guava, pear, tomato, passion fruit, grapead so on. The working capacity of these machines depend upon the size, type and quality of the product to be pulped. Our range of fruit & vegetable pulper machines are available from 80 kg/hr to 3 t/hr capacity also are also found in the following capacities

Twin Pulper

A wide range of fruit and vegetable pulper which can be utilized to extract pulps from fruits and vegetables. These pulpers are highly effective and also high on performance. These fruit an vegetable pulpers are used various purposes like skin removal, destoning, pulping and finishing of pulps from fruits and vegetables like mangoes, litchi, tomatoes, carrot, pineapple and many more. The fruit and vegetable pulper is furnished with parts like scraper rotors, spiral scraper and brushes which rotates at a very high speed thus separating the stone, skin and the pulp.

Fruit mill

The fruit mill crusher is a robust machine designed with a sturdy fixture mounted on an MS steel band. It is primarily used for crushing hard, seedless fruits for pulping or juice extraction. The machine operates by feeding the fruit into a hopper, where it is crushed by an SS rotor against stainless steel blades, powered by a high-performance motor. All parts of the fruit mill crusher are made from food-grade stainless steel, ensuring durability and hygiene in the processing of fruits.

Motorized Hydraulic Fruit Press

The Hydraulic Juice Press (Motorised) is a versatile and durable machine designed for extracting juice from crushed fruits such as pineapple, grapes, oranges, apples, and more. Manufactured using high-quality materials, it offers efficient durability and high tensile strength. The motorized version is equipped with a stainless steel tray with an appropriate depth, ensuring that juice does not spill from the filter cloth or wooden racks. This design helps retain the valuable nutrients left in the pulp, making it an effective solution for juice extraction while preserving the quality of the product.

Fruit Juicer

The Hand Operated Fruit Juicer is designed for efficient juice extraction from peeled fruits. It features a robust aluminum body and a stainless steel strainer, ensuring durability and longevity. This juicer is ideal for continuous operation, requiring no electricity or power, as it operates on a simple pressing mechanism. It is easy to clean, maintain, and use, making it a convenient choice for small-scale juice extraction. Available in various designs and models, it caters to different preferences and needs in fruit juicing.

Stainless Steel Pulper

These Stainless Steel 304 fruit and vegetable pulpers are designed for efficiently extracting pulp from a variety of fruits and vegetables, including mango, litchi, guava, pear, tomato, passion fruit, and grape. The working capacity of these machines varies depending on the size, type, and quality of the product being pulped. Our range of fruit and vegetable pulper machines is available in capacities ranging from 500 kg/hr to 3 tons/hr, catering to different production needs.

Variants of Fruit Pulper Machines

Fruit pulpers come in various models, each tailored for specific applications and capacities. The following are the most common types of fruit pulper machines used in the industry:

Manual Fruit Pulper Machine

Manual fruit pulper machines, as the name suggests, require human labor for operation. These machines are typically compact and cost-effective, making them suitable for home use or small-scale production. While they efficiently pulp small batches of fruit, they are less efficient for large-scale operations.

Semi-Automatic Fruit Pulper Machine

Semi-automatic fruit pulper machines are a step up from manual models, designed to handle moderate fruit volumes. These machines automate certain tasks, such as pulp extraction, while still requiring the operator to feed fruits into the machine. This type of machine is ideal for medium-sized businesses or food processing units.

Fully Automatic Fruit Pulper Machine

Fully automatic fruit pulper machines are ideal for large-scale operations. These machines can process large amounts of fruit with minimal human assistance. They are equipped with advanced features, such as automated fruit feeding, pulping, and waste disposal, making them perfect for professional juice producers. Large factories prefer fully automatic machines due to their high yields and consistency.

Continuous Fruit Pulper Machine

Continuous fruit pulper machines are designed for uninterrupted operation, processing a continuous flow of fruits for pulping. Unlike batch models, which work in discrete cycles, continuous pulpers can operate non-stop, ensuring high productivity. These machines are best suited for large-scale juice production and food processing plants that require continuous operation for extended periods.

Structure and Component of Fruit Pulp Extraction Machine

- A fruit pulp extraction machine is mainly composed of transmission system, bearing block, sleeve, drum, guard plate, back cover, front cover, spline shaft, screener, scraper or beating bar, rack.

  The fruit pulp extraction machine has single-drum and double-drum 2 types.

  Double-drum fruit pulper machine is equipped with 2 different rotors in each channel.

  - The first drum is for destoning,
  - The second is for peeling and pulping.

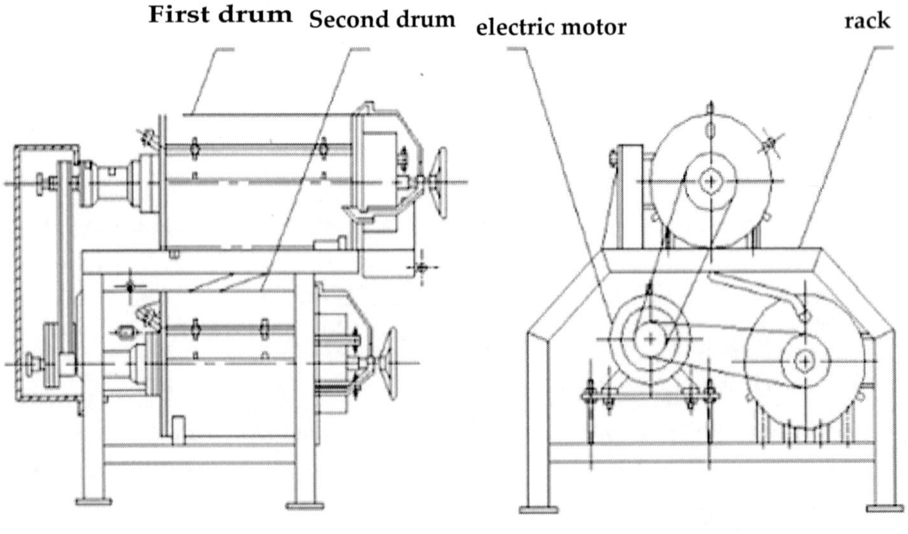

Figure.: 8.7 In single-drum fruit pulper machine, you need to replace the rotor of the drum to realize destoning and pulping separately.

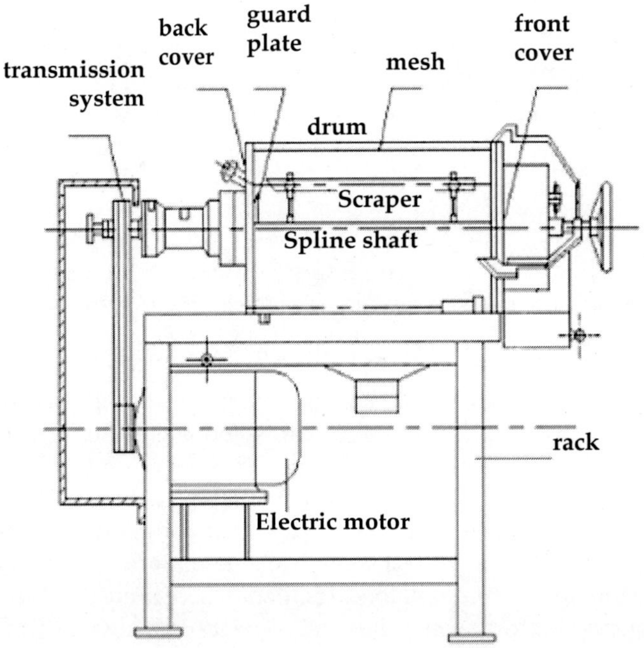

Figure.: 8.8 For berries and nuts, they only need the pulping drum. If you use a double-drum fruit pulper machine, just install the rotor for pulping in both drums.

Essential Features to consider in a Fruit Pulper Machine

When selecting a fruit pulper machine, it's important to consider several key features to ensure that the machine meets your specific needs. Below are the essential features to look for:

Material and Durability

The material used to construct the machine should be of high quality to ensure longevity and resistance to wear and tear. Stainless steel is the most commonly used material for fruit pulper machines due to its durability, corrosion resistance, and ease of cleaning.

Easy Maintenance

A good fruit pulper machine should be easy to maintain and clean. Machines with removable parts, such as screens and pulping chambers, make maintenance simpler and more efficient. Regular maintenance ensures optimal performance and extends the machine's lifespan.

Adjustable Pulp and Juice Separation

Some models allow you to adjust the pulp and juice separation based on the fruit type and your desired end product. This flexibility ensures that you can achieve the right texture and consistency for different fruit products.

High Yield and Efficiency

The yield of juice or pulp is a crucial factor to consider when choosing a fruit pulper machine. Machines with high extraction rates will provide better value for money, as they maximize the amount of juice or pulp you can extract from each fruit.

Energy Efficiency

Energy efficiency is another important consideration, especially for businesses that rely on continuous operations. Energy-efficient fruit pulper machines can help reduce operational costs by lowering electricity consumption.

Working Principle of Vegetable & Fruit Pulper machine

Pulper machines ranges with capacities ranging from 100 kg/hr to 3 tons/hr, designed for extracting pulp from various fruits and vegetables, including mangoes, guavas, peaches, tomatoes, bananas, and more. The pulper unit is equipped with two brushes that provide a combined beating and brushing action. The gap between the sieve and the beaters/brushes can be adjusted to accommodate different fruit and vegetable sizes and qualities. The sieve is available in various perforation sizes and is easily removable for cleaning. A food regulation screw ensures proper feeding of products, enhancing performance. All metal contact parts are made of stainless steel, while the pulper's frame is constructed using heavy-duty mild steel fabricated "L" sections. The machine is designed for easy dismantling and reassembly, facilitating inspection, cleaning, and routine maintenance.

Uses of Fruit Pulper Machines

The fruit pulper machine is not limited to juice production; its applications extend to a variety of industries. Below mentioned are some of the important uses:

Juice Production

The primary use of a fruit pulper machine is for juice extraction. It is widely used in the beverage industry to produce high-quality fruit juices and concentrates. The machine extracts juice from fruits like mangoes, oranges, apples, and more, with minimal waste.

Fruit Puree and Sauce Production

Fruit pulper machines are also used to produce fruit purees and sauces, which are used in the production of jams, preserves, and canned fruits. These machines ensure that the fruit pulp is processed to the desired consistency for smooth, flavorful products.

Baby Food Manufacturing

Fruit pulpers are commonly used in the production of baby food, especially fruit-based purees. The fine pulp obtained from fruits like apples, pears, and bananas is used to make nutritious and easily digestible baby food.

Cosmetics and Pharmaceuticals

In addition to food production, fruit pulp is used in the cosmetics industry to produce creams, lotions, and soaps that contain natural fruit extracts. The nutrients in fruit pulp are beneficial for skincare, making it a valuable ingredient in cosmetic products.

JUICER

Key Fetures of a Fruit Juice Processing Line

- **Complete System:** The fruit juice processing line covers the entire process from raw materials to packaged products. This includes fruit cleaning, elevating, sorting, crushing, juicing, preheating, enzymolysis, filtration, concentration, blending, degassing, homogenization, sterilization, filling, and packing. It is suitable for producing clear juice, cloudy juice, concentrate juice, and jam.
- **Device Independence:** Many of the equipment used in this system can operate independently or as part of the broader juice processing plant. The power supply can be separated, which helps to save energy.
- **High Technology:** The equipment used in fruit juice manufacturing incorporates advanced technology and superior materials. This ensures scientific design, compact structure, and attractive exterior.
- **Orderly Layout:** The layout of the system is carefully organized for ease of operation and presentation. The pipeline is arranged in an orderly manner, with each unit designed as a self-contained program to enhance efficiency.
- **Multiple Functions:** This system facilitates industrial production of fruit juice, demonstrating the entire juice-making process. It is also useful for research purposes, including juice processing formulas, the application of additives, and sample testing.

Figure.: 8.9 Juice manufacturing equipment

Emerging Trends in Juice Manufacturing Equipment

High speed, high quality and high precision

To adapt to large-scale production, and achieve better economic efficiency, juice production equipments are becoming more and more automated. The production capacity is hugely improved.

Multifunctional

Multiple use in one set of equipment. The fruit pre-treatment equipment is applicable to many types of fruits. Meanwhile, the sterilization and filling machine works well on tea, coffee and milk.

Mechatronics

This is the most important trend in juice manufacturing equipment. Programmable controller has been adopted in the controller system. Large-scale equipment controlled by computer can realize self-diagnosis and intelligent adjustment.

9

Operation and Maintenance of Canning Machineries

OVERVIEW OF CANNING MACHINERIES

Canning is a food preservation method where selected raw materials are prepared, packed into containers such as tin, glass, or plastic jars, and sealed airtight. The contents are then heated to a sufficient temperature to destroy spoilage and pathogenic agents within the container, followed by rapid cooling to prevent overcooking. Canning extends the shelf life of foods, ranging typically from one to five years, with some products like freeze-dried lentils lasting up to 30 years.

Can Manufacturing Machinery and Equipment

- **Can Body Reformer:** Can bodies are often supplied collapsed to save space and ease transportation. The can body reformer shapes them into cylindrical forms, preparing them for further processing.
- **Flanger:** The cylindrical can bodies are flanged by the flanger, which has two flanging dyes. These dyes form grooves at the edges, preparing the cans for sealing.
- **Seaming Machine:** The seaming machine is used to close the open end of the can. It features a base plate to hold the can and an upper plate that presses the lid onto the can. The machine uses two seaming rollers (first and second) to seal the can tightly.
- **Can Leakage Tester:** After sealing, the cans are tested for leakage by immersion in water. If any leakage is detected due to improper sealing, it indicates that the can is faulty.
- **Flange Rectifier:** Cans that have been bent, deformed, or crushed during the flanging process are rectified using the flange rectifier machine, ensuring the cans are in proper shape for sealing.
- **Can Coding Machine (Embossing Machine):** This machine embosses codes on the cans, which include the product name, manufacturer details, and production date. It ensures proper identification and traceability of the product.

- **Transfer Car:** The transfer car is used to move the cooker tray, which contains the cans, from one stage to the next in the processing line. It helps streamline the movement of trays between various machines, such as the cooker or retort.
- **Packing Table with Conveyor:** This system consists of a stainless steel packing table and a conveyor belt. It helps rationalize the canning operation, improving production efficiency. The corrosion-resistant packing table is used for organizing and preparing the cans for packing.

VARIANTS OF COMMERCIAL CANNING MACHINES

The canning equipment landscape is vast and diverse, with each machine designed to perform a specific task to ensure the canning process—from filling to sealing—is carried out accurately and efficiently.

Can Filling Machine

In the canning industry, precision is crucial, and the can filling machine plays a central role in achieving this. It is not simply a machine; it is a cornerstone of quality and operational efficiency, ensuring that every can is filled and sealed accurately, maintaining the integrity of its contents.

Defining Can Filling Machine

A can filling machine is an essential tool used to fill various types of containers with products. Depending on the application and container type, it may be referred to as an automatic tin can filling machine, oil tin filling machine, or jar filling machine. This equipment is key to ensuring that each container—whether a can, jar, or bottle—is filled consistently and accurately.

Usage of Can Filling Machines

In commercial canning, precision is vital. Can filling machines ensure that each container is filled to the exact level, playing a significant role in maintaining product quality and uniformity. Using the right can filling machine can significantly improve both production efficiency and the consistency of the final product.

Working of Filling Machine

The process starts with containers being fed into the machine via a conveyor. Depending on the machine's design, it may fill one or more containers at once. The product is stored in a hopper or cylinder and is dispensed into containers using either gravity or volumetric filling. The chosen filling method depends on the product's consistency and the required filling precision.

Can Seamer Machine

In the expansive field of commercial canning machinery, the can seamer machine plays a pivotal role. It ensures that cans are sealed tightly, which is essential for preserving freshness, preventing contamination, and extending shelf life. Whether for beverages, food products, or other items, a reliable sealing process is a fundamental aspect of maintaining product quality.

Figure.: 9.1 Can Seamer Machine

Defining Can Seamer Machine

A can seamer machine, also known as a can sealer or closer, is a specialized piece of equipment designed to create an airtight seal between the lid and the body of various containers. These containers can include paper cans, aluminum cans, tin cans, and even PET cans or jars. The primary function of the machine is to ensure that the contents remain uncontaminated and fresh for a prolonged period.

Usage of Can Seamer Machines

The importance of a secure seal cannot be overemphasized. A poor seal can result in products like beverages becoming flat or food products getting contaminated. A dependable seal guarantees product safety, quality, and consumer trust. In industries like food and beverages, where quality assurance is critical, can seamer machines are essential for upholding the promises made to customers.

Working of Can Seamer Machine Work

The operation of a can seamer machine can be intriguing. There are two main types: rotary and non-rotary. In rotary seamers, the can itself rotates while being sealed, and this design is typically used in automatic machines for high-volume production. Conversely, non-rotary seamers keep the can stationary while the seamer rotates, making them ideal for liquid-filled products as they reduce the risk of spills or disturbances. Regardless of the design, the ultimate goal is the same: a perfectly sealed can, ready for distribution.

Can Capping Machine

The journey of canning doesn't end once the product is inside the container. The next critical step is ensuring that the container is capped securely. Enter the can capping machine, a marvel of modern machinery designed to apply various types of caps to containers with precision and efficiency.

Define Can Capping Machine

A Can Capping Machine is a specialized piece of equipment used in the commercial canning industry. Its main function is to securely apply caps to containers, which can include plastic snap caps, metal threaded caps, fitments, and even some plug or cork types. By ensuring that each container is properly sealed, the machine helps to prevent spillage, contamination, and preserves the integrity of the contents.

Usage of Can Capping Machines

A cap isn't just a lid; it's the first line of defense against external contaminants. It also plays a pivotal role in ensuring the product's freshness and extending its shelf life. A reliable capping machine ensures that each container is sealed correctly, enhancing product safety and consumer trust. In industries where product integrity is paramount, having a dependable Can Capping Machine is non-negotiable.

Working of Can Capping Machine Work

The operation of a can capping machine combines precision with efficiency. Depending on its configuration, the machine can be either automatic or semi-automatic. Automatic machines feature a cap delivery system, providing a continuous supply of caps for seamless operation. On the other hand, semi-automatic machines require the operator to manually place the cap before the capping process begins. After the cap is positioned, the machine secures it tightly, ensuring a dependable seal to prevent leakage and contamination.

Can Labeling Machine

In today's competitive market, branding and product information are crucial. The can labeling machine ensures that products are not only identifiable but also compliant with regulatory requirements.

Figure.: 9.2 Can Labeling Machine

Defining Can Labeling Machine

A Can Labeling Machine is a device designed to print and apply labels to various containers. These labels, often the first thing a consumer notices, provide essential information about the product and enhance brand visibility. Whether it's a tin can, jar, bottle, or any other container, this machine ensures that each product carries the brand's message.

Usage of Can Labeling Machines

Labels serve multiple purposes. They provide consumers with vital information, from ingredients and nutritional facts to usage instructions and safety precautions. In many regions, regulatory bodies mandate specific labeling requirements, making Can Labeling Machines essential for compliance. Moreover, in a sea of products on store shelves, a well-labeled product can stand out, drawing consumers' attention.

Working of Can Labeling Machine

The process is a blend of precision and speed. Containers are fed into the machine, where they pass through a labeling station. Here, labels are either printed directly onto the container or applied from a pre-printed roll. The labeled containers then continue down the production line, ready for the next stage of the canning process.

Can Coding Machine

In today's fast-moving commercial canning industry, the can coding machine has become a vital tool. Experts agree that the growing demand for transparency from consumers, alongside the industry's need for traceability, has made these machines an essential asset.

Defining Can Coding Machine

A can coding machine is more than just another piece of equipment; it is key to fostering a transparent relationship with consumers. It effectively marks cans with crucial information such as manufacturing dates, expiration dates, barcodes, and QR codes. Recent industry data indicates that about 85% of consumers prefer products with clearly visible manufacturing and expiration dates. Additionally, QR code usage in supply chains has surged by 60% in the last five years.

Usage of Can Coding Machines

The push for transparency is not merely a consumer trend, but a necessity within the industry. With global supply chains becoming increasingly complex, traceability has become essential. Can coding machines assist brands in tracking their products in real-time, enabling efficient product recalls, accurate inventory management, and compliance with regulations. The data they provide, though small in size, is of great importance.

Working of Can Coding Machine

How do these machines operate with such high precision? Can coding machines integrate advanced technology with thoughtful design. They are usually connected to a centralized database or online system that generates unique codes for each product batch. With remarkable accuracy, the machines imprint this critical information onto cans, ensuring that every product leaving the production line is correctly labeled, reducing errors, and building consumer trust.

Can Rinsers

Before products reach the filling stage, ensuring the cleanliness and sterility of the containers is critical. The can rinser plays a vital role in the canning process, making sure that every container is free of contaminants.

Defining Can Rinser

A can rinser is a machine used to clean or sterilize containers before the filling process begins. Due to various industrial factors, containers can accumulate dust or other contaminants. Can rinsers ensure that containers are spotless and ready for filling with product.

Usage of Can Rinsers

In the world of commercial canning, cleanliness is vital. It's not only about meeting international packaging standards but ensuring that the products inside the containers are safe, of high quality, and trustworthy for consumers. A can rinser ensures these standards are met, ensuring that businesses deliver products that consumers can rely on.

Working of Can Rinser Work

The operation of a can rinser depends on the cleaning method it employs. Some rinsers use air, blowing hot, pressurized air into containers to remove germs and dust. Other rinsers may use ionized air, where negative ions bond with the positive ions in contaminants, making them heavy and easy to remove. Water-based rinsers spray containers with treated water at high pressure. After the rinsing process, containers typically go through a drying phase to ensure they are completely clean and ready for filling.

Steps for Canning Preparation

- **Selection of fruits and vegetables:**Fruits and vegetables selected for canning should be fresh. Fruits usedfor canning should be ripe, firm and evenly matured, and vegetables should be tender. Fruits and vegetables should be stored at cool place and free from dirt, mechanical injury and insect damage.
- **Sorting and grading:**Sorting for same kind of items is done by passing through series of moving screens. After sorting fruits and vegetables are graded for uniform quality of size and color. Different types of grading machines are used such as screen grader, roller grader, rope and cable grader. Hand picking methods is usually used for soft fruits and berries.
- **Washing:** Fruits and vegetables are washed through high pressure sprays, steam, by soaking or agitating in water. Vegetables soaked in a dilute solution of potassium permanganate and root crops soaked in chlorine water (25-50 ppm).
- **Peeling, Coring and Cutting:** Hand peeling, heat peeling, steam peeling, mechanical peeling and lye peeling methods are used. Hand peeling is done in case of irregular shape fruits and vegetables. In heat peeling fruits and vegetables are exposed to a high temperature of 40°C for 10-60 seconds. In steam peeling, steam is used to loosen the skin which is then removed by mechanical means. Fruit are immersed in 1- 2% lye solution for 30 seconds to 2 minutes in lye peeling. Mechanical peeling is done in case of fruits like peaches, apricots, sweet orange and vegetables like carrot, sweet potatoes. Coring is the process of removing centre of various fruits and vegetables such as apple, pears, pineapple, lettuce and cabbage, done by a hydraulic powered device with turbine wheels. A special blade mounted on the turbine wheel spins and removes the core. Cutting is done according to the requirement of process.
- **Blanching:** Blanching is done by dipping fruits and vegetables in hot water at temperature 82-90° C for 2-5 minutes and then immediately cooled by immersion in cold water. Main aim of blanching is to inactivate the enzyme,to soften the texture, to loosen skin, to reduce the number of micro-organism, to increase the green color of vegetables, to remove acid and astringent taste.

Hard water cause toughening of tissue and destroys the natural texture, so it should be avoided.

- **Cooling:** To keep fruits and vegetable into good condition, cooling is done after blanching.
- **Filling:** Before filling cans are subjected to steam jet or hot water to remove dust and foreign material. Automatic can filing machine is used by canning industry. Generally for fruits filling is done by hand to prevent the bruising. After filling syrup or brine is added.
    - **Syruping:** Syrup is a solution of sugar in water, done only for fruits. Syrup is added to improve the flavor and serve as a heat transfer medium for facilitating processing. Strained, hot syrup of concentration 20 to 55° brix is used and filled at about 79 to 82°C, leaving head space of 0.3 to 0.5cm.
    - **Brining:** Brine is a solution of salt of concentration 1-3%, used for vegetables. The brine should be filtered through a thick cloth before filling.

After Syruping or brining the cans are loosely covered with lids and exhausted. Lidding has certain disadvantages such as spilling of the contents and toppling of the lids. Hence lidding has now been replaced by clinching in which lids is partially seamed.

- **Exhausting:** Exhausting is the process of removal of air from the cans. It is very essential as it avoids the corrosion of tinplate and pinholing during the storage. Exhausting is done to minimize discoloration, to reduce chemical reaction between the container and the contents. It alsohelps in better retention of vitamin and prevents development of excessive pressure during sterilization. For exhausting heating method is generally used but can also be done bymechanical means. The can are passed through a tank of hot water at 82 to 87°C for 5-10 minutes. At the end of exhausting temperature at the centre of can should be about 79 °C.
- **Sealing:** After exhausting can are sealed immediately with the help of can sealer and temperature should not fall below 74°C during sealing.
- **Processing:** It is heating or cooling of canned foods to inactivate the bacteria. Processing time and temperature should be adequate to eliminate all bacteria and to reduce quality damage. Fruits and vegetables processed at temperature of 100°C as presence of acid retards the bacteria and their spores. Non-acid vegetables are processed at high temperature 115-121°C. Temperature and processing time vary with size of can and nature of food. Temperature at the centre of can, should be maintained for long period of time to ensure the destruction of most heat resistant bacteria.

Uses and Industrial Application of Commercial Canning Machines

Commercial canning machines have become indispensable in a wide array of industries, playing a crucial role in preserving product quality, extending shelf life, and maintaining high standards. Here are concise yet comprehensive descriptions of eight sectors where these machines are essential:

Figure.: 9.3 Canning Machine

- **Food and Beverage Industry:** In this sector, canning equipment is essential for preserving a variety of products, including fruits, vegetables, meats, and seafood. These machines help maintain the freshness, nutritional value, and taste of foods, while also ensuring that beverages retain their flavor, carbonation, and overall quality.
- **Pharmaceutical Industry:** In pharmaceuticals, canning machines are vital for sterilization and packaging. They prevent contamination, preserving the therapeutic properties of drugs. Accurate packaging and sealing are crucial in protecting medicines from external factors, ensuring public health and safety.
- **Cosmetics and Personal Care Industry:** In the cosmetics sector, these machines provide airtight sealing for products like creams and lotions. This process ensures product integrity, keeping them in optimal condition, while also extending their shelf life for consumers.
- **Chemical Industry:** Canning machines in the chemical industry are critical for preventing leaks, spills, or cross-contamination. Proper sealing ensures that chemicals are safely packaged, complying with industry safety standards and minimizing the risks associated with hazardous materials.
- **Agricultural Industry:** In agriculture, canning machines are used to preserve products like grains and seeds. These machines help maintain the freshness and nutritional value of the produce, reducing food waste and contributing to food security.
- **Oil and Lubricants Industry:** For oils and lubricants, canning equipment provides secure packaging to prevent leaks and ensure product consistency. This is vital to avoid environmental hazards and minimize resource waste.
- **Beverage Industry:** Canning machines are indispensable in the beverage industry, from carbonated drinks to juices. They ensure that beverages are canned under stringent hygiene conditions, maintaining their taste,

carbonation, and nutritional quality while extending shelf life and facilitating distribution.

- **Paints and Solvents Industry:** In the non-edible products sector, such as paints and solvents, precise packaging is critical. These machines ensure airtight sealing to prevent leaks, evaporation, and contamination, ensuring safe transportation and storage.

Guidelines for Canning Operation

Prepare equipment, Preheat the canner

- Assemble and wash equipment and containers before gathering fruit or vegetables.
- Fill the boiling water bath or pressure canner with the appropriate amount of hot water and begin heating it on the range.
- Boiling water bath – 1 to 2 inches of water above the tops of the jars
- Pressure canner – 2 to 3 inches of water in the bottom of the canner

This can be difficult to determine before jars are placed in the canner. Have an extra pan of water heating in case you have too little water in the canner. If you heat too much, be prepared to remove some.

- Examine jars and discard any that have nicks, cracks, or rough edges. These defects will prevent an airtight seal, allowing food to spoil.
- Wash canning jars in soapy water, rinse well, and keep hot. This can be done by using a dishwasher or by placing the jars in the water that is heating in the canner. The jars need to be kept hot to prevent breakage when they are filled with a hot product and placed in the canner for processing.

Ensuring jars and lids are safe for canning

You must sterilize jars that will be filled with food and processed for less than 10 minutes in a boiling water bath canner. This can be done by boiling them for 10 minutes (for 1,000 feet altitude). Add one additional minute for each additional 1,000 feet of altitude. Jars that will be processed in a boiling water bath for 10 minutes or more or in a pressure canner will be sterilized during processing. Always use new two-piece lids. Follow the manufacturer's instructions for treating them.

Preparation of food to be preserved

Wash the product carefully, a little at a time. Lift food out of the water, drain the water, and continue rinsing until the water is clear and free of dirt. Dirt contains some of the hardest-to-kill bacteria. Don't let the food soak; it will lose flavor and nutrients. The raw food should be as clean as possible to make the canning process as effective as possible.

Packaging food according to instructions

Fruits and vegetables may be packed raw or preheated and then packed. Some foods can be packed by either method, but always follow the directions given in the recipe. Hot pack often gives better color and flavor, particularly when foods are processed in a boiling water bath.

A jar funnel is helpful when you fill jars with small foods. There should always be enough liquid to fill in around the solid food in the jar and to cover the food – usually ½ to 1½ cups liquid for a quart jar.

Leave the specified amount of headspace in the jar. The amount depends on the type of food, so follow the directions in the recipe.

Closing the jars Correctly

- To release any air bubbles that may be trapped in the jar, run a bubble-freer or any plastic knife-like utensil around the edges of the jar, gently pushing the food from side to side so that any trapped air is released. Add more liquid, if needed, to ensure proper headspace.
- Wipe off the rims of the jars with a clean, damp cloth. Place the treated lid on the jar, center it, and hold it in place with your fingers while you tighten the screw band to fingertip tight. Tightening the screw band too tight will prevent air from escaping as necessary during processing.

Using Correct Canning Method

Choose the correct canning method. Use boiling water bath for fruits or high-acid foods. Use pressure canners for all other foods.

- Boiling water bath procedure
- Pressure canner procedure

Boiling Water Bath Procedure

- Fill the canner halfway with clean, hot water.
- Using a jar-lifter, carefully place each filled jar into the canner, ensuring it's positioned securely on a rack. Always keep the jar upright.
- Add additional boiling water as needed, ensuring the water level is 1 to 2 inches above the jar tops. Pour water around, not directly on the jars, to avoid breakage.
- Turn the heat to the highest setting, cover the canner, and heat until the water reaches a vigorous boil.
- Once boiling, set a timer to process the food for the required time.
- Keep the canner covered throughout the process. Adjust the heat if necessary to maintain a steady boil.
- Add more boiling water if the level drops below the jar tops.
- If the water stops boiling during the process, increase the heat to restore a vigorous boil, then reset the timer from the beginning.
- After processing, turn off the heat and remove the lid. Wait 5 minutes before taking out the jars.
- Using the jar-lifter, remove the jars and place them upright on dry towels or a cooling rack, ensuring at least 1 inch of space between jars. Avoid placing jars in a cold draft and do not cover them with towels.

- Allow jars to cool for 12 to 24 hours undisturbed. Do not tighten the lid rings or press down on the flat metal lid until fully cooled.

Pressure Canner Procedure

- Follow the manufacturer's instructions carefully, especially regarding venting or exhausting for 10 minutes before closing to pressurize the canner.
- Position the canner on the burner and add a rack with 2 to 3 inches of hot water. Begin heating, but prevent the water level from dropping.
- Use a jar-lifter to place the filled jars onto the rack inside the canner, ensuring space for steam circulation around each jar. Keep jars upright.
- Secure the canner lid. Leave the vent port open or the petcock open.
- Turn the heat to the highest setting and allow steam to flow freely from the open vent or petcock for 10 minutes.
- After venting, place the counterweight or weighted gauge on the vent or close the petcock. The canner will start to pressurize.
- For dial gauge canners, allow pressure to rise quickly to 8 pounds. Then, lower the heat slightly and continue to increase pressure to the correct level.
- For weighted gauge canners, adjust the heat so the gauge starts to jiggle or rock, indicating the correct pressure.
- Start timing when the recommended pressure is reached or when the weighted gauge begins to move.
- Adjust the heat to maintain a steady pressure. If pressure exceeds the recommended level, reduce the heat instead of opening the vent or removing the weight.
- If the pressure falls below the recommended level, bring it back to the correct pressure and restart the timing from the beginning.
- Once processing is complete, turn off the heat and let the canner cool down naturally. Avoid forcing the cooling process.
- Once the canner has depressurized, remove the weight or open the petcock. Wait 10 minutes before carefully removing the lid.
- Carefully remove the jars, ensuring not to tilt them, and place them onto dry towels or a cooling rack with at least 1 inch of space between them.
- Let the jars cool undisturbed for 12 to 24 hours. Avoid tightening the ring bands or pressing down on the lids until they are completely cooled.

10

Operation and Maintenance of Packaging Machineries

Packaging machinery is integral to all packaging processes, from primary packaging to distribution packs. It encompasses various stages, including fabrication, cleaning, filling, sealing, combining, labeling, overwrapping, and palletizing.Food packaging refers to the methods, materials, and technologies used to package food items. It serves multiple purposes, such as prolonging the shelf life of products. However, food packaging is not a recent innovation, and its history is quite fascinating.

Food packaging has existed in various forms throughout history. The Journal of Agricultural and Food Chemistry highlights that Napoleon played a major role in its development by offering a reward of 12,000 francs for anyone who could invent a method to preserve food for his army. This prize went unclaimed for 15 years until Nicholas Appert introduced the canning method. Appert's process involved boiling food and sealing it in airtight glass containers, laying the foundation for modern canned food as we know it today.

EVOLUTION OF FOOD PACKAGING THROUGH AGES

The history of food packaging dates back centuries! The Chinese were pioneers in developing paper and wrapping materials, which were utilized for storing food. In ancient Egypt, advancements were made in glass-blowing and molding techniques, allowing glass to be shaped into various forms for food and water storage.

Over time, innovations continued to evolve, with figures like Nicholas Appert leading the way. Appert's glass canning method eventually led to the creation of modern metal cans. In the 1880s, the food manufacturer Quaker Oats introduced cardboard cereal boxes as a packaging solution for their oats, further advancing food packaging technology.

Food packaging serves several vital functions beyond simply containing food.

Here are Some Key Roles of Food Packaging:

- **Preservation:** Packaging prevents exposure to air and moisture, which can cause food to spoil quickly. Proper packaging extends the shelf life of food, benefiting manufacturers by reducing waste.

- **Protection from Biological Agents:** Packaging safeguards food from pests, bacteria, germs, and other contaminants that could degrade the product or make it unsafe to consume.
- **Information:** Packaging provides important product details, such as brand name, expiration dates, and ingredients, allowing consumers to make informed choices.
- **Convenience:** Packaging makes it easier to use food products, like milk cartons or pre-sliced foods in cans, allowing consumers to store and use items as needed.

Different types of food packaging include:

- **Aseptic Packages:** Sterilized containers that don't require refrigeration, used for products like soups, milk, and liquid eggs.
- **Trays:** Commonly used for meats, fish, seeds, and cans, trays have high sides to prevent contents from spilling.
- **Bags:** Often used for snack foods like chips, crackers, or fruits.
- Boxes: Used for cereals, frozen foods, pizzas, and other items, available in various shapes and sizes.
- **Cans:** Versatile, durable containers, usually made from metal coated in tin to prevent corrosion, commonly used for beverages and canned food.
- **Cartons and Coated Paper:** Includes egg cartons and liquid food containers, like milk, made from coated paper or cardboard.
- **Flexible Packaging:** Made from flexible materials like plastic, foil, or paper, commonly seen in bagged salads.
- **Pallets:** Used by wholesalers or distributors to hold multiple boxes of food items for storage and transport.
- **Wrappers:** Used for products like candy bars or gum, with techniques such as flow wrapping to package confectionery items.

PACKAGING & LABELING EQUIPMENT

Packaging and labeling equipment play a important role in the food and beverage industry by ensuring products are properly packaged, labeled, and ready for distribution. Below are some key types of equipment and their functions:

- **Filling machines:** These machines measure and fill containers with food or beverages, with various types such as gravity fillers, piston fillers, and vacuum fillers designed for different products. Proper filling ensures product consistency, minimizes spillage, and reduces waste, resulting in cost savings and customer satisfaction.
- **Capping machines:** Capping machines seal containers with caps, lids, or closures, including screw caps, snap caps, and cork stoppers. Proper sealing

preserves freshness, prevents contamination, ensures safety compliance, and provides tamper-evident features for product integrity.

- **Labeling machines:** These machines apply labels to products, displaying important information like ingredients, nutritional facts, expiry dates, and branding. Accurate labeling is essential for regulatory compliance, establishing brand identity, and building consumer trust, while also aiding in marketing and product differentiation.
- **Coding and marking equipment:** Used for printing batch numbers, expiry dates, barcodes, and traceability details on packaging, this equipment ensures traceability for recalls, assists in inventory management, meets regulatory standards, and helps prevent counterfeiting.
- **Wrapping machines:** These machines wrap products in protective materials like shrink wrap, stretch film, or flow wrap, providing stability, protection, and tamper-evidence. Proper wrapping prevents physical damage, preserves product quality, and enhances shelf life.
- **Case packing and palletizing equipment:** These machines automate the process of placing products into cases and stacking them onto pallets for efficient transportation and storage. Automation boosts productivity, reduces labor costs, and ensures uniform packaging for easier handling during distribution.
- **Quality inspection systems:** Using methods such as vision inspection, metal detection, and x-ray scanning, these systems identify defects, contaminants, or inconsistencies in products or packaging, ensuring product safety and meeting regulatory standards.
- **Conveyors and handling equipment:** These systems move products through different stages of the packaging process, linking various machines into a streamlined production line. They automate the packaging process, reducing manual labor and improving efficiency.

Together, these machines enhance product safety, regulatory compliance, cost-effectiveness, and customer satisfaction, while ensuring high standards of quality and consistency.

Variants of Food Packaging Machines

The scale of modern food processing is so large that it is no longer feasible to pack every food product by hand. This job is now done automatically by food packaging machines.

Some common examples of automation in food packaging include:

Pick and Place Machines

These pick a food product from one place and place it somewhere else. Pick and place robots are commonly used for handling chocolates, snack crackers, and processing similar food products.

Figure.: 10.1 Case Packing Machines

Case Packing Machines

PWR has flexible packaging robots that can be used to pack food into any tray, case, basket, or crate. Case packing systems can also reject any defective product as programmed.

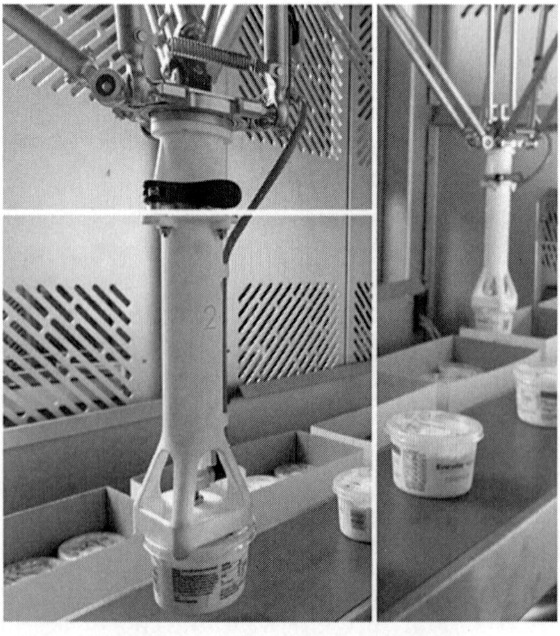

Figure.: 10.2 Cutting Machines

Cutting Machines

Cutting machines are used to slice bread or other food items into smaller pieces. Innovative cutting solutions like food cutting robots can create precise cutting shapes on food items.

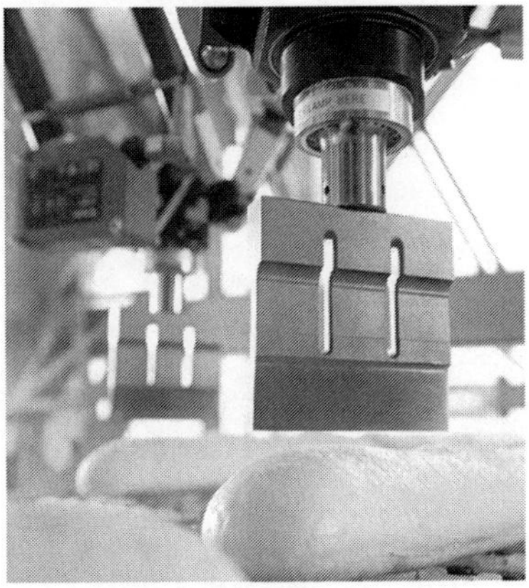

Fig : 10.3 Smartline

Smartline

Smartline is an economically feasible automation solution to speed up the workflow of your food packaging line while reducing labor costs. It has very low costs, and can do product loading, case loading, and loading into the flow wrapper.

Figure.: 10.4 Packaging Machines

Packaging Machines

These come in different types like blister, skin, and vacuum packaging. Each has a different application. For instance, blister packs are used for medicines, while vacuum bags are used for items that have a smaller quantity.

Figure.: 10.5 Cartoner

Cartoner

Cartoning machines handle making folding cartons and packing food items into them. Folding cartons generally come as flat cardboard pieces, and a cartoner converts the folding cartons into their intended shape.

Form, Fill, and Seal Machines

These machines are used to create pouches or sachets and pour the food item into them. For instance, milk pouches are made using form, fill, and seal machines.

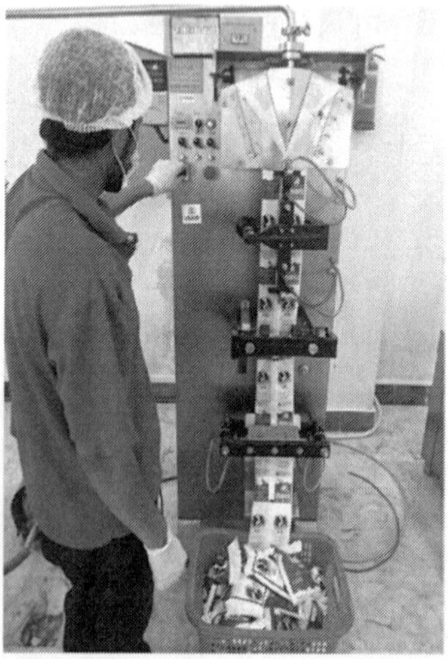

Figure.: 10.6 Check weighing Machines

Checkweighing Machines

These machines are installed at the end of a food packaging line. They check the weight of the final packed food item. If the weight is incorrect, the food item is rejected.

Autocoding Machines

These machines create and install labels on food packets. The labels contain details like manufacturing date, weight, relevant codes, etc. The food packaging sector is enormous and includes many niche machines. There are also a lot of different variations of the machines we mentioned above.

Key Fetures of Effective Food Packaging

Packaging professionals know that high-quality food packaging should have the following characteristics:

No-leakage

The material and packing method should ensure that no food leaks out after the packing is done.

Sturdy

The packaging should be sturdy enough to handle the stress it will undergo during transportation, loading, and unloading.

Food-grade

Some food packers use low-end materials to minimize costs. However, these materials can chemically react with food and harm the integrity of the food item. Therefore, the packaging material should be food-grade.

Airtight

While ensuring food doesn't leak, the food packaging should also guarantee that air or moisture doesn't enter.

Efficient

A good food packaging solution should minimize material wastage. It should use the precise amount of material required to efficiently seal the product.

Environment friendly

Today, there is more focus on environmental factors related to packaging. Efforts are being made to create packaging solutions for food that are environmentally friendly. Good food packaging nowadays contains recycling information on how to dispose of the used material.

Commonly used Materials for Food Packaging

Some of the most used food packaging materials are paper and paperboard packaging.

Paper and Paperboard Packaging

- Paper and thick paperboard material have an approximate market share of 34% when it comes to usage as food packaging materials.

- This material is used to pack dry food items like rice, lentils, and flour. It is cheap and biodegradable.

Plastics

Plastic packaging for food containers is divided into two types: rigid plastic materials and flexible plastic materials, holding market shares of 27% and 10%, respectively. The advantages of plastic containers include their affordability, versatility in shaping, lightweight nature, and ease of processing. However, plastic food containers often face criticism due to the challenges associated with recycling them.

Glass

- Due to their nonpermeable nature, glass bottles are the method of choice for many liquid food items.
- It is a chemically safe method and can be recycled endlessly.
- However, one downside of this food packaging is its heavy weight. It also breaks easily.

Metals

Metals are commonly used to package solid and liquid food products, such as beverages and canned foods. They provide similar advantages to glass but are lighter and less fragile. In the food industry, metals like tin-coated steel and aluminum are used, with aluminum gaining popularity due to its superior barrier properties.

FILLING MACHINE

Variants of Filling Machines

There are different types of machines used in the filling of different substances. These fillers are used in various companies as it makes it easy for factories to fill up the bottles & other containers.

- Liquid filling machine
- Digital liquid fillers
- Vial filling machine
- Powder fillers
- Ampoule filling machine

OPERATING PRINCIPLES OF DIFFERENT FILLING MACHINES

Liquid Filling Machine & It's Principles

The liquid filling machine works when the pressure is high. This can be classified as liquid pressure filling, which means the liquid flows into the bottle based on its own weight when the amount of pressure of the liquid reservoir is equal to the amount of air present in the bottle.

These liquid fillers are easy to control and to fill the exact amount of liquid into gallons or containers. There is a filling mechanism that allows the machine to adjust the different sized bottles without replacing parts and also have a "No Bottle-No Fill" mechanism which means the machine will automatically stop the process when there is no bottle available on the belt.

Working of Liquid Filling Machine

The liquid filling machine operates based on the principle of liquid pressure filling. When the pressure is high, the liquid flows into the bottle under its own weight, occurring when the pressure in the liquid reservoir aligns with the air volume inside the bottle.

To ensure accurate filling, liquid fillers are equipped with a filling mechanism that allows for precise control and adjustment of the liquid amount dispensed into containers or gallons. This mechanism enables the machine to handle bottles of varying sizes without the need for part replacements, improving efficiency and saving time.

A key feature of liquid filling machines is the "No Bottle-No Fill" system. This function automatically stops the filling process when no bottle is detected on the conveyor belt, preventing wastage and ensuring that only bottles present are filled.

In conclusion, liquid filling machines use liquid pressure to fill bottles, allowing the liquid to flow in due to its weight when the pressures are aligned. These machines offer accurate control over the filling process and accommodate different bottle sizes without the need for changing parts. The "No Bottle-No Fill" feature ensures efficiency by halting the process when no bottle is detected.

Principles of Digital Liquid Fillers

Digital liquid fillers are one of the most demanded liquid fillers in the current scenario due to operator-friendly features that make it easy for the operator to achieve the best results at an increased rate.

- Digital liquid fillers have an easy operative interface that accesses every filler function like indexing the diving nozzle and system control.
- The digital liquid filling machine works on a stable electricity supply & sometimes automatically adjusts itself withlow power supply under certain scenarios.
- These digital fillers scan if any error is occurred in bottles and pouches before reaching to the finalization of the product.

Working of Digital Liquid Fillers

Digital liquid fillers are highly valued in the current market for their user-friendly features, enabling operators to achieve efficient and fast results.

The core functionality of digital liquid fillers lies in their intuitive interface, which provides easy access to all machine functions. Operators can easily navigate through various options, such as indexing the diving nozzle and controlling the overall system.

These fillers operate on a stable electricity supply, ensuring consistent performance. Furthermore, they are equipped with the ability to automatically adjust to low power conditions, minimizing disruptions and ensuring continuous operation despite power fluctuations.

A standout feature of digital liquid fillers is their ability to scan bottles and pouches for errors before finalizing the product. Through advanced scanning technology, the fillers detect any defects or abnormalities, ensuring only products that meet the required quality standards proceed to the final production stage.

Digital liquid fillers offer a smooth and efficient experience for operators with their user-friendly interface and reliable operation. Their ability to adjust during low power situations and scan for defects enhances quality control, ensuring only flawless products reach the final stage. By incorporating digital liquid fillers, you can optimize your liquid filling process and achieve exceptional results.

Principles of Vial Filling Machine

The vial fillers are cost-effective, asthey require lesser area and can be installed in compact space depending on the size of regulators, and it just requires only a single operator to conduct the process. There are sensors in vials fillers that reject the vials that are not filled.

The weight checker mechanism in these fillers enables the feature such that the weight of every vial will be exact to the other. One of the mechanisms of these vial fillers is such that it loads the vials, which are then carriedthrough an isolated transport section.

Working of Vial Filling Machine Work?

Vial filling machines are an efficient and cost-effective solution, making them ideal for various industries. These machines are space-efficient, requiring minimal room and can be installed in compact spaces depending on the size of the regulators. Additionally, they only require one operator to manage the filling process, which reduces labor needs and boosts productivity.

Equipped with sensors, vial fillers play a key role in quality control by detecting and rejecting improperly filled vials. This ensures that only accurately filled vials proceed through the process.

To maintain precision and consistency, vial fillers incorporate a weight checker mechanism. This feature guarantees that every vial has the correct weight, ensuring product quality and compliance with standards. By monitoring the weight of each vial, these machines produce a consistent and reliable product output.

In operation, vials are loaded onto the machine and transported through a controlled, isolated section that ensures product integrity and minimizes contamination risks.

In summary, vial filling machines provide a cost-efficient, space-saving solution for vial filling. With their single-operator design and features like sensors and weight checkers, these machines enhance quality control, reject improperly filled vials, and ensure uniformity in filling. Choose vial filling machines for precise, reliable, and consistent results in vial filling operations.

Various Principles that are Used in Powder Fillers Machines

Powder fillers are most preferred to be utilized in pharmaceutical industries to ensure high productivity and efficiency in the production rate.As a result, they have a high demand in the market.

Some of the features that make these fillers for powder, a preferable choice for these industries.

- Powder filling machines work at a speed of in general, 108 strokes per minute.
- These powder fillers are semi-automatic or fully automatic, and these devices run efficiently to give the best results.
- The speed of filling in these machines is always higher in rate as most of the industries look for a machine that has a reliable rate of output during work.
- The drive mechanisms of the fillers are compatible & user-friendly as the motor allocates the satisfactory push that is needed by the rotating elements.

Working of Power Filler Machines

Powder filling machines are highly valued in the pharmaceutical industry for their ability to deliver high productivity and efficiency in production rates. These machines are in great demand due to their numerous features that make them the top choice for powder filling in various industries.

Operating at impressive speeds, powder filling machines typically achieve an average of 108 strokes per minute. This rapid operation enables the quick and efficient filling of powdered substances into containers, significantly enhancing production output.

These are available in both semi-automatic and fully automatic versions and these machines cater to different industry needs and preferences. Regardless of the type, whether semi-automatic or fully automatic, powder fillers are designed to operate with optimal efficiency, ensuring fast and accurate results.

The filling speed in powder filling machines remains consistently high, fulfilling the requirements of industries that need reliable production rates. This steady performance guarantees a smooth and continuous workflow, maximizing productivity while minimizing downtime.

The drive mechanisms in these machines are compatible and easy to operate. The motor powers the rotating components, ensuring smooth and dependable performance. These mechanisms are engineered to handle the demands of the powder filling process, improving overall efficiency and reliability.

In conclusion, powder filling machines are an excellent choice for the pharmaceutical industry, offering high productivity and efficiency. With their rapid operation speed, availability in semi-automatic and fully automatic models, consistent filling rates, and user-friendly drive mechanisms, these machines provide optimal results for powder filling tasks. Choosing powder filling machines will boost productivity and efficiency in your pharmaceutical manufacturing processes.

Operatin of Ampoule Filling Machine

Ampoule filling machines are preferred in pharmaceutical industries for the ampoule filling process. These machines are beneficial for industries looking to invest for a high productivity rate.

Various features that make these filling machines for ampoules as themost opted choice are as mentioned below:

- One of the most important principles of ampoule filling machines is, that it can cover the product entirely in the inert glass without having a rubber stopper or any other element that is in the direct exposure to the drug.
- Ampoule fillers are used to fill up the ampoules and the speed varies with the significant mechanism of these ampoule machines depending on the model of the equipment.
- Some of the ampoule coding machines imply the ring banding to finish the entire ampoule tips for the perfect identification of the vials.
- In general, ampoule filling machines have the filling range for these mechanisms normally around 1ml to 20ml.

Ampoule filling machines are highly sought after in the pharmaceutical industry for their efficient filling capabilities. These machines offer numerous features that make them the ideal choice for ampoule filling, ensuring high productivity. Here's a closer look at how ampoule filling machines operate:

A key feature of ampoule filling machines is their ability to completely enclose the product within inert glass, ensuring that the drug remains protected and free from any direct contact with rubber stoppers or other elements that could compromise the product's integrity.

These machines are specifically designed for filling ampoules, with the filling speed varying depending on the machine's mechanism and the model being used.

Many ampoule filling machines are also equipped with coding mechanisms that apply ring banding to the ampoule tips, allowing for proper identification, labeling, and traceability.

Ampoule filling machines typically have a filling range of 1ml to 20ml, making them versatile for a variety of ampoule sizes and providing flexibility during the filling process.

In summary, ampoule filling machines are engineered to ensure precise and efficient filling in the pharmaceutical industry. They utilize specialized mechanisms and principles to protect the product while maintaining high productivity rates. Opting for ampoule filling machines can offer pharmaceutical companies accurate and reliable filling processes.

These filling machines are used across various industries, including pharmaceutical, dairy, cold storage, and more. They are essential for filling containers such as bottles, pouches, vials, and gallons. Investing in these machines can yield significant results for businesses by enhancing the efficiency of their filling operations.

SEALING MACHINE

Sealing machines are important and essential in various industries. To prevent product damage during transportation, most items are sealed and packaged through a series of related packaging machines during production. This not only safeguards the products but also enhances their visual appeal.

The packaging industry encompasses a broad range of sealing machines, which include various equipment with different levels of automation for processes like filling, sealing, wrapping, and packaging. Depending on the specific packaging requirements for different products, the appropriate machine models can be selected. This process spans from the initial filling of materials into containers, packaging bags, bottles, boxes, etc., to the subsequent sealing and packaging stages, and ultimately the cartoning process, each involving specific packaging machine needs.

Working of Sealing Machine

The entire operation of a complete sealing machine system begins with the weighing and filling unit, which determines the appropriate metering and unloading method based on the characteristics of the ingredients. Once measured, the materials are transported by conveyor belts to the next packaging and quality inspection unit.

At this stage, various packaging methods such as box, bag, or bottle/can types can be selected. The inspection area automatically removes any products that fail weight or metal detection, enhancing the product's quality rate.

The packaged items are then efficiently moved via conveyor belts to the unpacking, packing, and sealing units. This area can be equipped with robots for flexible packing, enabling automated sorting and packing of products into cartons. This automation ensures that the process can be done without human intervention. Finally, the packed cartons are transported to the palletizing, wrapping, and storage units, where intelligent systems facilitate the completion of warehousing and transportation tasks, streamlining the entire packaging process.

Varieties of Sealing Machine

Bag Sealing Machine

Continuous band sealers are utilized to seal the openings of packages to ensure product protection. They are commonly used for sealing a variety of heat-sealable packaging, including aluminum foil bags, plastic bags, composite bags, kraft paper, freshness-keeping bags, tea bags, shrink films, and more. They are also capable of sealing thicker and heavier bags.

Depending on the application and product type, continuous band sealers can be categorized into horizontal sealers (placed horizontally) and vertical sealers (used for powders, granules, or liquids). They are also available in different models based on speed requirements, such as hand pressure sealers, semi-automatic sealers, and fully automatic sealers. Additionally, they can be tailored for specific packaging needs, such as sealing, capping, vacuuming, or pinch bag sealing machines.

Uses of Sealing Machines

These sealing machines offer numerous benefits, including strong, reliable seals, high efficiency, low operational costs, and versatility. They are widely used across various industries such as food, pharmaceuticals, chemicals, agriculture, and lubricants.

Vacuum Packaging Machine

The vacuum packaging machine uses a vacuum pump to extract the air from the packaging bag. If it has an inflation function, it first inflates the vacuum chamber, uses the pressure difference between the vacuum chamber and the outside atmosphere to compress and seal the bag mouth, and then cools it. The vacuum chamber is vented into the atmosphere to complete the vacuum packaging process. It is suitable for various food needs that require a delayed shelf life, such as meat, seafood, vegetables and other foods. It is necessary to better maintain the freshness and humidity of the food and reduce bacterial growth and decay of the food.

Tray Vacuum Packaging Machine

There are three types of box vacuum machines: Vacuum, MAP, and VSP. It works by removing the air from the tray and replacing it with an inert gas mixture.

When this gas mixture is injected into the tray, it slows down the growth of microorganisms to preserve freshness. It is usually used in various restaurants and supermarkets, and is suitable for today's popular pre-prepared foods (including ready-to-heat foods, ready-to-eat foods, and ready-to-eat foods), providing safe and efficient packaging solutions to maintain the quality and taste of pre-prepared foods.

Thermoforming Vacuum Packaging Machine

The fully automatic thermoforming vacuum packaging machine efficiently completes the entire packaging process, including film forming, automatic or manual product feeding, vacuuming, sealing, and cutting. It effectively packages the product with a protective outer skin.

Carton Sealing Machine

The carton sealing machine uses tape to seal the upper and lower boxes at one time. Printed tape can also be used to better enhance the product image. Carton sealing machines can be mainly divided into uniform sealer, random sealer, semi-automatic, full-automatic and other series. The following are the corresponding characteristics, advantages and applicable industries.

Table.: 10.1 Features and advanges of carbon sealing machine

Classification	Feature	Advantage	Industry
Uniform Sealers	Handle cartons of fixed size, suitable for packing cartons of the same size.	1. High stability 2. Simple operation 3. Consistency	Food, Electronics Manufacturers
Random Sealers	Automatically adjust to different sizes of cartons	1. High flexibility 2. Time saving 3. Strong adaptability	Logistics Services
Semi-automatic Carton Sealer	Manual assistance is required to complete the sealing action	1. Low cost 2. High efficiency 3. Easy to operate	Small and medium-sized enterprises, smaller factories
Automatic Carton Sealer	Automatically complete the sealing process without manual assistance	1. High automation 2. Reduced labor costs 3. High efficiency	Large manufacturers and producers

Shrink Wrapping Machine

The heat shrink wrapping machine operates through two main processes: sealing and cutting, and hot cutting.In the sealing and cutting phase, the product moves into the packaging area via a conveyor belt. The film roll automatically covers the product with packaging film, while the sealing and cutting systems use heat to seal and cut the film.In the shrinking phase, the sealed product enters the shrink furnace via a conveyor belt. Hot air circulation causes the packaging film to shrink rapidly, tightly adhering to the product's surface. This shrink-wrapped film protects the product, preventing contamination and damage, while enhancing its appearance. The completed process ensures sealed, cut, and shrink-wrapped packaging, ideal for use in food, pharmaceuticals, electronics, and other industries. This method boosts packaging speed, improves quality, and reduces production costs.

Strapping Machine

The strapping machine applies straps around items, then tightens them to secure the goods for transportation, storage, and handling. The straps ensure the items remain tightly secured, making them easy to load into cabinets. Commonly used in logistics, shipping, manufacturing, and warehousing, this machine offers various models, including handheld, semi-automatic, and fully automatic, providing stability and safety. Depending on speed and packaging volume requirements, equipment can be customized to fit specific applications.

Labeling Machine

The labeling machine performs a series of steps including label cutting, applying the label, pressing the bottle with a roller, and affixing the sticker to the bottle. Designed for high-precision, fast-speed labeling, it is ideal for applying self-adhesive labels or films to various sizes of round bottles. This machine is commonly used in the food, beverage, pharmaceutical, and other industries for marking production dates and batch numbers. It is compatible with PET bottles, plastic bottles, glass bottles, metal bottles, and slightly curved bottles.

Usage of Sealing Machine

To effectively use a sealing machine, it's important to follow the specific guidelines for the type of machine and packaging process you're working with. Here's a general step-by-step guide for using Hualian Machinery Group's sealing machine:

- **Unbox and Setup:** Begin by dismantling the wooden box (or carton) and removing the dust bag. Take out the manual to understand the installation guide and precautions.
- **Machine Installation:** Fix the machine in place and open the accessories bag to ensure all required components are present.
- **Accessory Installation:** Install the necessary machine accessories according to the manual.
- **Machine Startup:** Start the machine and configure the appropriate settings, such as temperature and time, based on the type of material you're sealing.
- **Preparation:** Prepare the packaging bags and materials in advance. Make sure they are ready for the sealing process.
- **Preheating:** Allow the machine to preheat, if necessary, to the specified temperature.
- **Filling and Packaging:** Once the machine is preheated, fill and seal the materials according to your packaging requirements.
- **Final Inspection:** After packaging, check the sealing quality of the packaging bags to ensure they are properly sealed.
- **Completion:** Once you've confirmed the sealing quality, the machine is ready for use.

Precautionary Tips

- Always read the operator's manual thoroughly before using any packing machine.
- Make sure that all safety guards are properly installed and functioning correctly.
- Perform regular maintenance on the machine, including cleaning, oiling, and inspecting for signs of wear and tear.
- Never attempt to operate a packing machine without proper training, or if any safety features are compromised.

Bibliography

Agarwal, S., & Verma, R. (2020). Technological Innovations in Agro-Processing Equipment for Indian Agro-Industries. International Conference on Agricultural Engineering, Pune, 80-85.

Agri-Tech India. (2020). The Role of Automation in Agro-Processing Equipment Maintenance in India. Retrieved from http://www.agritechindia.com

Bansal, R., & Singh, H. (2020). Equipment Maintenance and Operational Practices in Agro-Processing Industry in India. International Conference on Sustainable Agriculture, New Delhi, 112-118.

Bansal, S., & Joshi, K. (2021). Operational Practices and Challenges in Agro-Processing Units in India. International Agro-Tech Conference, Pune, 70-76.

Bansal, S., & Joshi, P. (2021). Mechanization and Maintenance in Agro-Processing Industries. Innovators Press.

Bansal, S., & Shah, V. (2021). The Role of Efficient Equipment Maintenance in Agro-Processing Industry Growth in India. International Journal of Agro-Technology, 12(6), 170-175.

Bhat, M., & Kaur, R. (2021). Equipment Maintenance and Troubleshooting in Agro-Processing Units in India. Food Processing Industry Journal, 12(1), 55-62.

Central Institute of Post-Harvest Engineering and Technology (CIPHET). (2020). Study on Agro-Processing Equipment and Operational Techniques in India. CIPHET Report.

Chauhan, N., & Verma, A. (2021). Equipment Operation in the Indian Agro-Processing Sector: Current Trends and Future Directions. Indian Journal of Agro Technology, 9(3), 99-107.

Chauhan, S., & Sharma, G. (2021). Automation in Agro-Processing: Maintenance and Operational Methods in India. Food Engineering and Technology Symposium, Delhi, 40-47.

Chopra, P., & Jain, S. (2021). Food Processing and Preservation: Methods and Techniques for India. AgroTech Publishing.

CII. (2021). Agro-Processing Equipment and Its Role in India's Rural Economy. Confederation of Indian Industry Report.

Deloitte. (2021). Improving the Efficiency of Agro-Processing Equipment in India. Deloitte Report.

Department of Food Processing, Government of India. (2020). Technological Advances in Agro-Processing Equipment for Indian Farmers. Report on Agro-Processing Innovations.

Deshmukh, P. (2021). Agro Processing and Food Technology: Equipment and Operations. Scientific Agri Publishers.

FICCI. (2021). Agro-Processing Industry in India: A Comprehensive Review of Methods and Equipment. FICCI Industry Report.

Food Processing India. (2020). Agro-Processing Industry in India: Trends and Maintenance Strategies. Retrieved from http://www.foodprocessingindia.com

Food Processing Ministry, Government of India. (2020). Report on Operational Efficiency in Agro-Processing Industries in India. Government of India.

Food Safety and Standards Authority of India (FSSAI). (2020). Guidelines on the Operation and Maintenance of Agro-Processing Equipment. FSSAI Report.

Food Safety and Standards Authority of India (FSSAI). (2021). Regulatory Standards for Agro-Processing Equipment in India. FSSAI Policy Document.

Government of India, Ministry of Agriculture and Farmers Welfare. (2021). Policy Framework for Agro-Processing Equipment and Operations in India. Government of India.

Government of India, Ministry of Food Processing Industries. (2020). Policies for Supporting Agro-Processing Equipment Operation and Maintenance in India. Government of India.

Government of India. (2020). Regulatory Guidelines for Agro-Processing and Equipment Operations. Government of India Policy.

Gupta, H., & Patel, M. (2020). Optimization of Agro-Processing Equipment Operations in India. Conference on Agri-Tech and Equipment Maintenance, Bangalore, 60-65.

Gupta, P. (2021). Maintenance of Agro-Processing Equipment in Rural India: A Sustainable Approach. M.Tech Thesis, University of Rajasthan.

IIFPT. (2020). Agro-Processing Equipment Technologies for Rural India. Retrieved from http://www.iifpt.org

Indian Agricultural Research Institute (IARI). (2021). A Comprehensive Review of Agricultural Processing Methods and Equipment in India. IARI Technical Report.

Indian Agro-Processing Association (IAPA). (2021). Maintaining Agro-Processing Equipment: Challenges and Solutions in India. Retrieved from http://www.iapa.org.in

Indian Food Processing Industry. (2021). Trends and Innovations in Agro-Processing Equipment for India. Retrieved from http://www.foodprocessingindia.org

Indian Food Processing Industry Federation. (2020). Technological Innovations and Maintenance Practices in Agro-Processing. IFPIF Report.

Indian Institute of Food Processing Technology (IIFPT). (2020). Agro-Processing Equipment Operational Efficiency: Challenges and Solutions in India. IIFPT Report.

Indian Institute of Food Processing Technology (IIFPT). (2020). Agro-Processing Equipment Technology Transfer and Innovation in India. IIFPT Report.

Indian Ministry of Agriculture and Farmers Welfare. (2021). Agro-Processing Sector Development in India: Policies and Guidelines. Government of India.

Indian Ministry of Rural Development. (2020). Supporting Rural Agro-Processing Units in India through Equipment and Maintenance Regulations. Government of India.

Jain, M. (2021). Sustainable Practices in Agro-Processing Equipment Operation. FoodTech India.

Joshi, A. (2020). Comprehensive Manual on Food and Agro-Processing Technologies in India. Indian Engineering Press.

Joshi, P., & Mehta, V. (2021). Agro-Processing Equipment: Challenges and Solutions in Indian Context. International Conference on Agro-Technologies, Mumbai, 122-129.

Joshi, P., & Sharma, M. (2021). Agro-Processing Technologies: Key Equipment and Maintenance Strategies for India. Global Agri-Tech Conference, Bengaluru, 100-106.

Joshi, P., & Singh, S. (2020). Technological Innovations in Agro-Processing Equipment and Their Impacts in India. Journal of Food Engineering and Technology, 19(4), 77-85.

Joshi, R. (2021). Automation and Operational Efficiency in Agro-Processing Units in India. M.Sc. Thesis, Indian Agricultural Research Institute, New Delhi.

Joshi, R., & Yadav, G. (2020). Emerging Trends in Agro-Processing Equipment Maintenance in India. International Conference on Agri-Tech and Innovation, Hyderabad, 99-105.

Joshi, S., & Gupta, V. (2020). Review of Maintenance Strategies for Food Processing Equipment in India. Food Technology Journal, 33(4), 147-152.

Kaur, S., & Yadav, R. (2021). Automation and Sustainability in Agro-Processing Equipment in India: A Case Study. Food Processing and Technology Journal, 30(4), 123-128.

KPMG. (2020). Agro-Processing in India: Innovation, Equipment, and Maintenance Challenges. KPMG India Report.

KPMG. (2020). Technological Developments in Agro-Processing Equipment in India: Challenges and Solutions. KPMG India Report.

Kumar, A., & Joshi, P. (2021). Recent Advances in Agro-Processing Equipment Technologies in India. Indian Journal of Agro-Processing Science, 15(2), 45-52.

Kumar, A., & Sharma, R. (2020). Emerging Trends in Agro-Processing Equipment in India: A Review. Indian Journal of Agricultural Engineering, 31(1), 58-64.

Kumar, M. (2020). Agro-Processing Equipment Maintenance Challenges: A Study of Rural India. Ph.D. Dissertation, Jawaharlal Nehru University.

Kumar, N. (2020). The Economics of Agro-Processing in India: Methods and Trends. Business Tech Publishing.

Kumar, P., & Patil, R. (2020). Food and Agro-Processing: Maintenance and Troubleshooting in India. Agricultural Research Journal.

Kumar, S. (2020). Operational Challenges in Agro-Processing: A Study of Equipment in India. Ph.D. Dissertation, Punjab Agricultural University.

Kumar, V., & Mehta, K. (2020). A Handbook on Agricultural Equipment and Processing in India. Techno Agri Books.

Kumar, V., & Shah, S. (2020). Emerging Technologies in Agro-Processing Equipment in India: A Review. National Agro-Engineering Conference, Chennai, 130-137.

McKinsey & Company. (2020). Opportunities in Agro-Processing and Equipment Maintenance in India. McKinsey Report.

Mehta, G., & Sharma, P. (2020). Agro-Processing in India: Review of Equipment and Operational Trends. Journal of Agricultural Engineering, 15(2), 90-97.

Mehta, H., & Sharma, G. (2021). Modern Agro-Processing: A Handbook for Engineers and Technicians. Innovations in AgriTech.

Mehta, V., & Mishra, S. (2020). Handbook of Agro-Processing: Methods, Maintenance, and Operations in India. Agro Solutions.

Ministry of Agriculture and Farmers Welfare, Government of India. (2020). Guidelines on Agro-Processing Equipment and Maintenance in Indian Agro-Industries. Government of India.

Ministry of Food Processing Industries (MOFPI). (2020). Policies for Enhancing Agro-Processing Industry in India. Government of India.

Ministry of Food Processing Industries (MOFPI). (2021). Policies for Supporting Agro-Processing Equipment and Maintenance in India. Government of India Policy Document.

Nadanassababady, T. (2015). Post-Harvest Technology and Processing of Fruits and Vegetables. Daya Publishing House, New Delhi.

Panesar, P.S., & Marwaha, S.S. (2010). Handbook of Fruit and Vegetable Processing. I.K. International Publishing House, New Delhi.

Ranganna, S. (2001). Handbook of Analysis and Quality Control for Fruit and Vegetable Products (2nd Ed.). Tata McGraw-Hill Publishing Company, New Delhi.

Sahay, K.M., & Singh, K.K. (1994). Unit Operations of Agricultural Processing. Vikas Publishing House Pvt. Ltd., New Delhi.

Singh, K.K., & Sahay, K.M. (2001). Unit Operations of Agricultural Processing (2nd Ed.). Vikas Publishing House Pvt. Ltd., New Delhi.

Verma, L.R., & Joshi, V.K. (2000). Postharvest Technology of Fruits and Vegetables – Handling, Processing, Fermentation and Waste Management. Indus Publishing, New Delhi.

Index